The Thief in the
White Collar

The Thief in the White Collar

by Norman Jaspan

with Hillel Black

J. B. Lippincott Company

Philadelphia & New York

To Jeanne and Miriam

Contents

Acknowledgments

WE would like to express our indebtedness to Nicholas O. Prounis whose command of the problem, his advice and unflagging patience have meant so much to us in the shaping of the book. We also want to thank Thomas P. Coleman, Daniel H. Greenberg, David Jaffe, Milton R. Moskowitz, A. H. Raskin, and the members of Norman Jaspan's staff for their help and invaluable suggestions. Finally, we wish to express our gratitude to Miss Elizabeth Otis, Corlies M. Smith and Alan Williams.

Preface

THE popular conception of the white collar criminal is the bank teller who steals from the "till" and then hides his thefts by doctoring the books. A white collar crime, however, would have to include not only embezzlement of cash, but stealing of merchandise, theft of company secrets, fraud to maintain job or community status, sabotage with or without financial gain, padded expense accounts, falsification of time cards and production records, and manipulating inventories to conceal stock shrinkage. The essential difference between white collar crime and robbery and/or burglary is that white collar crime is invariably concerned with violation of trust. The professional safe-cracker, for example, is not a white collar criminal, even though he may hang his penthouse walls with Picassos. However, the bank executive wearing his twenty-five-year service pin and stealing $200, may not only be a burglar but a white collar thief as well. He has violated the trust put in him by the bank's depositors, shareholders, the board of directors, his fellow employees, his community and the bonding company.

What makes white collar crime so important is the moral issue it raises. As Edwin H. Sutherland, the eminent sociologist, once noted: "White collar crimes violate trust and, therefore, create distrust; this lowers social morale and produces social disorganization.

"Many of the white collar crimes attack the fundamental principles of the American institutions. Ordinary crimes, on the other hand, produce little effect on social institutions or social organizations."

I. A. Jaspan, my father, who is founder and Chairman of the Board of our management consulting firm, started the company over thirty years ago. He was frequently called upon to advise or to take over the management of businesses, some of which were on the verge of bankruptcy. Although the Depression had caused many of these firms to flounder, a number of them, my father pointed out, could trace their financial difficulties to employee dishonesty, indifference and disloyalty. This was when I learned about white collar crime.

A large percentage of our clients are listed on the New York Stock Exchange. We represent one out of three major retailers, as well as manufacturers, hotels, hospitals, airlines, banking firms, mining companies and government agencies. Yet I have found time and again that, despite impressive-sounding control systems and business procedures and brilliant technological advances, one company after another is experiencing a serious drain in profits simply because of the thief in the white collar. That is why, in many cases, before we undertake the actual management of a business or initiate engineering projects whether they be the establishment of methods and systems, setting work performance standards, installing materials handling procedures or supervising trainee and executive development, we send in staff engineers from our fact-finding division, Investigations, Inc., to survey employee morale, performance and reliability. In fact, in more than fifty per cent of these assignments involving engineering projects with no hint of dishonesty, white collar crime was uncovered. In addition, in the last year alone, our staff has unearthed more than $60,000,000 worth of dishonesty, with more than sixty per cent attributable to supervisory and executive personnel.

I might add that most cases concerning white collar crime never see the light of public print. And the relatively few that do, lack the detail or depth to give the reader an understanding not only of the methods but the motives of the people involved. One of the main purposes in writing this book is to try to explain the nature of white collar crime and why employees, who are honest to begin with, and most of whom come from good homes, turn to theft. Since no purpose would be served by identifying the individuals and firms involved, names have been changed and locations omitted in cases derived solely from our files. A few of these cases have made headlines, however. Here we have attempted to go behind the scenes and give you a first-hand account of the story and how it came to be.

NORMAN JASPAN

Chapter 1

Are We Becoming a Nation of Embezzlers?

THIS BOOK is concerned with the alarming growth of a new kind of thief. Generally a member of the middle or upper class, he rarely has financial cause to steal. Often the product of a college education, he has been exposed to all the ethical values that western civilization holds dear. In many instances he has had a religious training that stresses the commandment: "Thou shalt not steal." Frequently he is the offspring of parents who are looked upon as hardworking, respected members of the community. Yet, despite his heritage and upbringing, he deliberately and consciously denies the very values upon which his existence is predicated. In the last decade he has become America's most resourceful and successful crook. He is the thief in the white collar.

According to insurance company figures, white collar employees, rank and file, supervisory and executive, are stealing about four million dollars in cash and property from their employers each working day. By the end of 1960, such thefts will reach the astronomical figure of more than one billion dollars per year. Compared to the white collar crook, the professional criminal is an amateur. The F.B.I. reports that the nation's burglars, pickpockets, armed robbers and auto thieves managed to steal 479 million dollars in 1957. This is considerably less than half the amount stolen by the country's white collar embezzlers.

11

Not only are the losses severe, but the rate of white collar crime is increasing ominously. And there is no sign of abatement. Indeed, the amount of loss is rising much faster than the amount of money in actual circulation. From 1946 to 1956 fidelity or "honesty" insurance increased about seventy per cent. During the same period "honesty" insurance losses climbed 250 per cent. Just consider banks, one of the largest sites of white collar crime. In the last two decades 105 were forced to close their doors because of embezzlement, and an average of one out of five has experienced at least one embezzlement in the past five years. Right now it is estimated that between ten and twenty-five million dollars is missing in thefts that haven't even been discovered.

The harm growing out of white collar crime cannot be measured. For the consumer it means higher prices, and for the worker decreased earnings. For numerous businesses it means the difference between success and failure. And in some instances it can mean bankruptcy for an entire community. But perhaps most dangerous of all, white collar crime portends the collapse of our ethical code of fair play and honesty. Indeed, the implication is that we are becoming a nation of thieves and embezzlers. If this statement seems too strong, consider the following facts.

In 1960 an estimated five billion dollars will probably change hands in kickbacks, payoffs and bribes. But that isn't the only area where dishonesty is an accepted fact of life. You will grant that most people try to cheat on their income tax if they think they can get away with it. To give you some idea of how many people try, and incidentally do not succeed, consider the amount paid in penalties, interest and back taxes for 1957, a record year. According to the Commissioner of Internal Revenue Service, the most recent figure reported comes to a whopping $1,661,354,000, an eighteen per cent increase over the previous year.

Frank Gibney, writing in *Life* recently on white collar crooks, took a look at an active, if somewhat compact, day of a reputable New York state businessman. During the day, the businessman bribed a cop, cheated on his income tax, entertained his wife at the expense of his company, bribed a building inspector, took a kickback in the form of a TV set, juggled his books, issued a misleading ad, lifted an office desk set for his personal use and advised his wife to forget the maid's social security tax. Writes Gibney: "Laying aside the cares of the day, he settles down to watch the news on his souvenir TV set—and fulminates about the dishonesty of the 'union racketeers' he sees on the screen."

If this solid and respected member of the community had been successfully prosecuted for his day's activities, he could have received thirty-three years in jail and a fine of $26,500. Yet, if he had been brought to court on any of these charges, he undoubtedly would have been filled with righteous indignation. You can hear his wail. "Why pick on me? Everybody else is doing it." Frankly, he would have been right.

This apparent national indifference to dishonesty is not limited to our private lives. It extends to the very life blood of our society, the nation's market places. The core of our independence is the free enterprise system under which a businessman is supposed to compete fairly and honestly with his competitors. But does he? Of course, in many cases he does. But in too many instances his only aim is a quick and easy profit, no matter what ethics are involved. His methods of gaining such profit have degenerated into a nefarious activity called business espionage.

The purpose of business spying is to steal secrets from your competitor without regard to fair play or the law. The result is subterfuge, lies, hypocrisy and dishonesty. Richard Austin Smith, writing in *Fortune,* says that in the opinion of some business spies, "there is more industrial espionage going on in the U.S. today than in any other period in our history." He notes that their operations range from spying out a competitor's multimillion-dollar bid on a government contract to paying a supermarket clerk five dollars a week for an advance copy of the Thursday Specials. Business espionage helps mold an atmosphere in which stealing from the competitor leads to the next step, embezzling from one's own employer.

This atmosphere of dishonesty and ethical laxity is not limited to the business world. During just the first year of its investigations the Select Senate Committee unearthed outright

theft or misuse of $10,000,000 by the leaders of seven interna-
tional labor unions, an average of $5 out of the pocket of each
rank and file member. Government, our most sacrosanct area of
public trust, has witnessed the departure of nearly a dozen top
federal officials during the Democratic and Republican administrations of Truman and Eisenhower. These officials have
either been jailed, fired, or they resigned under charges ranging
from fraud and influence peddling to conflict of interest.

These facts and figures, as shocking as they may appear, only
skim the surface of white collar crime. Examine, for a moment,
just one case from our files, that of a large private hospital. The
institution's pharmacist decided to go into business for himself.
His stock, the hospital's drugs. His clients, neighborhood drug-
gists. His yearly profit, $40,000. Nurses and volunteer service
workers not only stole thousands of dollars' worth of sheets
and pillow cases but sent all their dirty linen to the hospital's
laundry. Members of the staff bilked their own hospital of
thousands of dollars in drugs. They simply had the drugs requi-
sitioned in the names of the welfare patients who were supposed
to get them free. It reached the point where the family of a
paying patient was billed for drugs that had been prescribed ten
days after the patient died.

The tragedy of white collar crime is not just the cost in dollars and cents, but the corruption of our most respected citizens,
the professional worker, the executive, the top government and
union official.

The final irony is this: With the threatened obliteration of
our standards of honesty and fair play, it actually has become
easier for the dishonest white collar worker to steal. Since World
War II, business has expanded tremendously. This growth has
made it increasingly difficult for management to know what is
going on in its own house. The days when the boss knew everyone in his plant or office are well past. As a result, those who are
prone to steal have more opportunity to do so.

Indeed, the dishonest employee is literally given the opportunity to steal. Unlike the burglar, he doesn't have to jimmy his
way into the office and blow the safe. He already has the key
and the right combination. Often he handles company mer-

chandise, records and funds as part of his job. There's no chance that he will be shot while committing his crime, and he has the time and opportunity to falsify records and cover up. Many dishonest employees have fooled their employers for more than ten years, and some for as long as twenty-five years while pocketing loot well into the seven-figure bracket.

To sum up: With the rapid and extensive increase in white collar crime and the abasement of our ethics of fair play and honesty, we are inexorably heading toward that final denouement, a nation of embezzlers.

But who is this thief in the white collar? What does he look like? What are his motives? Where and how does he operate?

Chapter 2

The Embezzler Type: Everyman

THE MOST shocking aspect of white collar crime is neither the losses involved—and they can be huge—nor the number of people who turn dishonest. What is most frightening is that the white collar thief is often the last person anyone would believe capable of committing fraud. Indeed, as far as his friends, neighbors and employers are concerned his honesty is above reproach—until, of course, he is exposed.

In many instances the knowledge that your neighbor is a crook can be a shattering experience. Such was the case of an executive and a co-worker who lived next door. The two men and their families frequently visited each other. Their wives were close friends and their children attended the same school. When the executive learned that his neighbor, friend and fellow worker had stolen over $30,000 in merchandise during the last three years, he had to be forceably restrained from hurling himself down a flight of stairs. When I talked to the executive several months later, I found him still in a state of shock. He kept repeating, "I knew him. I trusted him. I was so good to him."

The executive felt that he had lost the ability to judge the honesty of his fellow man. At the same time his faith and trust in others had been shattered. The executive's disillusionment can be multiplied many thousandfold when you consider that the situation he found himself facing occurs with alarming frequency. Furthermore, not only isolated individuals but whole communities have been rocked by the exposure of astronomical thefts committed by the communities' leading citizens.

Take the case of Collingdale, Pennsylvania, a suburb of Philadelphia, and Faber E. Stengle, one of those big, heavy-jowled, jolly men who lived like most other members of the community in a modest row house. Stengle, sixty-seven, and his rotund and equally pleasant wife, Ethel, sixty-two, were childless. Stengle, though, loved children and devoted his life to them. For twenty-four years he served as superintendent of schools. And twenty of those twenty-four years were spent teaching Bible lessons at the Presbyterian church. Those who knew him, and almost everybody in the community of 8,400 did, had fondly nicknamed Stengle, Casey. Casey was honored, trusted and generally well-liked.

One bleak day in December, 1957, Angelo LaBuono, a pharmacist and newly elected member of the board of school directors, dropped in at Casey's office for a get-acquainted chat. Casey happened to be out at the time. And this proved to be his undoing.

LaBuono, finding Casey absent, started chatting with the superintendent's three clerks. During the conversation the clerks repeated rumors and suspicions about Casey showering attention on a pretty West Philadelphia redhead and the juggling of school checks.

The pharmacist passed on what he had heard to the board of school directors. When Casey flew to Florida for a vacation, the school directors and the police started an investigation. It wasn't long before they learned that there *was* a redhead in the life of their jovial superintendent of schools. Her name was Mrs. Margaret Barnes, thirty-six, a twice-married divorcee with two children. Casey had met Mrs. Barnes, whom he called Bonnie, at a picnic in Lebanon, Pennsylvania.

A week after he met her, Casey decided that Bonnie, who had been living in a trailer, should have better quarters so he moved her to a luxurious apartment in West Philadelphia. He not only furnished the apartment, but showered her with expensive gifts, a diamond bracelet, a mink coat and a car.

Where did he get the money? It was simple. He would dip into the school funds, taking as much as $300 a week. In fact, Casey had been pilfering school funds for the last ten years or for nearly nine years before he ever met Bonnie Barnes. During that time Casey, who as superintendent received a yearly salary of $9,400, had taken at least $125,000.

As one official of the school board of directors put it: "Casey was a 'take-charge' man. The bookkeeping? He took that over too. He seemed to like the job."

Casey managed to leave the school system poorer and himself richer by drawing checks on a special revolving "high school fund." He took the double precaution of using personal blank checks instead of official checks with serial numbers and made them out to cash instead of himself. He was able to draw the checks by forging the name of the school board's secretary as co-signer. At the end of the month Casey made out a check for the money he had stolen. The source for this check was the school district's tax fund. He was able to tap the tax fund by simply forging the names of the school board's three officers, the president, secretary and treasurer. He would then take the check drawn on the school district tax fund and put it in the high school fund, thus replacing the money he had stolen from the high school fund with money he had swiped from the school tax fund.

Once a month Casey received the school board bank statement. And each time he altered it. Over the years there were three elected auditors who examined the statements. Not once during that period did they find anything wrong with them. Everything balanced and Casey, as far as the school directors were concerned, was the epitome of efficiency.

When Casey's activities were finally uncovered, the people of Collingdale were dumbfounded. And their shock was compounded when it was learned that as a result of the school superintendent's violation of trust, there was only about $15,-000 left in the coffers of the community's school district, hardly enough to last the rest of the school year.

Casey, of course, is not the only civic leader who has stunned an entire community. There was Miss Minnie Clark Mangum, assistant secretary-treasurer of the Commonwealth Building and Loan Association of Norfolk, Virginia. Over a period of twenty-three years, Miss Minnie helped herself and friends to nearly $3,000,000, probably the largest haul in the annals of embezzlement. The sum was more than twice the amount stolen by armed robbers in the Boston Brink's case. Miss Minnie's only weapon was her fountain pen. The late Governor Harold Giles Hoffman of New Jersey embezzled $300,000. Others who have been accused of misapplying funds include a civic league's choice of Man of the Year in a large southern city, a veteran New York Internal Revenue agent and a Massachusetts congressman. Probably at least once a week the members of some community in the United States pick up their local newspaper to find that a personage they had believed, perhaps since childhood, to be a civic pillar, has betrayed their trust.

The effect on young and old alike can be twofold: (1) If this man whom my community has called a paragon of virtue, is dishonest, then who isn't? (2) And if he is dishonest, why shouldn't I take a little myself? With such a prevalent atmosphere of corruption, it is not surprising that white collar theft has become the largest and most costly crime.

In part, the typical white collar thief does not make the headlines because the pond is too big and the fish when caught is too small. But since dishonesty is communicable the average white collar worker is frequently infected by the muddy waters of his own environment. Indeed, to expect an individual to be honest when dishonesty is rampant is often asking too much. Perhaps, most appalling is the corruption of the young, who are actually trained on their very first job to believe this is the way things are done.

Consider the case of a girl called Jane who received an M.A. in retailing from a large university. Her first job was that of an executive trainee in a department store. Jane was on the job no more than a week when she noticed a lovely cashmere skirt and sweater set. She would have loved to buy it, but the sweater set cost $49.95 and her weekly take-home pay was $51. One day her superior, the assistant buyer, noticed that the young girl was admiring the cashmere costume.

"Do you really want this badly?" she asked.

"Oh, it's out of this world," Jane moaned, "but I can't afford it."

Jane's superior smiled and picked up the cashmere sweater set. "My goodness. Can you imagine that. Why, this button is falling off." And she ripped off the button. "How clumsy of me," she added as the sweater fell to the floor.

The assistant buyer sadly shook her head. "Isn't that too bad. I guess we'll have to mark it down now that it has been damaged."

And Jane's superior proceeded to do just that, marking the sweater set down to $30. Since Jane had not worked for the store for thirty days, she was not allowed the employee's twenty per cent discount. However, the assistant buyer solved that problem by writing up the sale to herself. Jane had just purchased the $49.95 cashmere sweater set for $24.

Several weeks later she received a wedding invitation from a college friend. As Jane passed the housewares department, she noticed a perfect gift, an electric coffee percolator which retailed for $13.95. A friend in the housewares department quickly realized that Jane was admiring the coffee percolator. She removed a bobby pin, made a tiny scratch on the percolator's chrome finish, and Jane acquired just the right gift for a sizable markdown plus a twenty per cent discount. Now Jane not only had a Master's in retailing, but a Ph.D. in stealing.

In Jane's case her school for dishonesty was the job. Add to that the passive acceptance of dishonesty in the home. The combination—and it occurs more often than you would believe possible—results in the inevitable corruption of the innocent.

One of the most startling cases we ever handled involved a young fellow I'll call Roger, the son of a minister in a large mission. Roger and his parents had recently moved to a comparatively small community where Roger's father had been assigned to open the town's first mission. It was rough going at first for the whole family, what with making ends meet and their friends a thousand miles away. To ease the family financial strain, Roger went job hunting. Although he was twenty-four, the only other work he had done, except to help his father, was in the Navy where he served a three-year hitch.

After several weeks of searching Roger finally landed a position with a wholesale drug and variety company. Roger's classification was stock card clerk and his principal duty was to check the inventory cards to see if the company had certain merchandise on hand and where it was located. This gave Roger the freedom of the entire warehouse where the goods were kept.

Roger's job was the first rung on the white collar ladder. His take-home pay was $172 a month or $40 a week. Out of this he paid out $81 a month for a secondhand Pontiac, $50 a month to his parents for room and board, and $40 a month for gas and oil. This left him one dollar a month for spending money. Roger was far from rich. Yet he was happy. Deprived of many of the things that most of us would call necessities, Roger looked upon the vast warehouse with its drugs and electric appliances and incidentals as Solomon's mine.

Roger began stealing. But the merchandise he took was not for himself, that is, not at first. He would pocket free samples like vitamins and medicines which he would give to the itinerant charges who passed through his father's mission. This soon developed into a routine and it didn't take long before he began taking other merchandise. Each day he would go home with his pockets loaded and eventually he began to feel that if they were only half full he had been cheated. The next step, of course, came easy.

Instead of handing out his largesse just to members of the mission, he would keep some items for himself and give the remainder to his family. His excuse at home was that the goods had been damaged or that they were free samples which had been given to him. Pretty soon he began swapping stolen merchandise with his fellow employees. In turn he would receive items like cameras and prescription drugs which were considered valuables and not accessible to Roger. Eventually Roger was acquiring more than he could actually use. So he started to hand out gifts to his neighbors, friends, his girl friend and her parents. In less than two months this son of a minister had advanced from the ranks of a clerk who took an occasional free sample for his father's mission to the plateau of the professional crook. The thrill of getting something for nothing had become a disease. Roger began stealing merchandise and selling it to fences who in turn would dispose of the goods to drugstore owners.

But as Roger began taking sizable amounts of merchandise he found his job of stock card clerk taking on new complications. Fearing that some of the stolen goods would be missed, he destroyed or falsified the figures on the stock cards. There was one factor, though, which was working in Roger's favor. His supervisor, a man of about sixty, was afraid to admit he couldn't control the young clerks who worked under him. The clerks in turn neither respected him nor feared him, and could, if they wanted, have walked out with a third of the warehouse.

Roger's undoing came when an honest store owner complained to the wholesale firm that other retail stores were selling the wholesale company's goods at a much lower price. It wasn't long before an investigation showed that Roger had become deeply involved. In a period of six months, Roger's thefts totaled more than $6,000. He had been averaging more than $1,000 a month.

"My father," Roger related, "told me that it's none of my business to discuss with the company what the other boys were doing and that the company should handle their own problems and that it wasn't for me to tell them anything other than what I, myself, personally took. My mother knew that I was stealing. She only told me last night that she knew the stuff I was bringing home wasn't given out for nothing by the company. *She is a little disturbed, but my father is used to these things and it doesn't seem to bother him!*"

The warping of community ethics typified by "Casey" Stengle and the indifference exemplified by Roger's parents and his supervisor and by Jane's fellow workers form the swamp in which white collar dishonesty is being spawned. It is a swamp without geographical limitations and can be found in large cities and crossroad villages, in polyglot communities and towns where the inhabitants' roots have grown generations deep in American soil. Indeed, take a map of the United States, close your eyes and point to any city or hamlet and you probably will have discovered an attic hiding the skeleton of a white collar thief.

According to the United States Fidelity and Guaranty Company, which has made two studies of 1,001 embezzlers, one pre-war and the other post-war, the white collar thief can be found in every one of the fifty states from Alabama to Wyoming, as well as Washington, D.C., the Canal Zone, and Puerto Rico. The insurance company adds, ". . . all types of business are represented; manufacturers, jobbers, wholesalers and retailers of every description, building and loan associations, social and beneficial societies, banks and governments."

The United States Fidelity and Guaranty Company goes on to break down the occupations of 845 men and 156 women in its post-war study. "Some," says the insurance company, "worked in large establishments, others were the sole employee of their employers. And they were in a position of every degree of importance, from handyman to heads of establishments." The following tables, taken from the post-war study, dramatically point up that no position is immune from the white collar thief.

In addition to occupational distribution, the current study includes the marital status of both men and women, their ages, length of service, period of embezzlement, salaries and total amounts embezzled. Of the men, two thirds were married, less than one third were single, about six per cent were divorced or separated, and a little more than one per cent were widowers. Their ages ranged from fifteen to seventy-five and length of service varied from less than one year to forty-eight years. Some men embezzled only once, while one man worked at it for seventeen years. The total amount the 845 men stole including 150 blue collar workers came to $3,544,222.89.

From these figures and case histories, the insurance company was able to etch this composite picture of the average male embezzler. He's thirty-five, married, has one or two children. He lives in a respectable neighborhood and is probably buying his own home. He drives a low or medium priced car and his yearly income is in the top forty per cent of the nation's personal income distribution. He's been employed by his firm for three years and he's been stealing for eight months. On the average his total take exceeds his annual salary by twenty per cent.

Occupational Distribution

MEN

Position	Number	Percentage
Executives, Managerial & Professional	261	37.6
Sales	190	27.4
Clerical	142	20.4
Government	52	7.5
Labor Officials	50	7.1
Total	695 [1]	100

WOMEN

Position	Number	Percentage
Executive, Managerial & Professional	26	17.2
Sales	37	24.5
Clerical	73	48.3
Government	7	4.7
Labor Officials	8	5.3
Total	151 [2]	100

[1] This excludes 150 blue collar workers.
[2] Excluded are five blue collar workers.

In sketching the portrait of the average female embezzler, the insurance company runs into difficulty as the result of varied marital status, home conditions and motives. Of the

156 women studied, most were or had been married. The average female embezzler is comparatively young, a little over thirty-one. Her average yearly income is in the bottom third of the nation's personal income. She has worked for her current employer less than two and a half years, and has been embezzling for six and a half months. She has been stealing at a rate equal to her annual salary.

The insurance company takes special note of the fact that there were four times as many women found in the post-war study as were reported in the pre-war period. And it draws this conclusion: "The increase in the number of women appears to reflect the more wide-spread employment of women in the years of World War II and immediately thereafter and their increased importance in positions of trust." To put it another way, given the opportunity, women are just as dishonest as men.

A general comparison of the pre-war, depression times embezzler and his post-war counterpart proves interesting not so much because of the similarities, but the differences. The post-war embezzler is younger, earns much more money, is less often married, and has fewer dependents than the depression times embezzler. His character and past record are less good. He lives faster and less normally. The percentage of absconders is higher and those whom remorse led to suicide are fewer. In addition, liquor, gambling and domestic troubles played greater roles as causes of embezzlement and no less than eighteen per cent stole throughout the whole term of their employment or at the first opportunity.

The study goes on to conclude that "When the first group operated, the nation was in the throes of a depression, with mass unemployment; hence embezzlers were mostly employees of long service, with records fully known to their employers. Jobs were scarce and employees had no reason to take their service lightly. Furthermore, those were sober times, with gambling and dissipation at a minimum, and the handling of money and commodities was carefully supervised. All of this militated against easy defalcation."

The post-war boom period, however, with its business expansion and decentralization made it easier for the dishonest employee to operate. The great demand for white collar workers resulted in lax selection of employees. At the same time, management didn't have to be as careful when it came to watching its profits and losses. It thought it could afford to lose more and thus its controls or supervision of its employees became even more inadequate.

I would include another factor and that is the emotional tensions of the last two decades. From 1939 to 1949 alone an estimated fifty million people moved from one place to another. Add to the rootlessness of the last twenty years, the insecurities of a decade of ricocheting boom and recession plus increasing world tensions. It is not surprising that today's white collar worker is frequently unstable and that his concept of right and wrong is somewhat blurred.

For the future, I would predict that whether we find ourselves in a period of prosperity or depression, white collar dishonesty—indeed dishonesty in general—will continue to flourish. The question arises what, if anything, can be done to minimize white collar crime, which has spread from an occasional fester to a dangerous wound that could prove fatal. But before suggesting any cure it is necessary to examine how the white collar thief operates, his methods and motivations. Through an understanding of the forces that drive him, as well as how he functions, it may be possible to detect the first symptoms of the disease, and perhaps, in many instances even prevent the original infection.

The typical white collar thief leads two lives. On the surface he appears to blend with the crowd. Generally friendly, he would seem to be the first person you would trust and the last you would suspect of wrongdoing. Above average in intelligence, he usually is the hardest worker in the establishment. Once involved in fraud, he seldom suggests new methods of business operation for fear that a radical change in procedure would result in his exposure. Except in rare instances, his home life is exemplary. He is, in the phrase of the mid-twentieth century, the ideal organization man, or so he seems.

But there is another world which the white collar thief

inhabits. Fraught with darkness, secrecy and fear, it is a world in constant turmoil. It is the world of the white collar thief's conscience. In most cases his greatest fear is exposure and the ridicule and loss of status that would invariably follow. Once he has begun his peculations, he will continually be on his guard. Often he is the first employee in the office and the last to leave. He may even eat his lunch at his desk. In short his fate is a constant damnation, for he is inexorably tied to the scene of his crime.

Sometimes the tension is so great that the relief of being caught far outweighs the fear of exposure. One woman who had been stealing for several years developed a pronounced facial tic because she felt that she was being watched. But she had become so deeply enmeshed in her thievery that she couldn't stop. When she was eventually confronted with her acts of dishonesty, she wept. Her tears were those of joy.

This dramatic internal struggle is typified by the case of a man whom we shall call Harold who resided in a small Midwestern community. As soon as he graduated from high school, Harold became a clerk in one of the community's largest banks. By 1920, three years after he had started with the bank, Harold was promoted to teller and his salary was raised to $20 a week.

Everybody respected Harold. A bit too proper perhaps, but a hard worker, Harold was the exemplary citizen. He joined all the right organizations, the Rotary Club, the Masons, the Chamber of Commerce. Although he could hardly afford it, Harold even found a way of giving some of his salary to charity. Seven years after he became a teller, Harold married. It was at that point that Harold discovered he couldn't make ends meet, even though he had been rewarded with an $8 a week raise for ten years of hard and efficient labor. Harold, if he had wanted, could have asked for more money. And he probably would have got it, but somehow Harold couldn't bring himself to share his problem with his employer. Instead, he began to embezzle.

During the next fourteen years Harold stole $7,541. The largest amount he ever took at one time was no more than

$100. He managed to hide his thefts of cash deposits by juggling the individual ledger cards so that the books always balanced. Although there were 150 bank examinations during the period, Harold's thievery went undetected.

From 1941 until the summer of 1952, when Harold's defalcations were discovered, the hard-working bank teller had embezzled nothing. He was making a little over $36 a week and he felt that he and his family could afford to live on it.

Harold was caught when the bank missed several old ledger cards which Harold had hidden and apparently forgotten about. When he was questioned about the missing cards, Harold readily admitted his crime. But his employer, who was more strait-laced than Harold, not only fired him but reported the thefts to the authorities. Harold, who pleaded guilty and was out on bond, found himself unable to obtain another job. The man who for the last twenty-five years had carried within him the terrible secret of his crime would tell the story of his wrongdoing to each prospective employer.

Harold's day of reckoning came when he appeared in court for sentencing. Harold expected the worst. But instead the judge reviewed Harold's case and decided not to sentence him. Instead his Honor said: "The bank ought to be indicted here. I have no power over these men who were members of the board of directors of this bank, but if I had I would sentence them to read Dickens' *Christmas Carol* every Christmas and to think of this defendant." Harold, stunned at first, listened to the judge in silence. Then he began to cry. For the first time in twenty-five years Harold was free.

Unlike the Harolds, there is a group of white collar thieves who act almost as though they courted exposure. Boastful and immature, they seek attention as assiduously as others insist upon anonymity. Many are young, in their late teens or early twenties. They feel that by playing the role of the big shot who has just pulled a fast one they will gain the respect and admiration of their friends and elders. Some eventually mature and find healthier ways of winning the admiration that all of us covet. Others, however, remain the perpetual adolescent. Continually seeking adulation, they live spectacularly. Always in the public eye, they are the Walter Mittys, eternally searching for glory.

Such a one was Harry R. Dash, a forty-seven-year-old Brooklyn insurance broker whose collection of baubles included a yacht, a Cadillac sedan and plaques from testimonial dinners. Dash made himself as conspicuous as a suit woven out of thousand-dollar bills.

Living well, however, wasn't sufficient for Dash. After all thousands of people owned Cadillacs. But how many could boast a siren, a flashing red light and the emblem of an honorary New York deputy fire commissioner? And Dash managed to do just that. Dash, though, wasn't satisfied with speeding to big fires, passing through police lines, and sporting his official white rubber boots and coat. His next step was to get himself a major's commission in the Marine Corps Reserve. Assistant District Attorney Jerome Kidder later described Dash as "something of a mystery man." For it turned out that the Brooklyn insurance broker had never served with the Marines.

When Dash was finally arrested he had become an executive director of the Marine Corps War Memorial Foundation, a group which was raising funds for the erection of the monument to the Marine Corps heroes of Iwo Jima. At the time Dash was caught the foundation had collected $150,000, most of it from former servicemen. Of that amount, Dash himself had pocketed $41,000 by simply signing foundation checks for his own needs. Dash said he considered the money as a "loan" and that he was using it for other business purposes. In sentencing Dash to two-to-five years in prison, General Sessions Judge Saul S. Street consigned him to "the category of the meanest thief," adding that "the house of fraud and deceit finally toppled on your head."

Although there are many personality variations among white collar thieves, the everyday performances of Harold and his extreme opposite, Harry Dash, typify in the broadest sense the two kinds of people who are responsible for much white collar crime. Their acts of dishonesty were committed without conspirators, a standard form of behavior among white collar thieves. However, in recent years the increasing complexity of business operations plus an increase in the theft of merchandise and supplies has resulted in a growing amount of collusion. This is particularly true among the lower echelons where white collar crime is rarely an individual affair, but takes on the trappings of organized gang activity.

No case better illustrates this point than the activities of a supervisor of a large department store. The supervisor headed the store's rug department, whose sales volume came to $2,000,-000 a year. Working under him were sixteen rug and carpet installers. Although the installers were employed and paid by the store, they spent three fourths of their actual on-the-job time helping the supervisor carry out a fantastic scheme that cost the store directly and indirectly more than $1,000,000 over a five-year span. This is how the supervisor, whom I'll call Bob, and his workers operated a racket that almost rivaled the haul made by Miss Minnie Mangum, who embezzled almost $3,000,-000.

As supervisor, Bob was responsible for the assignments of his skilled mechanics. He would arrive at his office by 8:00 A.M. and by 9:30 all sixteen rug installers would have their day's work cut out for them. Bob would then depart, ostensibly to supervise the day's major installation job. Actually, he would head for home, a plush $30,000 house whose basement housed enough rug cutting, binding and sewing equipment to fill a small factory. Bob's working day had begun in earnest.

And for whom was this trusted twenty-year employee working? His own department store's chief competitors. A number of discount houses, which had sprouted after World War II, had gone into the rug and carpet business. They had asked Bob to recommend a good rug and carpet installer. He, of course, knew just the man for the job—Bob. He not only could supply the mechanics but had all the necessary equipment, which had been sold to him by his own firm during the war years, when there was a scarcity of skilled labor. Bob, who had helped his employer at the time, kept the equipment.

While the rug supervisor busied himself cutting and binding the carpets for the discount houses, his own mechanics installed them. Both the installers and Bob worked on company time, so that the department store was actually paying the wages for work their own employees performed for the store's own competitors. As business mounted with the discount houses, Bob found himself faced with a problem. His mechanics spent so much time installing rugs for the discount houses that they were unable to keep up with the orders placed at the department store. Angry customers began canceling their purchases because of the delays in installation. Bob was to turn this bottleneck into a bonanza.

As soon as an order had been canceled, Bob would call the irate customer, proffer his apologies, and then offer to install the rug over the weekend. The rest was easy. Bob already had a copy of the exact measurements of the room where the carpet or rug was to be laid. He also knew the kind of material the customer desired. Sometimes he would order it from the mill or discount house. But in most instances he would simply send one of his own mechanics to the department store's warehouse. The mechanic would put through an order for matting, an inexpensive item for which the supervisor paid. The mechanic would then remove the carpeting by wrapping the matting around it. Next he would bring the material to Bob, who would cut it and bind it, and then install it for the customer. Unwittingly, the store not only paid the installers' overtime but supplied free of charge the material Bob used for the store's former customers.

As a result of this scheme the carpet and rug installers were nearly trebling their salary. Starting with a base pay of $6,000 a year, they received an additional $3,000 each in overtime plus $5,000 to $6,000 apiece more from the supervisor's profits. Including his base pay of $9,000, Bob found himself netting as much as $32,000 a year, almost as much as the president of the store was earning. The yearly theft in merchandise cost the department store from $200,000 to $250,-000. And it took management five years before it even suspected that someone was cutting corners in the rug department. The supervisor had successfully forestalled any detailed questions from management by falsifying inventory records, overestimating yardages and manipulating prices. In addition he had claimed that operating costs were higher than similar operations because of the quality of the work performed by his department.

When management finally looked under its own rugs, it found that it had no other choice but to fire not only Bob, but all of its sixteen carpet installers, most of whom had had more than ten years' service with the company. Ironically, Bob's wife had been badgering him to quit and set up a carpet and rug installation business of his own. After all, she reasoned, he had a fully equipped workroom in the basement of their home, and what could be more convenient? Bob, though, had been with the department store for twenty-six years. And in four more years he could retire on a company pension. The man who had cost his firm some $1,000,000 had decided he would serve those four years so that he would be eligible for retirement pay. But what troubled Bob more than anything when he was fired was that the store took away his pension. (As you read on you will become aware of a startling fact. White collar thieves are rarely prosecuted. The reasons why will be spelled out later.)

White collar crime has mushroomed to the point where the dishonest employee often is physically incapable of carrying out his thefts by himself. In many instances he simply can't carry all the loot in his briefcase. Where once he concentrated on manageable items like cash, he is now taking everything in sight. With the help of his fellow workers one man employed by a wholesale grocery firm stole enough canned goods to feed his own family of three plus his mother and in-laws for more than three years. When he was caught he readily admitted he could just about enter his cellar; it was stacked with everything from peas to ham.

The gag that has now become a classic concerns the employee who approached the factory gate every night pushing a wheelbarrow filled with sand. Each night the guard filtered out all the sand but could find nothing amiss. At the end of the month the guard couldn't take it any more.

"Look," he told the employee, "I know you're stealing something. But for the life of me I can't figure it out. Before I go crazy please tell me what it is. I swear I won't turn you in."

The employee winked and replied, "Why, wheelbarrows, of course."

The problem of pilferage hits not only small- and medium-sized concerns but the giants as well, and sometimes involves collusion between white collar and blue collar workers. *Newsweek* reports that at the Ford Motor Company criminal rings of employees have been detected and smashed at least three times (the last in 1951). In one instance the "bucket brigade" walked off with roller bearings, ignition points, carburetor parts, distributors and crankshaft bearings in their lunch pails. In addition, truck drivers whom the gangs called "plutocrats," drove away with truckloads of parts. The stolen goods were unloaded in cities throughout the country, including Detroit, Chicago and New York. The F.B.I. eventually stepped in and stopped the biggest haul, "somewhere between $5,000,000 and $10,000,000."

A second reason for the increase in collusion is the general deterioration in the white collar worker's attitude toward white collar crime. In part, he reasons that since everybody else in the place is doing it, why shouldn't I? And then carries his reasoning one step further by adding: Think of how much easier it would be if all of us worked together. And that is frequently what happens. Often collusion is unspoken. Although two employees may be working in entirely separate operations, they often stumble on each other's wrongdoing. In order to protect themselves, they will, of course, say nothing that would cause their exposure.

Take the case of the control clerk who was troubled by his own petty thefts. After spending several sleepless nights, he finally approached his superior, the credit manager, and blurted out the details of his malpractices. Then, resigned to a jail sentence, he waited nervously for his superior's verdict.

The credit manager carefully closed the door for privacy and said calmly, "I'm not going to turn you in. Forget this conversation. And don't discuss it with anyone else. You see, this department just can't afford a scandal—I've been embezzling for years, myself. We're in this thing together."

I would estimate that as much as fifty per cent of the white collar crimes committed now involve overt collusion. This only increases an already dangerous situation. It is not just that so many people are doing it, but that they are doing it together.

Equally alarming is that management rarely has the slightest glimmering that it has a thief or even a gang of thieves on its hands. In fact, most white collar crimes are discovered, not as the result of an alert and overzealous employer or employee, but simply as the result of chance, such as an innocent question or a misplaced invoice or voucher, or a sudden intrusion.

This point was brought out by Herman W. Bevis, a partner in the worldwide accounting firm of Price, Waterhouse & Company. Bevis made a thorough study of one hundred cases of white collar fraud and came up with the following:

"It is interesting to review a recapitulation of the manner in which the frauds under discussion were brought to light. A little less than one third of these were uncovered by auditors (internal and external); this figure is undoubtedly too high to be representative, the distortion being brought about by the fact that an independent public accountant's files would be unduly weighted by the number in which auditing figured prominently. The routine operation of internal controls was responsible for detecting eleven defaulters. Management inquiries led to the discovery in sixteen cases, *and circumstances for which no one can claim particular credit—fortuitous events —led to discovery in the remaining thirty-six cases involving $3,400,000.*" [3] (Emphasis supplied.)

Although the number of cases studied by Price, Waterhouse is comparatively small, a startling fact emerges because it exists in the thousands of cases that occur in the surveys made by our engineering staff. Most of the white collar crime which is detected would never have been uncovered except for happenstance. Here are just two examples of how luck led to the

---

[3] The relatively poor performance of internal controls and the efforts of auditors to detect defalcations does not necessarily reflect on their technical competence. In too many instances controllers are provided neither with the funds nor staff to do the job they know needs to be done. And in the case of outside auditors, their primary responsibility is to attest that financial statements are fairly stated; if they discover fraud it is a by-product rather than an objective.

catching of dishonest employees. The first, related by Bevis, involves a rank-and-file employee and the second an executive.

A mechanic in a large department store started tapping the pneumatic tubes which led from the sales clerks to the cashiers. He would extract the cash and sales slips, stamp the slips, make change when needed and then pop the container into the pneumatic tubes, returning it to the sales clerk who originally sent it. He probably would have continued pocketing thousands of dollars except for one error. Unfortunately for him he once made the wrong change which the sales clerk sent back to a very puzzled cashier, who began asking questions. If the mechanic had been more accurate in arithmetic, his dishonesty would probably have gone undetected.

The other case is typical in that the dishonest employee involved was caught not by alert management or even a puzzled fellow worker. Fate in the guise of a newspaper photo and a brilliant, red fire engine resulted in the detection.

The chairman of the board and founder of an old, established company that sold musical instruments died. The general manager, who had been with the firm more than twenty-five years, was given the responsibility of running the firm. Capable and experienced, he appeared to be a perfect choice to carry on the old man's business. But as the years progressed business began to fall off. The founder's two sons, who owned substantial shares in the concern, decided to step in. The general manager felt that since the two sons had little experience in selling musical instruments, they would only be a nuisance. As far as the general manager was concerned profits were down because competition was keen and if the two sons would stay away business would eventually pick up. But the two sons were adamant and they called in my firm of management consultants to analyze the company's operation.

In the process of establishing a unit control of inventory, we discovered that the current records were missing. We called in the general manager who said that when he had instructed his staff to destroy all the old records, they had accidentally thrown away the records of the last three years. Although the general manager's story seemed questionable, other employees testified that what he had told us was true. It had happened and it had been an accident.

Several weeks passed before a bizarre turn of events broke the case. The local paper had appeared that day with its usual quota of international thievery. Tucked away in a back page was a photo which at first glance seemed to remove the gloom from the day's report. In the background was a large country home surrounded by a lush, green lawn. On the lawn stood a fire engine, a little obsolete perhaps, but apparently in good working order. The fire engine was crammed with neighborhood children and their parents.

But as I glanced more closely at the picture I noticed a familiar face grinning back at me. It was the general manager of the firm we were helping reorganize. He was sitting in the driver's seat, a fireman's hat placed jauntily on his head. The caption went on to explain that the fire engine belonged to the general manager who had acquired it as plaything for the youngsters in the area. He would take them on rides through the countryside, sirens screaming, bells clanging. The general manager, in a short space of time, had obviously become the most popular man in the county.

As I looked at the photo, one question kept disturbing this idyllic scene. How, I wondered, did the general manager acquire the fire engine?

I began checking around and came up with an interesting bit of information. Like Nero, the firemen stationed nearest the general manager's home would spend their spare time fiddling, providing, of course, nothing was burning. In fact, this particular fire house not only had the best band in the neighborhood, but the finest musical instruments. The fire fighters had acquired them in a barter deal with the general manager. In return for cornets, clarinets, trumpets, bugles and drums, he had been presented with this somewhat obsolete fire engine. There was only one sour note in the trade. The general manager, I eventually learned, had stolen the musical instruments from his own firm.

When confronted with this information, he went on to confess numerous other peculations which eventually totaled more than $100,000. His most lucrative scheme was to make out vouchers which listed payments to musicians for instruments that they were either trading in or selling back to the firm. The catch was that in many cases the musicians were figments of the general manager's imagination. He was simply stealing the money from the firm and making out false vouchers.

Ironically, the general manager's exposure turned out to be the luckiest thing that could have happened to him. Fired from his job, he turned to his brother, a wealthy retired executive, who lent him enough money to set up a roadside ice cream stand. The former general manager did so well that within two years he owned a chain of ice cream bars and was earning more money honestly than he could have possibly earned or stolen from the company that had once employed him. And what's more he was working only half as hard. He also had peace of mind as far as his own business was concerned. Knowing all the gimmicks, he was completely protected against any of his own employees turning dishonest and stealing sizable amounts of his own profits.

The fact that luck and chance are responsible for the detection of most white collar thieves points up an amazing paradox. On the one hand, management spends a great deal of time and effort seeing that its stockholders receive a decent return on their investments. This is done by continually pushing sales with the hope of harvesting handsome profits. Indeed, management is so often concerned about sales and profits that it spends too little time trying to minimize its own internal losses. Yet these internal losses can be so disastrous as to shove a firm into the red or over the brink into bankruptcy. This is especially true whenever there is a squeeze on profits.

Supermarkets, for example, will suffer an estimated one hundred million dollars' loss due to employee malpractices in 1960. This loss will cancel every penny of profits that would result from five billion dollars' worth of sales—ten per cent of the grocery industry's entire projected volume for the year.

Or examine, for the moment, the problem as it affects department stores. According to the National Retail Merchants Association, stores doing between twenty and fifty million dollars a year business in 1957, made a 1.85 per cent profit on sales. Shortages averaged 1.2 per cent of sales. Profits for stores doing more than fifty million dollars a year business came to 2.55 per cent of sales. Yet shortages averaged 1.4 per cent of sales.

Management will go to great lengths to increase sales volume, feeling that for every increase in sales, a significant increase in profit can be expected. But often a comparable increase in profit can be realized at relatively little cost to management and with only a fraction of the headaches that accompany every effort to increase sales volume. Using the most recent N.R.M.A. figures, *a reduction of a half of a percentage point in shortage figures related to sales volume* can have the same effect on profits as a:

$1,428,570 increase in sales for a $10 million store
$5,454,540 increase in sales for a $20 million store
$6,250,000 increase in sales for a $50 million store
$7,258,085 increase in sales for a $75 million store.

Thus, when management is able to reduce shortage figures by another half of one per cent, their profits increase by approximately what might be expected from opening up a suburban outlet with the above sales volume, without the merchandising, advertising, employment and overhead involved. Yet I have found one concern after another planning to start more stores or factories in order to increase their sales and profits, while they could earn an equal amount of profit by simply cutting out internal losses and thefts.

But before attempting to cut the heart out of white collar crime, it is necessary to examine what makes that heart tick. Although we now have a general picture of what the white collar thief is like, we need to know his motivations and needs. Some may shock or amuse you.

Chapter 3

The Non-Sharable Problem

THE WHITE collar thief constantly fears exposure and the obvious social censure that would follow. Yet the white collar thief steals. Indeed once he has begun he frequently will repeat his thefts until he is caught or absconds. Why?

Several sociologists have tried to find the answer to that question. Perhaps the most incisive theory offered so far is the one suggested by Dr. Donald R. Cressey in his book *Other People's Money* (The Free Press, 1953). Dr. Cressey is a professor at University of California at Los Angeles where he teaches criminology. Leaving behind the airy atmosphere of the academic white tower, but not its strict methodology, Dr. Cressey went behind the walls of three prisons, the Illinois State Penitentiary at Joliet, the United States Penitentiary at Terre Haute, Indiana, and the California Institution for Men at Chino. He interviewed frequently and at length more than 130 inmates, all of whom had violated positions of trust. And he came up with this theory of what conditions must be present when trust is violated by the white collar thief.

"Trusted persons," writes Dr. Cressey, "become trust violators when they conceive of themselves as having a financial problem which is non-sharable, are aware that this problem can be secretly resolved by violation of the position of financial trust, and are able to apply to their own conduct in that situation verbalizations which enable them to adjust their con-

ceptions of themselves as trusted persons with their concep-
tions of themselves as users of the entrusted funds or property."

Stripped of its academic complexities, Dr. Cressey's theory
can be broken down into three parts. (1) The embezzler has
an unusual economic need, and he may be ashamed to ask
anyone to help solve it. Thus, his problem is non-sharable for
he feels that if others know about it he will look like a fool
or a scoundrel. (2) The embezzler must have the opportunity
and technical knowhow to commit his fraudulent act. Generally the white collar thief has been aware that he could
commit a dishonest act, but hasn't done so because either his
problem did not exist or it was not sufficiently pressing. Once,
however, he finds it overwhelming then he sees his opportunity
and knows a way to use it. (3) The embezzler still must overcome the final hurdle, his conscience. He does this by ration-
alizing, by saying to himself for example that he is only
borrowing the money and will return it. According to Dr.
Cressey all three factors must be operating for a violation of
trust to occur.

Using Dr. Cressey's theory as a guide, I would like to probe
further into what makes a man or woman whose entire upbringing emphasized respect for the law violate that law and
risk the shame that would occur if the violation were exposed.
How does an individual get himself in such an awkward position that this financial problem becomes all encompassing? At
first glance the answer seems obvious. Examples that quickly
come to mind include the lawyer who has lost his client's
money while gambling, the married man who is keeping another woman, the employee who finds his accounts short because of an honest error and feels that he must manipulate
funds to hide the shortage, the businessman who has made a
bad investment with someone else's money.

There are, however, subtler causes for pressing financial
need, the kind the sociologist and criminologist do not investigate. They are, indeed, the subject of novels and short
stories. Here are three examples from my own files. They are
the kind of stories that lie behind the police blotters and
bonding company statistics. And they are the basis for the

generalization that acute financial need could happen to any of us if fate had treated us differently. Let us begin with loneliness.

Her name was Adelaide. She was twenty-eight and plain. Her hair was a mousy brown and her eyes were too close together. Her figure was average. But her clothes were dull and whatever promise she held had been muted. Adelaide lived at home with her mother, her father having died some years before. Her two younger sisters and brother had married.

During the day she worked in a large store, where she had started as a clerk at the age of seventeen when she graduated from high school. She worked hard and well and now, eleven years later, she could boast that she was the general manager of the technical book department and earned a salary of $75 a week. But she was too much alone for the world to hear of her accomplishment.

Her nights and weekends seemed to drop from the calendar of her life like dead leaves from a dying tree. She truly lived only when she slept. For then she could dream. And under the spotlight of her sleep she would awake as a beautiful bejeweled queen, her court filled with the lovers who in real life never appeared.

So it passed, the days and the nights and her heart ached. The loneliness was suffocating.

Then one day a co-worker stopped to chat about her vacation in Bermuda. She had had a lovely time, swimming, picnicking, dancing. Her only chaperone, the moon looking over her shoulder. The manager in charge of the technical book department smiled a private smile and wondered if she, too, could go to this island of romance. She acquired several travel folders that spoke of sand that was as white as pearls and stars that glittered like diamonds. The picture showed strong men with gleaming teeth riding the surf, ordering the best champagne and strolling in a golden sunset.

Adelaide knew that she would visit this enchanted isle. She decided it was her only chance. Because of her seniority she would have the time, a three-week vacation which was due in two months. But a trip to Bermuda can be expensive. Her co-worker told her that she would need evening dresses as well as several chic costumes for the daytime. And then there was the cost of staying at a good hotel, and the luggage, and the plane fare. Since Adelaide had been supporting her mother as well as herself, she simply didn't have enough money. And then the opportunity, which had always existed, presented itself.

Adelaide worked in the basement which housed her own technical book department, the mail order department and the main cashier's desk. Unlike the busy first floor where the general books were sold, the basement had compartively little traffic. Adelaide thought she could do what she wanted without fear of being observed. A good part of her department's business was with certain "sensitive" government agencies. Unlike other government agencies which insisted that all their purchases be billed to them, these organizations would pay for their merchandise in cash. This way they could be assured that no permanent record was kept of what their employees were reading and studying.

Adelaide's first theft involved $18 in cash which one of the government agencies had left in payment for a number of volumes. After the purchaser left, Adelaide rang up a $2 figure on the cash register, deposited $2 and kept the rest of the money. As the weeks passed Adelaide repeated the process several times, taking over $8,000, enough to get her to Bermuda and back several times over. She planned to return it just as soon as she got the chance.

Finally vacation time arrived and Adelaide left for Bermuda. She had a suitable wardrobe and her fare was first class. She stayed there three weeks but had a miserable time. Although Bermuda proved to be enchanting, Adelaide was not. Sharing the day's community activities, Adelaide found herself alone as soon as the moon came out. It was, to say the least, disappointing.

When Adelaide returned home, she was struck by a disturbing thought, one that had lain dormant during her vacation. Now it burst through the protective skein of her subconscious, a terrifying fear that while she was absent the store might have discovered her thefts. Quickly she called her friends at the

store. All of them asked her about Bermuda. No one had mentioned anything unusual like a shortage. After the third phone
call, she regained her self-assurance.

When she began the new working year the next day, a
Monday, Adelaide was determined to return the money. But
as time passed she felt that somehow she had been cheated
on her Bermuda trip and that somebody would have to pay for
it. It turned out to be her employer.

For the next six months Adelaide never took a penny. Then
one day she found herself with a new assistant, a young man
who was earning some extra cash while studying international
law and diplomacy. His ambition was to enter the State Department and become a man of importance, indeed internation-
ally famous. Although his father was a leading surgeon, he gave
his son an allowance sufficient for just his minimal needs. The
boy, whom I'll call Nicholas, was a little over nineteen and
five hundred miles from home. His first time away from his
parents and having few friends, he was soon unbearably lonely.
So lonely in fact that he found himself whiling away an occasional lunch or afternoon Coke break with Adelaide. Adelaide, in turn, began coming to work in some of those chic
outfits she had purchased for her abortive journey to Bermuda.
And as Nicholas' interest seemed to increase, Adelaide bloomed
with a new personality, fresh, gay, even at times coquettish.

Adelaide had fallen in love. Nicholas responded and they
began going out together at night. Realizing that his allowance
and earnings were small, she would insist upon a dutch treat,
slipping her share under the table. As their nightly meetings
became more frequent, Adelaide found herself paying the
whole bill. She raised the money the only way she felt she
could, by stealing from the store. As it turned out the store
unwittingly had gone into the business of romance. A person
in love has few secrets and soon Adelaide was confiding in
Nicholas. She would sweeten her admissions by saying that
what she was doing was normal practice. Besides, she said, the
company could afford it. Nicholas accepted both her explanations and money.

Adelaide was now taking as much as $600 a week, happily

ringing up no sales and pocketing the money. The couple soon became familiar figures at the plush restaurants and nightspots. They were known by all the head waiters and were eagerly catered to. They began going to the race tracks and spent as much as $100 a week just on tips and cab fares. To keep up appearances during their nightly outings, they equipped themselves with expensive wardrobes. Adelaide's closets began to bulge. She had bought $3,000 worth of clothes.

A year and a half had passed since Adelaide and Nicholas had begun their love idyll when management, unaware that it was being two-timed, called on us for help. The store decided to open several new branches and felt that it needed more extensive controls. There was also a minor problem concerning the location of certain books. They were supposed to be in stock but they couldn't be found. It didn't take long for two of our staff engineers to discover what Adelaide and her boyfriend were up to.

But before questioning them, we felt there was one mystery that had to be solved. The main cashier, a woman in her late fifties, had been with the store for more than twenty-five years. Although she worked within a cage, she was located no more than twenty feet from where Adelaide had her own cash register. We felt that, with her experience, the main cashier should have had some knowledge of what was taking place. Yet she had never said a word to management, or anyone else. We decided to check her background and this was what we learned.

Some ten years previously she and her husband had bought a new home. But when he became afflicted with a permanent illness, the couple found they were unable to keep up payments on the house. At the same time they were supporting their daughter and her two children, their son-in-law having died in the service.

An investigation of the cashier's operations turned up the following. She sold gift certificates for cash and pocketed the money. The certificates proved a phenomenal success and management was very pleased. They would frequently compliment the main cashier who had pushed the idea from the first.

She too was very happy. For unknown to management the gift certificate operation had made her a silent partner in the firm. Her profit over a ten-year period—$50,000.

The cashier, of course, was aware of Adelaide's peculations. But, she reasoned, if she questioned the operations of the technical book department, a probe would follow and her own thefts would be uncovered.

When Adelaide and Nicholas were confronted with the evidence of their own thefts they readily admitted their guilt. Together they had stolen nearly $40,000 within a year and a half. Three days after the couple was fired, Nicholas in a fit of despondency, went on a drinking spree. In the early morning he drove at sixty miles an hour through the city streets. His heart heavy and his head light, he didn't much care where he was going. As he sped though a darkened street, Nicholas was blind to the figure that stepped from the curb. His brakes screeching, he finally stopped, but five seconds too late. Nicholas had killed a pedestrian. He now faced charges of manslaughter as well as embezzlement. Before he had reached his twenty-first birthday, Nicholas had irreparably shattered his life. Ironically, the car that he was driving and the liquor that he had drunk had been paid for with the money he and Adelaide had stolen from the store.

On the surface loneliness would seem improbable as a cause for the commission of a criminal act. Yet Adelaide as well as Nicholas became white collar thieves because of circumstances that were beyond the control of others as well as themselves.

The point that needs to be stressed here and one that is vital in the understanding of white collar crime is that the complete spectrum of human failing or tragedy can serve as the cause of white collar crime. Indeed, if the need is great enough and non-sharable and the opportunity is present, almost all of us would be able to rationalize the dishonest act.

To put it another way, it is questionable whether a complete listing of motivations could ever be made. Virgil W. Peterson, writing in the *Journal of Criminal Law and Criminology* on "Why Honest People Steal," lists five main causes for embezzlement: gambling, extravagant living standards, unusual family expense, undesirable associates and inadequate income. However, he adds, "Many other factors also contribute to embezzlement. Surety companies have attributed employee thefts to such factors as financial pressure due to losses in other business activities, a past criminal history, mental irresponsibility, low morals, improvident investments and revenge." Although Mr. Peterson could surely add numerous other factors, instances of the ones presented would prove infinite. For example, here are two cases of unusual family expense, both of which are perhaps unique because of the family situations or personalities involved.

The first case concerns a woman whom I shall call Dorothy and her husband, Joe. Although they had been married for more than ten years, Dorothy was the chief breadwinner. Over the past five years Joe had averaged no more than ten weeks' work per year. Joe couldn't hold a job because he was too lethargic. Joe's problem? He ate too much because he had glandular trouble. Joe was so overweight that he completely lacked the stamina to do much more than sleep.

For seven years Dorothy faithfully worked as the manager of a specialty store. Not once during that time had she asked for a raise, although she certainly had the right to do so since she was a hard and efficient worker. The impression that Dorothy left with her fellow workers and management was that she really didn't need the money, or the job for that matter. Her husband, she said, was a successful salesman and had an excellent income. "Joe keeps after me to quit this job," she would go on. "But I don't know what I would do at home. I think it would drive me crazy. There're only the two of us."

Then Dorothy became ill and had to spend several weeks away from the office. During her absence, management held its semi-annual inventory and discovered sizable discrepancies in the accounts. When Dorothy returned she was confronted with the shortages. Tearfully she admitted stealing nearly $35,000 during the seven years she had served as store manager. "I just needed this job," she said. "Not only couldn't my husband hold a job, but he had such a ravenous appetite that my salary was not enough to feed him."

The cause of Dorothy's illness? The fear that some day she would be caught plus the strain of having to support her overweight husband resulted in a serious loss of her own appetite. She had become ill as the result of undernourishment.

The next case, like Dorothy's, concerns unusual family expense. Although the basic factors are similar—in each case the wife, who is the main breadwinner, steals to maintain the family unit—the personalities and individual motivations are markedly different.

Ruth came from a typically small town where secrets were few and every neighbor was his brother's keeper. Ruth herself was the youngest of three sisters. Pretty, gay, alert, she brought joy and pride to her parents and family. Shortly after her twentieth birthday, she asked her parents for permission to move to a large, near-by city where she could attend nursing school. Her parents, though saddened at her leaving home, readily agreed. During all the years that Ruth had lived in this small town, the pages of her life were open and unblemished. Her parents had no fear that Ruth would get into trouble. Besides, Ruth's older sister, who had married, already was living in the same city. So suitcase in hand, Ruth left home with her parents' blessings.

Her first few months at school were hard and demanding. So much so that she had no time for anything else. Without waiting to graduate, Ruth quit school before becoming a registered nurse and took a job in a doctor's office. She remained there for seven months, learning through experience what she would never have been taught in class. Then one of her former classmates got her another job at a small, private hospital. Her social life became a kaleidoscope of young doctors and interns. Then something happened to Ruth which tragically changed her way of life. She became pregnant.

It shouldn't have happened. The man who was responsible was a young doctor. Ruth was a nurse. Yet with all their knowledge, someone was careless. Since Ruth's lover was already married, she decided to have an abortion. A short time later another doctor called Ruth. He asked her to help him with a case like hers. It wasn't long before she found herself assisting in all his illegal operations. In fact, they had established a brisk and successful trade, which lasted about eight years. During that time Ruth married and divorced twice. Somehow the men she picked always turned out to be tramps.

Then one of the women she helped operate on died and a scandal threatened, although in this case neither the doctor who performed the abortion nor Ruth herself was directly responsible for the death. To protect the people involved Ruth agreed to plead guilty to the charge of performing an illegal operation. The physician's counsel promised her that she would receive only a suspended sentence. He claimed that the mayor's right-hand man and the physician were close friends and that Ruth would be protected. The judge, though, had a different viewpoint and Ruth was sentenced to from one to four years. After serving thirteen months, she was paroled for another two years and four months.

When Ruth was released she was close to thirty. Her life had become a living nightmare. Although she had been promised by the authorities that no one at the jail would know why she had been imprisoned, it became common knowledge even before she had arrived.

Now that Ruth was free again, she made a firm resolution to avoid trouble. But a curse seemed to hang over her. Again she married. This time to a bartender. When he worked, his take-home pay was $75 a week. But this wasn't too frequent. Instead, he spent his time gambling and running after other women. Ruth, though, was determined to make her marriage a success. She had reached the point of desperation where, no matter how weak the promise, she would keep the faith.

Through her older sister, Ruth obtained a job as a clerk in the jewelry department of a large department store, which was unaware of her prison record. Ruth's older sister, who headed the children's wear department, felt that she could insure that no harm would befall her young sister. What's more she was in a position to supply Ruth with clothes for her young son by a previous marriage.

The store called on us for help because current inventory figures indicated shortages in several departments, including children's wear. Although we soon became aware that the younger woman was receiving merchandise from her elder sister, no one suspected that Ruth had done anything dishonest.

To learn more about her older sister's operations, we decided to talk to Ruth. According to the records before us, she had been working at the store for about seven months. Management had consented to Ruth's two weeks' leave of absence without pay because she had requested it during the slow season. The day she returned from her vacation she was called into the president's office for questioning. As far as we were concerned it would be routine. Indeed, her appearance, her neatly bobbed black hair, her bright print dress and relaxed smile gave no hint of the disorder of her day-to-day existence. Ruth herself was completely unaware as to why she had been called into the office. We passed the usual pleasantries. No sooner did we ask Ruth her name and address, innocuous, routine questions, than her manner changed. She suddenly drew back, her eyes glistening with anger, her voice hard and indignant.

Somewhat taken aback, we told Ruth that she could leave if she wished, that there was no reason for her to become angry. No one had suspected her of wrongdoing. My only concern was possible irregularities involving favoritism in her sister's department.

"I thought you people were going to leave me alone," Ruth snapped. It was apparent the woman before me was in some difficulty. Her jaunty appearance when she first entered the office had been a veneer. I began questioning her further and the threads of her life and fears unrolled before me. She concluded by telling me that her present husband, accompanied by another woman, had gone to Las Vegas two weeks ago to gamble and that he had needed money to come home, and that she had sent it to him. For the last seven months, she said, she had taken over $5,000 in cash and jewelry which she either gave to her husband or used to support her family. A further investigation showed that her older sister had done nothing dishonest, except to give Ruth a few cut-rate bargains on clothes.

As Ruth ended her story, I posed one last question. I guess I asked it more out of curiosity then anything else. With her husband away, I had wondered why Ruth took a two-week leave of absence.

Ruth paused, apparently struggling over how to answer me. Finally she blurted, "I performed two abortions." Then after a moment's hesitation, she brightened and added proudly, "The mayor's assistant (the man who had recommended her as an abortionist) says I do the best abortions in town. I got $700 for them."

The irony was both apparent and tragic. The only thing at which Ruth could now succeed, indeed for which she was well paid, appreciated, and of which she was proud, was her ability to extinguish the seed of life.

Although the aims of Dorothy and Ruth were almost identical, the personality needs of each and the individual motivations that caused them to commit similar acts of dishonesty are obviously different. And what is true in both cases can be found in white collar crime in general. Indeed, the cases that you have read and will continue to read document the fact that white collar crimes are seldom committed as the result of identical motivations.

While the motivations of the white collar thief are different, the opportunities for dishonesty repeat themselves over and over again. In the Price, Waterhouse study of one hundred cases, Bevis notes that the shortages rested in 140 different account classifications at the time of discovery. He makes the following breakdowns: "Sixty-six of these were balance sheet items, exactly the same number had been passed through to profit and loss; 5 involved memorandum accounts such as employee savings bond contributions; and 3 involved employee funds not on company books. It might be added that in 13 different cases the shortage had been cleared through an intermediate account en route to its final resting place." (An intermediate account involves items like inventory or cash deposits which can easily be verified by an auditor.)

Although the opportunities are numerous and repetitive, the techniques used by the white collar thief are various and at times ingenious. Bevis himself points out, "One of the most impressive and frightening aspects of the modern defaulter's technique is the facility and extent to which documents are falsified and books and other records are altered and manipulated. In the one hundred cases under discussion, it is estimated that more than one hundred different types of documents and records were manipulated."

Bevis adds these somewhat dramatic words, "An auditor must conclude, after he examines the documents which have been falsified by defaulters in a wide variety of cases, that the modern embezzler may be assumed to be sufficiently clever to fabricate the documents which the auditor expects to see. Whenever the transaction requires an appearance of legitimacy, he will forge vendors' invoices, receiving reports, correspondence, title policies, mortgages, physical inventory sheets, and so on. If approvals on the documents are required, he will supply them. (Incidentally, he will, and has, forged the customer's name to the auditor's account receivable confirmation if he can either intercept the request or persuade the customer to hand it over to him.)" [1]

While probably all employees no matter what their position can find the opportunity to steal, those who will do the most damage usually have attained the supervisory or executive status. The reasons are twofold. For one their opportunity is greater because they are least suspect. To reach an executive position an employee will often rise through the ranks. He will have served his firm for many years and consequently will be viewed with greater respect and trust. At the same time an upper echelon employee will be in the position to handle larger funds or quantities of merchandise with more opportunity to manipulate them.

This point was emphasized in a five-year study of 2,651 claims made by the Liberty Mutual Insurance Company. Sales personnel, for example, were responsible for 1,289 thefts or

---

[1] For example, an auditor sends a form letter to a bank to see whether the client has made a deposit claimed on the client's books. An embezzler can forge such figures to hide his thefts. He can then obtain the auditor's confirmation and alter the bank's answer.

forty-nine per cent of the claims. The total amount stolen by the salesmen came to $271,628 or nearly twenty per cent of the total loss of $1,374,719. Contrast these figures with thefts perpetrated by nine treasurers, one corporate secretary, three firm presidents and 276 department and branch managers. The total amount stolen adds up to $484,419. In other words ten per cent of those listed in the study stole nearly twice as much as about fifty per cent of those who committed dishonest acts. A further breakdown shows that while the average take of the 276 managers totaled $1,171, the average theft of the three presidents came to $40,883.

The study concludes: "As might be expected, the most severe losses are those created by employees in the positions of greatest trust and responsibility, such as paymasters and corporate officials." To put it another way, any white collar employee is in the position to bite the hand that feeds him. The difference is that while the ordinary worker may nibble on a finger or two, the executive invariably swallows the arm and sometimes the whole corporate body.

Although the opportunity to steal is almost always present, it does not follow that all white collar employees will eventually turn dishonest, if they haven't already. Besides a non-sharable problem and the opportunity to steal, the white collar thief must overcome the final barrier, his conscience. He must justify to himself that his dishonest act is not really dishonest, especially because of the circumstances that he feels "forced" him to steal. Indeed, in some instances the white collar thief is not even aware that he or she has committed a dishonest act. In one case a dishonest employee was confronted with the evidence that she had stolen more than $27,000 from the accounts receivable department. Her first reaction was: "Is this going to cost me my job?"

Whatever the rationalizations used by the white collar thief they are always chosen prior to the theft. The most common justification used by the dishonest employee is that he is only "borrowing" his employer's funds to tide him over. Usually he never repays the sum he takes. One exception, though, is this case related by *Fortune* magazine. A white collar employee in New York carefully calculated that he needed and deserved an income of $4,500 to live decently. He methodically proceeded to "borrow" the difference between that sum and his actual salary of $2,500. As his salary increased over the years, he reduced his thefts proportionately. The day his firm started paying him $4,500 he stopped stealing. His salary continued to climb and he began returning the difference between what he was making and the figure of $4,500. When he was caught, he had paid back all but $3,000 of the $25,000 he had stolen.

The rationalization that the boss or firm "owes it to me" has several variations and is used almost as often as the excuse "I'm only borrowing this, but will repay it." Some white collar employees feel that they must keep up appearances although they have been demoted or management has passed them by in favor of someone else. Their rationalization usually is, "They can't do this to me. They owe me more for what I have done for them." By "more" he will mean recognition and prestige. To recoup his lost or dwindling status the white collar employee will dip into the company till. For status is a commodity that can be bought on the open market. The man who finds that he is slipping on his job can bolster his ego by purchasing a larger house, entertaining regally or by playing the role of the rich uncle to his neighbors and community.

Such was the case of a man we shall call Arthur. Arthur had been the plant manager of a manufacturer of small appliances. When management reorganized, they decided to keep Arthur, despite his advancing age, and give him what for many would be a coveted executive title, vice-president. At the same time, though, they cut his responsibilities and salary. Arthur was still on the ranch but he had been put out to pasture.

Arthur felt that he was on an elevator that was going in only one direction, down. The title he figured was a farce. By cutting his salary and undermining his responsibility they put Arthur in a position where he could not afford to keep up appearances.

One of the jobs Arthur retained was the disposal of rejects

and salvage. Salvage is damaged merchandise which many manufacturers and distributors either sell to junk dealers or give to charities. The policy of Arthur's firm was to donate the damaged goods to some worthy cause. And Arthur continued to do just that, giving most of the salvage to his church. As time progressed he began to include goods that were in perfect condition and salable. The firm's stock handlers and office clerks knew that Arthur had been with the company for over thirty years. To them he was Mister, a man who had the authority to do pretty much what he pleased. The church, too, was unaware that he was doing anything dishonest. The merchandise which Arthur gave away, was sold by the church at its semi-annual bazaars. As the result of Arthur's kingly generosity, he was given a testimonial dinner where he was acclaimed Man of the Year. When he was finally caught two years later, Arthur had given away nearly $85,000 of perfectly salable merchandise. When asked why, he replied, "I wanted to win the respect of the community."

He had rationalized that since the company had not given him the respect he felt he deserved he would acquire it by becoming a big shot somewhere else. The firm, he claimed, owed it to him.

The final variant of the rationalization "the boss owes it to me" is used by the white collar employee, invariably of long standing, who feels that because of his years of service and the power that he wields, he deserves to be a partner in the firm's operation. Like the employee who has been demoted or passed over, the silent partner envisions a higher living scale and status level then he can actually afford.

Joe had been with a department store in his town for thirty-six years, where he rose to the position of supervisor of non-selling personnel of four floors. His authority, significant to begin with, increased when he took over supervision of the central stockroom. The manager of the stockroom became seriously ill and it appeared that Joe would continue in that position too. Although his take-home pay totaled $69 a week, he managed to buy a rundown farm with fourteen rooms. The home was located near a new highway.

Joe decided that the only way he could make ends meet was to go into business for himself. But he needed capital or stock. The solution was obvious. Joe had been with the firm so many years that he felt that in a way it belonged to him. And pretty soon a good part of it did.

One of the floors which Joe supervised carried antiques, knickknacks, lamps, occasional furniture, glassware, china and housewares. Such goods if chipped or damaged even slightly would lose most of their value. The merchandise would be marked down to a nominal price. Joe took advantage of this situation by having marked down not only damaged goods but merchandise that was in excellent condition. Joe, though, had a problem. It is general policy in most retail outlets that no employee is allowed to write up a sales slip for a sale to himself. It must always be done by another employee. Joe solved this problem with ease. Since his authority as floor supervisor carried considerable weight, he would simply approach a salesgirl and tell her to mark down a piece of merchandise because it was "salvage" or "damaged." She would then write out a sales slip for fifty cents for an item that retailed at $19.95.

Joe himself explained it this way: "I admit that all merchandise that is below the full price should be entered into the markdown book (price change records) or, otherwise, it is illegal. Also that all old-season goods (old stock) or any merchandise that is below the full price must first be okayed by the buyer or assistant buyer and put into the book and then should be okayed by the merchandise manager. Also, that no prices can be changed by anyone other than the buyer, assistant buyer or merchandise manager. I am aware of the fact that this is the company policy and that deviation from it would be dishonest or, certainly, subject to dismissal for cause.

"As a rule, you can have any merchandise that you wanted with the cooperation of the buyer or assistant buyer, and they will give me the preference of things that I could use for sale. However, in many cases, about once a month or more, the china department and the housewares department which are on the fourth floor, connecting, have truckloads of mer-

chandise that should go back to the vendor for credit or exchange or back to the selling floor as in most cases the goods
are good but have been returned for one reason or another.
As a matter of fact, in several cases, they are returned because
they are duplicate shipments to the customer. Then the girl
from the marking room and the assistant buyer would mark
the prices, and we would all be around there at that time.
Then, we would all help ourselves and load it up in baskets or
boxes and just walk out with it and there would be no
supervision of any sort whatsoever so that I could have anyone
write up the sale at the prices I told them. . . . You could
pay $10, as I did, and walk out with merchandise valued at
$250."

By the time Joe was in full swing, he was using eight
methods, some devious, others not, to steal goods from the
store. Indeed, every day had become bargain day for Joe.
And how did he dispose of the goods? The solution blossomed
right under his nose. He had just purchased a big home, in
fact too big. Now that a new highway loaded with tourist
and vacationing traffic swept by Joe's farm, he realized he possessed the ideal site for a business of his own. He opened a
gift shop, and sold woodenware, aprons, artificial flowers,
housewares, indeed anything he could lay his hands on. By the
time a year and a half rolled by, he found he was doing an
excellent business. Consider his overhead. For one, his wife by
staying at home was minding Joe's store. Secondly, the store
where Joe was employed was not only supplying him with his
stock but actually shipping it to his home without his paying a
cent for its transportation. The shipping cost, of course, was
borne by Joe's employer. For example, in one instance he
"bought" five boxes of goods worth $100. Joe paid a total of five
dollars. It cost his employers $14 to deliver them.

And Joe was very businesslike too. He got a sales tax certificate, paid state and federal taxes and kept a perfect set of books.
Although he paid only pennies for most of his merchandise,
he would enter each item with the normal wholesale price
for first-rate merchandise. He would mark up each item by
thirty per cent and then as his wife sold the item she would

enter the sale or retail price next to the so-called purchase or wholesale price. Finally, she would record her margin of profit and the sales tax that was due.

During the first six months of business, the gift shop netted an income equivalent to the money Joe was receiving after thirty-six years of service. Inventory on hand was worth $13,-000. The cost to Joe, $400.

Joe, when confronted with the thefts, explained that if he hadn't taken the merchandise, somebody else would have received it. Besides, he added, because of the time he had put into the firm and the length of his seniority, he deserved it. The company, as far as Joe was concerned, owed it to him.

Not all employees, of course, are like Joe. They neither claim that they are borrowing the goods or money, nor do they feel that it is owed to them. One of the most frequently used rationalizations is: "Everybody else is doing it." In this instance, the justification itself can also be the cause for dishonesty. "After all," says the dishonest employee, "if I do *not* steal, won't I look the fool." Indeed, management itself is often resigned to a certain amount of dishonesty. The trade newspaper *Supermarket News* recently quoted one food store executive as saying that his chain loses between four million and five million dollars a year through stealing, "half by our own employees." The executive added that workers furnish themselves with all the cigarettes they smoke and most of their nylon hosiery needs from stock. "Even the best people," he said, "don't seem to think of the things they take in a food store as stealing." What is the chain store doing about this huge loss? The executive replied that management writes off these thefts "as one of the costs of doing business. It would cost more to put in a total protection system."

A corollary to the rationalization "Everybody else is doing it" is the excuse, "Well, my friend asked me to help him. It all started as a favor." This road to dishonesty is often difficult for most people to avoid. Even though Fred Green knows that his friend, Sam Brown, is doing something dishonest, Fred is put on the spot when Sam asks him a favor like providing an invoice or saleslip he shouldn't or acting as a lookout. If Fred should deny Sam's request for help, he may lose a drinking companion. Besides, Fred will rationalize, Sam is a good friend and I will do anything for a good friend.

Usually the so-called "good friend" will find some way of involving his companion to the point where he, too, has permanently joined the conspiracy. After Fred has done several favors for Sam, his mentor will then suggest that if they worked together Fred himself could also have some of the smart money. If Fred is greedy, the temptation may prove too much. Sometimes Sam, "the good friend," will try a little blackmail. After Fred has done Sam a few favors, Sam will be quick to note that lack of co-operation could mean Fred's exposure. Faced with such a situation, Fred may well change his concept of friendship, but, unfortunately, not his new code of ethics.

The opposite of the "friendship" rationalization is the justification "the world is against me." The problem here is the imaginary slight. All of us suffer from it to varying degrees. For example, have you ever arrived at work to find that your co-worker or superior has neglected to offer his customary greeting. "I wonder," you say to yourself, "if Oscar is mad at me." And an hour or two later, you find yourself in Oscar's office saying, "Oscar, are you mad at me?" The look in Oscar's eyes should tell you that he positively loves you. But you are not satisfied until he actually tells you so in so many words. A common occurrence indeed. I would say that three fourths of most so-called slights are simply a figment of someone's imagination. Yet such situations arise frequently. In most instances, they mean no more than a few bruised feelings. However, if a white collar worker is suffering from a persecution complex then the results can be devastating. A wise employer, supervisor or executive will do well to go out of his way to see that such an employee has few if any grievances, real or imaginary. If the persecution complex is acute, and you can easily recognize the symptoms, then it would be prudent to release the individual and, if you can, suggest psychiatric treatment.

Take the case of the secretary, whom I'll call Mary, who

worked in the sales department of a large metal-working firm. Although Mary made no profit from her misdeeds, she still cost her employer at least a quarter of a million dollars. The sales manager had been repeatedly warned that Mary believed the whole world was against her. She herself told him in so many words. Her complaint was that she was the last to hear of any office gossip. She was sure that there was a conspiracy to shut her out from the scuttlebutt and chitchat which makes secretarial work bearable. In one instance a salesman who worked in the office told her he was unhappy and that he was thinking of quitting. When a new man arrived to learn the salesman's job, Mary decided that the salesman had been fired. She went to the sales manager and asked somewhat heatedly why she hadn't been told. Although such information was really not Mary's business, the sales manager informed her that the fellow in question had been transferred to an outside sales job. In fact it was a promotion. Mary, though, was sure that the sales manager was lying to her. "Nobody tells me anything," she mumbled and walked out. As the months passed, Mary was sure that a conspiracy of silence existed. Brooding and suspicious, she decided that if the world was against her— and her world was the office—then she would fight back, do something that would make them sorry.

Her chance came when one of the other secretaries went on a two-week vacation. Mary was told to take over her duties. As far as Mary was concerned the secretary she was replacing was the ringleader of the conspiracy. Mary waited for the propitious moment. It came with a huge order for one million pounds of specially processed aluminum. The firm that Mary was working for had only recently gone into the manufacture of this expensive metal. The order was particularly important because it would help the firm break the stranglehold that the nation's three largest producers had on the industry.

When Mary received the order, which was sent in by a major airplane manufacturer, she simply neglected to send it over the company's teletype to the firm's plant, a thousand miles away. She then faked a message on the teletype from the plant to the district sales office, acknowledging receipt of the order.

When the other girl returned, Mary went back to her own secretarial duties.

Mary waited. She could afford to. Six months had passed when the aircraft company decided to check on its order and called the plant. Initial delivery on one million pounds was expected in a week and the aircraft firm wanted to know if the plant would meet its commitment. "What order? What aluminum?" choked the plant manager.

For the next few hours the communications lines between the sales office and the plant crackled with more messages than at any other time in the firm's history. Finally, the sales manager found the phony message that Mary had made on the teletype. Although it was in a file kept by the secretary Mary had replaced, the sales manager soon learned that it was Mary who was responsible. Checking back on his calendar he found that the date on the phony acknowledgement coincided with the period Mary had replaced the vacationing secretary.

The cost to the firm totaled over $250,000 in lost sales. Not only did they lose most of the order, but their prestige was badly damaged. A neophyte in the field of aluminum production, they found themselves handicapped with the reputation of being unreliable. In addition, the airplane manufacturer was now six months behind in his production and had to lay off seven hundred workers. For the first time, Mary could truthfully say that she wasn't really wanted.

Mary had not personally profited from her actions. However, her motivation of revenge is the cause of much white collar crime. And the damage that resulted was greater than if she had walked off with a million dollars in cash. Mary's case brings up an unusual aspect of white collar crime. Like Mary, many employees profit not one cent from their dishonest acts. The harm, though can be disastrous. For Mary the motivation was vengeance. In the case that follows, the motivation was altruism. The result was the destruction of the faith of an entire community.

Chapter 4

The Helping Hand

WHEN SOME people conjure up a picture of a typical banker, they usually envision a man with rimless glasses, a bloodless Grant Wood face and an adding machine for a brain. Confront this fictive character with an orphan waif, and the heart of this imaginary banker would never skip a beat. But substitute a seductive profit and loss statement, and his eyes will gleam with the joy of a proud parent. If this is your image of the typical banker you couldn't be more wrong, especially if he is a white collar thief. For of all the white collar thieves, none has been so eager to help others without profit to himself. Indeed, in recent years no one has matched the selfless beneficence of the banker. There is only one hitch, most of the money given away belonged to others.

One of the most prominent white collar Robin Hoods is William Richard Rose. Unlike Miss Minnie Mangum, the Norfolk, Virginia, embezzler, who played fairy godmother to friends, relatives and the needy, Uncle Bill tried to underwrite almost a whole community. Over the years this portly, sandy-haired, ruddy-faced man ran through $1,400,000 of his bank's money. Yet he never profited one cent from his manipulations. In fact as the result of his generosity he lost over $200,000, his entire personal fortune. As the benefactor of his community, Uncle Bill became the idol of the whole village. But like all worshipers of idols, the people turned their backs on him when they found he had committed the cardinal sin of having failed them.

The tragic story of William Richard Rose begins naturally enough with the town in which he was born and raised. Ellenville, a village of 5,000, lies about eighty-five miles from New York. To the east stand the Shawangunk Mountains. The rest of the community looks out on the undulating foothills of the Catskills, where numberless summer resorts offer the big city's vacationers calories, comics and culture. And for more than three decades New Yorkers by the tens of thousands have loved it. During the summer months the residents of towns like Ellenville have benefited richly from this stampede for frenetic relaxation. But there is one problem. Shortly after Labor Day some resorts close their doors until the next season begins six to nine months later. Cut off from the holiday dollars, Ellenville and other communities must rely on their own industry if they want to thrive year round. The Rose family had faced this problem, the bête noire of the Borsht Belt, for three generations. But it was William Richard Rose who took it upon himself to end the problem for Ellenville.

Rose was born into a family of bankers. His grandfather had started and his father continued to head the town's leading bank. Rose himself was groomed to follow in the family tradition. Born in 1906, he was a sickly child until he was twelve.

Those early days for Bill Rose were pleasantly spent either in the country with his nurse or at his parents' seventeen-room home of gingerbread Victorian architecture. The house rests atop a knoll on South Main Street and there Bill could romp in the front yard with its stone fountain of nymphs. Although Bill was a scion of the town's leading family, his upbringing was relatively simple and unpretentious. At the age of sixteen Bill began working summers in his father's bank. During the remaining months he attended the local high school, and then Harvard, returning each summer to Ellenville and the Home National Bank. By 1929, at the age of twenty-three, Bill was awarded a permanent position in his father's bank. He had become a clerk.

His rise after that was somewhat more rapid. By 1933 he

was advanced to assistant cashier and in 1940 he became executive vice-president, and then president of the bank. The mantle had finally fallen on the shoulders of William Richard Rose. But no one could say that he hadn't worked for it.

Then came the war and Bill Rose at the age of thirty-six went off to serve his country. On October 18, 1942, he joined the Navy as a lieutenant commander in Air Intelligence. For the next three years he served in the Pacific aboard an aircraft carrier. They were good and exciting years for Bill. A close associate says that the war years were the happiest in Bill Rose's life. Freed from the dull routine of the bank, Bill was seeing the world for the first time.

When Bill Rose returned to Ellenville he was looked upon as a hero. A few people are born to great expectations. Bill Rose was one of the few and he had lived up to them. Rose, however, wasn't satisfied. As soon as he returned, his father, who had served in his absence as bank president, stepped down and once more his son took over command. Gold pouch in hand, Bill charged forward.

The Home National Bank, under Bill Rose, had initiated an extraordinary, liberal credit policy which contrasted sharply with the conservative banking practices of the community's second and older commercial bank, the First National Bank and Trust Company. While the First National restricted loans to fifty or sixty per cent of deposits, Rose had no such inhibitions. At one time the Home National's proportion rose to ninety per cent. Rose also encouraged installment loans until they grew to a total of nearly $3,000,000. Almost everybody in the community was to become indebted in one way or another to William Richard Rose and the Home National Bank. But no matter how high the total indebtedness ran, the bank seemed to flourish until it eventually was to do seventy per cent of the area's commercial business. The byword in Ellenville was: "If you need money, see Uncle Bill." For hardly anybody was ever turned down and many small businessmen conceded that without Bill Rose they would have gone bankrupt. In turn most of these merchants kept faith with Rose by making their loans good.

With the bank doing so well, Rose, like the modern knight that he was, had only one other interest in life, civic affairs. The most eligible bachelor in town, Rose dated occasionally, but never married. Instead he lived alone in that big ginger-bread house with his aging mother, his father having died. But Rose kept himself busy. At one time or another he was district president of the New York State Bankers' Association, a member of the Chamber of Commerce and president of the Shawangunk Country Club. As the most prominent veteran in town, he was always grand marshal of the military parades. He served as a member of the Scorsby Volunteer Hook and Ladder Company, rarely missing a fire. At any time he was ready to leave his desk in the red brick colonial bank and run out to the corner of Canal and Main streets to swing aboard the fire apparatus as it passed. During the floods of 1955, Rose, dressed in hip boots, helped battle the rushing waters. He was also leader of the Empire State Music Festival. Local merchants and townspeople annually provided $50,000 as a guarantee of festival expenses. Rose's interest in the festival was so great that he would grant loans to Ellenville residents so that they could pledge part of the guarantee. He would personally count the number of cars attending the festival and then boast about the number of people and variety of states that had been attracted to Ellenville and the famous cultural event.

How did the Catskill banker manage to do so much? He worked hard, almost like a man possessed. His average working day lasted a grueling fourteen hours. In addition, he would spend Saturday afternoons and Sundays going over the bank's accounts. A familiar sight for the early riser would be a non-descript man wearing an inexpensive blue suit strolling from South Main Street to the bank. Under his arm he would carry a homemade fried egg sandwich and a container of milk. He would arrive at the bank at around seven in the morning, eat his lunch at his desk and remain there until late in the evening. Even to the most casual observer it was apparent that no one worked harder or cared more than Ellenville's leading citizen. Perhaps he cared too much.

A chief concern of Rose's was the employment problem mentioned earlier. If Ellenville could maintain industry of its own it would not be dependent on the summer resorts. Uncle Bill tackled this problem in part by loaning money to almost anyone in the area who asked for it. Sometimes he would lend the money outright. Other times he would make the loan in a devious way. Instead of making a cash loan he would allow an overdraft in a depositor's checking account, when the depositor did not have enough to cover his check. An Ellenville grocer explained it this way: "He'd just telephone and say he was putting the check through, anyway. 'You owe me $200 like you owe any other bill,' he'd say. 'Pay me when you get it.' " Most eventually paid. Two accounts, though, didn't. And that was Rose's undoing.

The largest account involved a man named Joseph DiCandia and the Anjopa Board and Paper Manufacturing Company. Joseph with his father, Anthony, and his younger brother, Paul, came to Ellenville in 1949. Previously they had worked in the wastepaper business in New York. In 1945, they purchased a paper mill in York, Pennsylvania. Known as the York Paper Manufacturing Company, Inc., it lasted about four years before failing. The DiCandia family, though, was convinced that it could make a go of the paper manufacturing business and they began casting around for a mill that could be bought cheaply. They found it at Napanoch, just two miles from Ellenville. The mill itself was little more than a shell. During the last quarter of a century it had been in operation only one or two years. Weather and neglect had turned it into rotted ruins. But the DiCandia family was determined.

A reporter for the Ellenville *Press* described the situation this way: "When the DiCandias arrived they had a very small amount of capital. In no time it was gone. There was not even enough money for hotel rooms or food. They slept, by turn, on the floor or on a bench in the office. Meals were few and far between but Mrs. Turk, who operates a diner in Napanoch, heard not only of their plight but of their refusal to quit. She gave them meals to keep them on their feet so they could carry on. Not one single pound of paper had been made before the original DiCandia funds were gone.

Because the credit of the mill had been questionable for some time previously they were forced to pay cash for anything they bought.

"Working night and day with the loyalty of five employees who at times were weeks behind in receiving their pay the mill began to take shape again. There were no funds for plumbers, electricians and specialists so Joe DiCandia did the major part of that work with his earlier training as a guide. When the mill started to run it continually broke down. Maybe it would run for two or three hours, sometimes it might go along for twelve hours before something happened. But it always did happen and it was one great discouragement after another."

The family, operating on a shoestring, was desperately in need of shoes. The DiCandias decided to call on Uncle Bill for help. Paul was picked as the emissary. Around September, 1949, Paul climbed aboard an old truck and chugged into town to apply for a loan. Paul's knowledge of the mill's operations, however, lacked the details that a good banker prefers to receive. So Rose suggested that Joseph, the older brother, come in for a chat.

Rose later testified, "Well, Mr. [Joseph] DiCandia explained that he and his brother and his father had come here, had come to Napanoch and had reopened the mill. They needed help and I think I told them at that time that we would try and help them, we were anxious to have the mill reopened, we were anxious to have industry come to the community and we would do what we could. I think that is more or less the conversation."

Question: "And in fact hadn't that been your policy while you were president of the bank, to help new industry that came in?"

Rose: "That is correct."

Question: "Will you tell us whether or not it was your purpose to see that new employment was developed?"

Rose: "Yes, that was very definitely a part of it."

Joseph DiCandia's request for a loan amounted to $2,500, a minute figure compared to the sums William Richard Rose

The Helping Hand

and the Home National Bank were to put in the Anjopa mill. The first loan itself was made by the bank and was perfectly legal. A few days later Uncle Bill, as was his habit, went out to visit the DiCandias' and the bank's collateral. And as usual he became vitally interested in the mill's operations. By 1951 he was visiting the mill every day, sometimes twice a day, even on Sundays. He learned how waste paper is boiled, treated chemically, dried and made into a new salable commodity. He knew how much a paper boiler and a dryer cost. He learned the current cost of waste paper and the price of the finished product. In part, he was curious. And he also had to learn these things, for the paper market at the time was fickle with the price per ton jerkily rising and dropping like a Yo-yo on a knotted string.

Between the first loan in the fall of 1949 and May, 1951, Anjopa squeezed by, partly as the result of the hard work by the DiCandias and the mill's employees and through the help of the Home National Bank and Uncle Bill. During that period the Home National, through the good offices of Rose, loaned Anjopa between $18,000 and $19,000. In addition, Uncle Bill himself personally loaned Anjopa $13,717, plus $2,000 to $3,000 to Joe DiCandia. These loans were above the legal limit allowed to any one borrower and a national bank examiner in May, 1951, told Rose he had gone above the legal limit.

At that time Rose could have quit. But instead he continued to support Anjopa with the bank's funds. A month or two after the bank examiner told Rose that he and the bank had lent more money than was permitted under the Federal Reserve Act, Uncle Bill began honoring Anjopa's overdrafts. As Rose later explained it:

"We (Joseph DiCandia and Rose) had many conversations about the financial affairs of the company. At about that time in June or July of 1951, Mr. DiCandia needed additional moneys in order to keep his mill in operation. Collections were not coming in as fast as he had expected and in order to keep the mills in operation it seemed necessary for him to draw certain checks that would overdraw his account. And

I agreed that they would be honored with the expectation shortly sufficient collections would come in to pay the checks to cover the overdraft."

During the succeeding months Rose began juggling funds. On the one hand Anjopa had been loaned more money than the bank was legally allowed to extend. On the other hand, to continue in operation, Anjopa needed more money, which Rose either supplied personally or by having the bank honor the firm's checks, despite the fact that Anjopa did not have the money to cover those checks. At the same time Rose would have the bank honor Anjopa checks made out to "petty cash." Of the $500 to $1,000 in "petty cash" turned over to Anjopa each week, $200 was deposited in the personal account of William Richard Rose in payment of the personal loans he had made to Anjopa. But no matter how much money Rose and the Home National Bank gave to DiCandia and Anjopa, the paper mill continued treading backwards, always going deeper in debt. Rose refused to give up. DiCandia, of course, had no reason to. So they decided to try drastic action. Rose, testifying at DiCandia's subsequent trial, said:

"Well, at that time, in the fall of 1951 he [DiCandia] had been making what is known as nine point corrugated paper, and the price of nine point corrugated paper had slumped very badly. It had gone from $130 a ton back to $60 a ton and it was obvious to Mr. DiCandia and myself that it would be rather difficult to pay back the bank the money unless something was done to correct this situation.

"The solution to the situation was a conversion to what is known as board paper. Board paper is the kind of paper you make boxes out of, cigarette boxes and things of that nature. And we had many discussions at that time as to whether it was wise to convert to board paper or whether it was wise to stop or what the best thing to do under the circumstances would be.

"We ultimately reached the decision that it was better to convert and go on with the board paper."

The decision proved fatal. The conversion process lasted from December 1, 1951, to about April 1, 1952, a period of four months. During that time the mill was closed and completely unproductive. Rose had figured that the total cost of the conversion would be between $40,000 and $60,000. He was wrong. The final cost was $175,000. Rose had stepped into a pit filled with quicksand. But as amazing as it may seem, Rose was convinced that Anjopa, which had pushed him into the quicksand, would actually pull him out. Always a romantic in business, he had joined the mystics.

As the overdrafts kept mounting, Rose himself continued to hand out more of his own money to Anjopa until his personal loans eventually totaled $40,000. In turn, he continued to take out $200 weekly from the mill's "petty cash" checks and to deposit the money in his personal account as repayment for the loans made to Anjopa. He used $25,000 of that amount to buy additional stock in the bank. In effect, Rose was investing the bank's own money in the bank.

While trying to keep his and the Home National's accounts straight, Rose personally took over the financial operation of the mill itself. Every check that Anjopa had to pay for expenses, no matter how small, was passed on to Rose for his approval. If the mill had to have a dryer fixed, pay for fuel oil to run its machines, repair the Anjopa trailer truck, purchase wastepaper—every item was approved by Rose. Each Friday Mrs. Margaret Brush, the firm's bookkeeper, and Joseph DiCandia would meet Uncle Bill in his office at the bank. There they would discuss the amount of paper that had been shipped the previous week, the amount that was to be advanced on those shipments, the amount of checks that had been withdrawn the previous week, the number of checks which might be sent out the following week and the problems that the mill's operation presented. Mrs. Brush would then hand Rose a memorandum showing the checks that Joseph DiCandia and Anjopa wanted to pay within the following week as well as the overdrafts in the account at that time. Frequently emergencies would arise during the week and Uncle Bill would find himself approving more checks for unexpected expenses. Meantime, the overdrafts kept soaring like a flock of missiles. By the fall of 1956, Anjopa owed the Home National Bank

$940,978.64. The only insurance Rose had that the bank would be repaid was a $9,000 mortgage on the mill which had been acquired three years earlier.

Unlike Rose, DiCandia found himself in an enviable position. Uncle Bill and the Home National Bank had turned out to be an oil well that never ran dry. From 1951 to 1956, the Home National Bank had honored a total of $195,000 in petty cash checks. Although Joseph DiCandia was president of a business that had gone bankrupt, he received a salary of $150 a week, plus a $300 a week expense allowance. In addition he owned a $45,000 home, a Cadillac and a power boat. Joseph DiCandia had started with a ten-cent candy bar and found a winning Irish sweepstake ticket under the wrapper.

How did Uncle Bill get away with it? During all this time the bank's board of directors met monthly. Yet never once did they suspect that such a shortage existed. Federal bank examiners made surprise visits to the Home National Bank about once every six months. Yet they too were fooled by Rose for over five years. In addition, the bank had eight bookkeepers. Yet not one ever mentioned any irregularities. A combination consisting of good fortune and a chain of circumstances allowed Rose to get away with hiding shortages totaling $1,400,000.

The first thing Rose tried to do was to bring down the total amount of overdrafts. An overdraft, as you recall, occurs when checks are drawn on an account in which there are insufficient funds to cover them. As of December 31, 1951, the overall overdraft in the Anjopa account was a piddling $5,937.21. A year later, the overdraft had soared to $323,-904.59, an increase of more than $300,000. It was during that period that Anjopa made its costly conversion. By the end of 1952, Rose decided to start a new Anjopa checking account. The old one had been on pink checking paper. The new one was on tan paper. Once a week Mrs. Brush, the bookkeeper, would bring in a check drawn on the new checking or tan paper account. This check would then be deposited in the old or pink checking account. As a result the overdraft in the pink checking account decreased. But contrary to Rose's plan the overdraft in the current or tan account increased at a faster rate than the decrease in the old or pink checking account. In essence what Uncle Bill had wanted to do was deposit enough money from the mill's earnings in the tan account so that it would serve as a catchall reserve, making up the deficit in the pink account as well as to pay for current expenses. But the mill's expenses always were greater than its earnings. As a result Rose was unable to have Anjopa build up the tan account. Soon, it, too, was nothing more than a growing depository of overdrafts. In fact by December 31, 1953, the total Anjopa overdrafts had increased to $433,160.44 or an additional $100,000 in one year's time. During the next three years Rose had Anjopa open four more accounts ranging in color from yellow to green to blue to gray. But the overdrafts kept climbing. The Home National Bank had been left holding an empty pot suspended at the end of a rainbow of fraudulent checks.

Although the overdrafts were reaching a staggering figure, not one member of the bank's board of directors was aware that they even existed. At the monthly meeting each director would be given a booklet with his name on it. The booklets would include an agenda for the day, statements showing comparative earnings and expenses, new accounts and regular and installment notes. In addition, there would be a list of overdrafts. They were for odd amounts like seventeen cents, $37, $200, $500. The highest total would come to $3,000 or $3,500. Not once were the Anjopa overdrafts mentioned. Rose had simply neglected to include them, or any other overdrafts that would have raised a financial eyebrow. And since the bank, according to Rose's figures, was doing well nobody ever asked any questions.

A second problem that Uncle Bill had to contend with concerned an examining committee consisting of three members of the board of directors. The committee was expected to make a surprise examination of the bank's accounts once every six months. And they did, except that their examination covered all the areas where Rose had nothing to hide. They would start off by counting the cash on hand. The remainder of their time would be spent checking the loans the bank had

made. As Rose himself later explained: "The examining committee in a small country bank is more largely concerned with
the loans than anything, and they spend a great majority of
their time on that. They are not trained examiners, but they
are local people who know the individuals and that is why they
concentrate their attention on the loans." Never did they ask
to see the one item that really mattered, a true list of overdrafts.

The final problem that Rose had to overcome and the one
that proved most dangerous was a semi-annual examination
made by a federal bank examiner. Like the examination made
by the bank's own committee, the federal bank examiner's
check was also supposed to be a surprise visit. Although Rose
was never sure of the exact date that the examiners would
arrive in Ellenville, he could make a pretty close estimate by
keeping track of the time that had elapsed since the previous
visit and by ferreting out the information that the examiners
were in the general area visiting neighboring banks.

The knowledge that the bank examiners were on their way,
however, would not have been sufficient to give Rose the
protection he needed. Again circumstances in the form of an
inadequate federal regulation extended a helping hand to
Uncle Bill. The Home National Bank, like thousands of others
in the country, is chartered by the federal government. Under
the federal system the examiners must rely on records, statements and information supplied only by the head of the bank
and the bank's employees. Thus, if the examiners are given
false information they have no way of checking whether it is
accurate except by comparing it to other records in the bank
itself. If those records also are misleading, the federal bank
examiners are simply unable to prove or even know that a fraud
has been committed. These regulations contrast sharply with
New York State charter laws, under which the bank itself or an
outside agency must conduct periodic audits. Now, an audit is
different from an examination in that an auditor not only
checks the records of the bank itself but goes outside the
bank to verify whether those records are true or false. For
example, John Jones borrows $100,000 from a bank. He
writes out a statement in which he claims he can repay the

$100,000 because his factory earns that much. A bank examiner would only be concerned with the statement. An auditor would not only read the statement but would talk to John Jones, visit his factory and make other inquiries he thought necessary. Since the Home National Bank was chartered by the federal government and not New York State, Rose had no fear of the more thorough examination that an auditor would make.

A third factor working in Rose's favor was the fact that the federal examiners were short staffed. In many instances they couldn't make as many probing examinations as they would have liked. There simply weren't enough men to do the necessary work.

The usual procedure was for the bank examiner to arrive at the bank several hours after it had opened. They would count the cash, spot check ledger cards where individual savings and check deposits were listed, look over the bank's general records and examine the list of overdrafts. On occasion the federal bank examiners would be a little more thorough. Instead of just making a spot check of the individual ledger cards, they would total them and then compare the final sum against the total overall figure kept in the bank's separate, general ledger book. This is known as running and proving the ledgers. Of course, even this examination could prove inadequate providing someone altered either the figures on the individual ledger cards or more simply the overall figures in the general ledger book.

Rose himself managed to fool the bank examiners for more than five years by two simple tricks. He would prepare a false list of overdrafts which showed fewer overdrafts than actually existed. This false list, of course, left out whopping shortages like Anjopa and the Hotel Zeiger which eventually overdrew its checking account by the munificent sum of $255,000. Once Rose narrowly missed detection when a new employee accidentally was about to hand the bank examiner a complete list of overdrafts. Fortunately for Rose, she was stopped just in time. Rose's second gimmick was a bit of hocus-pocus that an ordinary bank clerk could have managed. The individual ledger cards which kept an accurate picture of each person's overdrafts were kept in tubs in a drive-in bank which Rose, who always believed in trying something new, had constructed. The drive-in also housed the bookkeeping department of the Home National Bank. While the federal bank examiners were busy counting the cash in the main building, Rose would jauntily walk out the front door of the bank and scoot around the corner to the drive-in, where he would pull out the individual ledger cards that showed the large overdrafts and hide them in a supply closet. He would then go to the block sheets which contained the overall figures for the bank and make a few pertinent alterations. When the bank examiners ran the ledger cards and compared those figures with the general ledger, the books invariably balanced.

Except for the ten days during the year when the bank examiners were present, the records of the bank accurately reflected the institution's impoverished financial status. A further irony is that the clerks who posted or listed the individual overdrafts were certainly aware of the sizable amounts involved. In addition, Rose told the bookkeepers where he had hid the ledger cards in case they needed them. Yet not one employee in the bank ever told a bank examiner that they suspected so much as a penny was missing. The explanation for this silence was amazingly simple. Nobody had ever bothered to ask the bank clerks, bookkeepers and tellers if they thought anything was amiss.

Eventually Rose's free-wheeling and haphazard banking methods caught up with him. And the men who found him out were the bank examiners whom he had been fooling for so many years. If they had been psychic, they would have had a hint of things to come two years prior to their discovery of the bank's monumental shortage. The warning took place at the Methodist church Uncle Bill attended. Like his father before him, he had become head usher and treasurer of the church. But in 1954 Bill Rose had to give up his job as treasurer. As the Reverend Ralph E. Spoor Jr. gently put it: "It was impossible to have Bill continue. He was too busy to make the kind of reports necessary for the church to know whether it was or was not in good financial condition." The Home National Bank was not so fortunate, for Bill Rose continued to be as active as ever.

The candle of Uncle Bill's career of infinite beneficence began to sputter in May, 1956. The cold breath and analytic eye of a bright, persistent bank examiner named George A. Monahan was the chief cause of Bill Rose's undoing. Monahan and two assistants paid a visit to the Home National Bank on May 21. It was Monahan's first examination of the Home National. Although everything appeared to be in order, the overall condition of the bank seemed to be somewhat anemic. Specifically three things troubled Monahan. One, the Home National Bank was strapped with what he felt was a high delinquency rate in the installment loan department. Two, the overall loan rate had reached ninety per cent of deposits. Three, the bank lacked a sufficient amount of government bonds which form a bank's secondary reserve.

As far as Monahan was concerned the condition was "serious" and something should be done about it. Following the usual procedure he sent a report of his examination to his superior in New York which, in turn, was forwarded to the Comptroller of the Currency in Washington. Even more important a few weeks after the May examination, Monahan called on the directors of the bank. He explained the situation as he found it and made a number of recommendations. Rose himself was present at the meeting, but it was the directors themselves who took up the cudgels in defense of the bank's policies. The loans, they felt, would be repaid. After all, the Home National Bank was a country bank, not a monolith like the Chase Manhattan in New York. Everybody knew everybody else. Besides, in the country life was informal. There was no need to be as strict with the folks who banked at Home National. If some of them were fifteen days behind in their installment loans, as Monahan pointed out, there was no need to become worried. They would pay.

However, the directors felt there was at least one thing they could do. Uncle Bill looked tired and they would try to get him an assistant to carry some of the day-to-day load of running the bank. In fact Bill Rose had been working too hard for years, and this had troubled at least three of the directors for some time. A couple of years previously, they had held a private meeting in New York with Rose's uncle, a former Long Island banker. They wanted to get Bill Rose's uncle to convince his nephew that he should take on an assistant. But Rose rejected the idea. He didn't mind the work and besides he was training and promoting personnel within the bank. After Monahan's examination, the bank directors tried again to convince Rose that Home National should hire an assistant. Three or four people were interviewed for the job. But all of them were rejected. Rose simply couldn't afford to have a stranger constantly looking over his shoulder.

Oddly enough, the directors also contemplated buying an excess fidelity insurance policy through the Bank-Share Owners Advisory League. That policy would have insured the bank up to $1,000,000 beyond a surety bond of $200,000 which the bank already had bought to protect itself against losses. The additional $1,000,000 policy would have cost a piddling $1,200 a year. If the bank had purchased that policy $1,200,000 of the $1,400,000 shortage would have been covered. But Rose turned down the directors' suggestion. He said the bank didn't need it.

Meanwhile, Monahan and his superiors continued to have misgivings. The next examination they decided would be one the likes of which the Home National Bank had never experienced. At 7:30 A.M. Friday, November 30, 1956, George A. Monahan and a squad of six assistants, four more than usual, appeared before the doors of the bank. A few minutes later Uncle Bill came trundling down the street, his daily fried egg sandwich tucked under his arm. By noon Rose would have lost his appetite entirely. Recognizing Monahan from his previous visits, Rose exclaimed, "You are not going to examine my bank, are you?"

"Yes, Mr. Rose," Monahan replied, "we are going to examine your bank."

"Well," said Rose, "you are not going to find everything approved. You are going to find things in a hell of a shape." Rose, who had a gift for underestimating a situation, had just made the greatest understatement of his life.

As soon as Rose opened the door to the bank, the examiners swept by; their main objective was to gather the individual ledger cards and prove them. Twenty minutes later Rose again told Monahan that the ledger cards were in terrible shape and that they wouldn't prove. He claimed that several girls in the bookkeeping department had left the bank to get married and that as a result of this shortage of help his records were not in order. And once more Rose requested that Monahan and his men defer running the ledgers until another day. Rose explained that he just wanted the opportunity to get things straightened out. But Monahan only shook his head and his men proceded to examine and total the individual ledger cards. The presence of the bank examiners in the bookkeeping department prevented Bill from hiding the ledger cards that showed the damaging overdrafts.

By 10:30 A.M., three hours after their arrival, Monahan's men found the first damaging piece of information. It was one of the Anjopa ledger cards showing an overdraft. The date on the ledger card preceded the May examination. Monahan immediately went into Rose's office for an explanation. During the May examination the bank examiners had come across a small loan to Anjopa. Monahan had discussed the loan with Rose. But Uncle Bill had made no mention of an overdraft in Anjopa's checking account. "Well," shrugged Rose, "it must have been an oversight." Monahan returned to his work with renewed vigor.

Uncle Bill realized that his time had come. At noon he sent a girl to tell the bank examiner that he would like to see him in his office. This time Monahan found two other directors with Rose. Uncle Bill quietly and calmly announced: "There is no need to look any further for that difference you are looking for in the bookkeeping department because I know what it is."

"Well," said Monahan, "what is it?"

Rose went on to explain that the difference was caused by overdrafts in several accounts which did not appear on the books. The chief offenders were the Anjopa Paper and Board Manufacturing Company and the Hotel Zeiger. Rose had

squeezed the bank like a sponge until it was dry. It was now
in the hands of the bank examiners. By 5:00 P.M. they discovered shortages totaling $580,000.

That weekend was, no doubt, the most frenetic in the small
community's history. When the people of Ellenville heard
about what Uncle Bill had done, they did an amazing thing.
Instead of going to the bank to withdraw their savings, they
rushed to the tellers' windows to make deposits. Although it
was open only until noon Saturday, the day after the examiners
had arrived, the bank had one of its heaviest business days. And
most of the business consisted of people putting their own
money into the bank's vaults. One depositor, Ben J. Slutsky,
owner of the Nevele Country Club, which already had a
$100,000 account in the bank, pledged another $100,000 by
Monday. And good to his word he took out $102,000 from other
banks and deposited it in Bill Rose's bank. As Ben told a
reporter, "I'm not a bit worried. I feel we will get all of that
money eventually. We all feel bad. But we are not resentful.
Just confused." Then he added thoughtfully, "You know I
don't know anything bad about Bill."

On Saturday night directors of rival banks joined other
businessmen, industrialists, hotel owners and representatives of
every civic, fraternal and veterans' group in Ellenville to work
out some way of helping the portly banker who had done so
much for the community. The group worked out a personal
letter which they sent to Bill Rose. It reaffirmed the "unique
affection and regard that we hold for you." The group also
drafted a petition which was to be signed by all 5,000 of
Ellenville's citizens. In part the petition said, "We know that
Ellenville is a finer place to live in because of his progressive
and unselfish leadership." It was to be used by Bill Rose's
attorneys. On Sunday a hastily built booth for the petition
was placed beneath the barren cover of a leafless tree in the
center of Ellenville. The people in the town needed no urging
to sign it. One by one they interrupted the routine of their daily
rounds, silently stepped up to the booth and added their names
to the swelling list of those who knew in their hearts that a
man like Bill Rose could do no evil. Perhaps an Ellenville cab

driver summed up the village's sentiment when he said, "You could talk to me from now to doomsday—and you'd still have to do a lot of talking to prove that man ever did anything wrong."

While the people of Ellenville proudly rallied to Rose's defense, there was one tiny group that remained aloof. The group, consisting of four Protestant ministers, issued a statement which read: "The question of guilt or innocence of any individual is to be established by the courts of the land. We cannot condone activities which are a breach of God's commandments or the law of the land. We, therefore, are not in a position to condemn or condone the activities of William R. Rose or any individual before the due process of law." One of the signers of the statement was the Reverend Ralph E. Spoor Jr., pastor of the Ellenville Methodist Church where Rose had proved so inadequate as treasurer.

Rose himself was kept busy by various branches of the law. Early Saturday he was taken to nearby Kingston, charged with manipulating bank funds and making false entries and released on $25,000 bail. He was also questioned extensively by the F.B.I. which, along with investigators from the Federal Deposit Insurance Corporation, had entered the case. Later, he was brought to New York City for more questioning by the United States District Attorney. Through it all Rose firmly denied that he had benefited in any way from the bank manipulations. Whatever he had done, he added, was for the good of the town. The people of Ellenville remained steadfast in their belief in Uncle Bill. Their agony came on Monday night.

Ironically, the shattering of their faith occurred while 1,000 townspeople were holding a mass rally at which hundreds arose to sign the petition supporting Uncle Bill. At 9:05 P.M. that Monday the National Board of Bank Examiners, with the approval of the board of directors, ordered the doors of the Home National Bank closed. Twelve F.D.I.C. investigators and eight bank examiners had unearthed shortages that finally reached the staggering total of $1,400,000, nearly twice the capital the bank had on hand to meet day-to-day obligations. Of that amount, over $900,000 had been traced to the Anjopa account, another $255,000 to the account of the Zeiger Hotel at Fallsburg. The remainder rested in 181 other accounts, all of which were overdrafts. The Home National Bank, which had seemed to every Ellenville citizen as solid as the earth on which it stood, had failed.

The announcement of the bank's closing came after the rally. But by the next day the booth which had been built to house Bill Rose's petition had been torn down. Some 3,000 depositors had been caught in the ruins. Despite federal insurance on deposits up to $10,000, a number of them faced stiff losses. But the big question on most people's lips was: "What'll we do about Christmas?" About three-fourths of the town's merchants banked with Uncle Bill. Hundreds of residents kept their savings there. Now with the bank closed no one knew how the weekly pay roll would be paid or where folks could get money for their Christmas shopping. And Christmas was just three weeks away. Where there had once been only confidence and an unshakable faith, there remained in its stead confusion, anger and hurt. On the eve of the holiday season Ellenville's Santa Claus had turned out to be a cheater and a liar. The town's most respected idol had fallen.

In the days that followed Ellenville slowly began to rally. The blow turned out to be mostly psychological. As one observer put it, "a sudden and incredible destruction of confidence." Although the town's faith had been shattered, no one went hungry. Food merchants and utilities extended credit. Christmas shopping was nonexistent at first, but the opening of the new Ellenville National Bank on December 21 restored the yuletide spirit. The new bank is in the same red brick colonial building that housed the Home National Bank. The $1,325,000 needed to start the new institution came from 465 residents in the area including housewives, high school students, businessmen and farmers. The people could believe again. Not in one man perhaps. But in themselves.

On March 13, Rose was indicted by a grand jury on thirty counts including misappropriation of the bank's funds and credit and making false reports to the Comptroller of the Currency. Also indicted were Joseph DiCandia; Mrs. Margaret

Brush, his bookkeeper; and the two sisters who owned the Hotel Zeiger. Rose eventually pleaded guilty to all thirty counts and received a five-year sentence. He served twenty months at the Federal prison in Danbury, Connecticut, where he worked seven days a week in the institution's hospital. Trials were held for the others. All were found guilty but only Joseph DiCandia was sent to jail. He was given a three-year sentence.

Why did Uncle Bill do it? Rose was a man, who, as columnist Max Lerner points out, had an image of himself which required him to play God with human destinies. Selfless, he wanted to do good deeds. But those deeds were more than just occasional favors. Rose was concerned with supporting others in the one area in which they would be eternally thankful and dependent—their very existence, the means by which they earned their bread and butter. The gratitude that resulted made Rose almost a God in their eyes. That Uncle Bill had at his command almost unlimited funds made his mission possible.

It was doubtful whether Rose ever felt a moral guilt in that he was using and manipulating money that didn't belong to him. For Uncle Bill felt that he was not just the chief officer of the Home National Bank but that the bank itself and all that it held was his to do with as he pleased. Often in his dealings with DiCandia Uncle Bill would write notes in which he would say that money was owed to "William Richard Rose." Actually he meant the bank. But the man and the institution had become synonymous in his mind.

Finally, Rose had a mystic faith in his own ability to make sound business judgments. That the investments made through the bank generally were successful only proved to Rose his infallibility. In his dealings with DiCandia and Anjopa, Rose eventually became aware that he had gone way out on a limb. But the reason he did, he added, was to get the bank's money back. And Rose fervently believed even after the bank's shortages had been uncovered that if the authorities had not interfered, the paper mill and all his other losing ventures would have succeeded.

Whether Bill Rose will ever understand that what he did

was wrong, if not to the bank, then to those who believed in him no one can foretell. And maybe Uncle Bill understands now. For a whole year before Rose went to prison he spent much of his time working in and around Ellenville, the place of his shame. The people there would stand and watch him in silence as he labored. William Richard Rose, whose father and father's father were bankers, was working as a plumber's helper. Perhaps he was atoning for what he had done to the village that bred and reared him. Perhaps he was doing the only thing he knew, just helping.

Chapter 5

The Honest Crook

MORALITY IS a complex thing. The commandment: "Thou shalt not steal" is continually broken. In many instances those who have stolen have been tried before their peers. Yet on numerous occasions the juries have refused to convict. In effect they have said: "The crime this man or woman has committed was justified. The pressures faced were beyond human endurance. There was no other recourse."

The most tragic kind of human being whom I have ever known is the white collar employee turned thief as the result of dire need. Paradoxically, he inevitably experiences the most seering conflict over his own dishonest acts. More than any other white collar thief, he is aware that he is committing a crime. Yet at the same time his conscience is so deeply troubled that the exposure of the wrong he has done serves as a purgation and release. Although the world has denied him decency, his is the greatest humiliation. And yet he is often the humblest of men.

This is the story of a man I shall call Waldo, who, after working for the same employer for more than thirty years still couldn't make ends meet. Waldo's only job was with a store that originally sold notions and gimcracks. The store was located in a small community of white clapboard houses, elm-lined streets and families whose ancestors once knew the fever of the American Revolution and the Civil War. In the succeeding years, the town and store where Waldo was to spend most of his life experienced a new kind of excitement, a subtler flame whose heat was unnoticeable unless you happened to live in the community.

The new excitement was the fire of prosperity. Industry began coming to Waldo's town and the town started to expand. The shop where Waldo worked grew, until it eventually became a large department store that sold everything from pianos to pinafores. Waldo, too, benefited from the fat years. Where once he made $25 a week, his salary climbed to $30, $35, $40 and finally reached $70 a week. It took Waldo years to double his earnings. And there was opportunity too. Waldo had started as a clerk. He eventually was promoted to head the draperies, slip covers, upholstery sales and installation department. This promotion was a special sign of favor. All supervisory and executive personnel in the store were given the privilege of supplementing their income by being allowed to work overtime. Waldo, like the others, could now join the custodial staff late at night, and with broom and mop, dust and empty trash. Waldo had arrived.

At first Waldo didn't complain. His boss had always been good to him and the rest of the employees at the store. Once a year he would take them out on a weenie roast. And people looked up to Waldo. He had a title too. His neighbors could say, "I knew Waldo when he was only a clerk. Now he heads a whole department in our biggest store." Waldo had responsibility and status. But there was one drawback. Waldo also had to support a family of three, a home and a eight-year-old car. He paid $50 a month on his home and $25 a month on the car. In addition there was a $13 monthly debt on a new furnace and a $14.44 monthly payment on a new refrigerator. These appliances had broken down and Waldo either had to incur the extra expense or permit his family to restrict their diet to canned goods in a cold house. So Waldo took the final step. He began stealing. Here is Waldo's story in his own words:

Through the years my salary was raised to $71.50 per week gross and has stayed at that figure for close to six or seven years. In the meantime with the increasing cost of living, I have tried

different times to have my salary raised. On one occasion my
mileage figure was raised from six cents to ten cents per mile
and cheerfully paid. In the meantime a few years ago, I don't
have the exact date, the company discontinued my parking
obligation which was and is at the present $5 per month. Ap-
proximately six or seven years ago I was promised, along with
another department head who since had a heart attack and died,
a bonus of $500 per year, payable every six months. At that
time I was able to secure a $10 per week raise for my mechanics
which numbered three or four; but only the promise of the
bonus for myself which was a wonderful outlook; but never
was forthcoming and to date I never received a dollar as a bonus.

A good many sales are charge accounts but naturally we do a
cash business also. I admit that many incidents, that items were
paid me at times when it did not seem convenient or necessary
at that moment to write up a sale and send [it] to the office with
cash. Finally I would eat into the money, and [it] would then
be impossible to turn in the money, so I would merely forget
about it and not write up the sale.

I admit that I have done several jobs for people in order to
satisfy outstanding debts which I owed them. I would treat
it as if they were regular customers, shift the goods from the
store and have the mechanics install the job. The mechanics
would not know that the customer or I were not paying for
the material or the labor. And that I was actually stealing to pay
off my debts. [He then lists slip cover and upholstery installa-
tions which went to pay for debts that included money owed
on purchases of coal, a storm door and a parking lot debt.]

It is very easy to conveniently forget to turn the money in.
Not only because of the pressure of time but I suppose subcon-
sciously some of this money should have belonged to me, for
the extra work, transportation, parking and towards the bonus
which I never got. It is very easy to hold back on the labor
alone which the store would never know about, although the
mechanics were paid overtime. Labor would be $20 or so per
job and it would finally wind up being used for personal purposes. For the past year and a half it has been very difficult to
collect my mileage due to indifference and sarcasm on the part
of my merchandising manager who doubtless does not see the

necessity of one's receiving all that which is justly due. I have put in many extra hours for the company, both in earlier starting times in the mornings to see that my men were properly starting the daily duties and many nights, calling on and making sales which I never receive overtime for. Living fifteen miles from the store, and in a community where everyone knows everyone else, I have gotten a great deal of business for the store.

I really have worked hard for many years for the store and feel that I have been responsible for a great deal of business through my own acquaintances and general dealings with customers.

I have been personally responsible for the training of at least a dozen mechanics which have been doing fine work for our company.

Reluctantly but willing to admit to the irregularities which I have been party to, I must say that I feel that I have been most unfortunate in having been held back in a financial way in our company. Sincerely, I have been for the past number of months praying for guidance from above and financial help for the future, which I believe is in sight. To say the words, "I am sorry," seems to mean so little, yet in reality I meant no harm and hope for relief.

Unfortunately, management felt it had no choice but to fire Waldo. His main source of income now had to come from odd jobs. Waldo began to feel like a man who had lost his will to swim after being dragged by an uncontrollable current to deep water. Besides his bare subsistence income, he had to face an even greater terror, gossip. His neighbors and customers soon learned that Waldo had lost his job. And it wasn't long before some busybody found out that Waldo had been stealing. Waldo became desperate and did the thing that he should have done long ago. He took a job as a foreman in a furniture factory in another community. Leaving the town that nursed him and watched him grow wasn't as hard as Waldo thought. For the first time in his life he was making a living wage. Waldo at last could walk with dignity.

Management too often takes the white collar employee's services for granted. Despite the widespread existence of personnel programs under which the employee is questioned about any problems he may have, there are many employers who show little or no interest in their employees' needs. Of course, I am not suggesting here that all employees' problems can necessarily be solved by management. But many can.

Although it may appear from reading Waldo's case that employers are Scrooges, this is far from true. Many would, if they were aware, help an employee in distress. The only trouble is they do not learn about their white collar workers' problems until it is too late. Such is the tragic case of a woman we shall call Jenny.

A widow in her early forties, Jenny had been forced to take a job as a salesclerk in a large eastern bookstore when her husband died. Although it was not an easy time for Jenny, she had the satisfaction of watching her two sons grow into manhood. The oldest son had his heart set on a military career and joined the Air Force. The younger son remained at home. Although Jenny was saddened to see her first-born leave, she felt that eventually a youngster had to try his own wings, so she couldn't blame her oldest for doing just that. Besides Jenny still had the fledgling to care for and watch. She did not think of the time he, too, would leave home. Jenny had been working at the bookstore for five years when that awful day of fear and tragedy arrived. At the age of seventeen her youngest son had contracted cancer, and the doctors knew of no way to save his life.

Jenny, who so far had been able to manage the upkeep of her home, found herself in a hopeless situation. Her salary came to $41 a week. Out of this sum she paid rent, gas and electricity and bought food for both herself and her youngster who was soon to spend all his living moments in the prison of his bed. Because she had no medical insurance, she also had to pay most of her boy's doctor and drug bills out of her salary. Sometimes her medical bills would eat up half her week's earnings. So for the next three years she stole company merchandise. Some of the books she took she marked down to half price. Others she just walked out with. Later, after I talked to her, she was to write down this account of what she did:

"I admit that I have stolen company merchandise on many occasions. I stole books for the following reasons:

"Whatever books that my son would enjoy reading would be that added comfort to him as he is home in bed alone while I work.

"I stole dictionaries and medical books so I could look up and know more about my son's sickness.

"I took books pertaining to cooking and food and fruits as my son has lost a lot of weight and I wanted to make the food as appealing as possible.

"I took books from the bookstore as several people have been so kind to me and my boy. As a token of appreciation I would give them some of the items that I took.

"I admit that on occasion when my friends came into the store I would give them a reduction in price without permission. As a rule I would give them 25 per cent off.

"It is impossible for me to evaluate how much I took from the bookstore. I realize that a few dollars at a time over the weeks adds up. I have no excuse for my behavior and I am ashamed of myself. The store has always been good to me."

Management found itself faced with a dilemma. Although Jenny over a three-year period had stolen several thousands of dollars' worth of merchandise, the reasons for her dishonesty were such that she really didn't deserve punishment. Yet management decided that it had to dismiss her. For one, the store could not have continued Jenny's surety bond with the insurance company. Secondly, the store found there were other dishonest employees whose reasons for stealing were, to say the least, more pecuniary. If management discharged the others and not Jenny they would claim favoritism. So the bookstore fired Jenny. But they helped her get another job.

The head of the store told me later that if Jenny had only informed management of her problem they would have been more than happy to give or lend her the money to pay for some of her son's medical expenses. But Jenny had never said a word about it. And I might add the store was not close enough to its employees to be aware that Jenny had reached the point of desperation. If they had they would have been able at least to ease a tragic situation.

The second type of honest crook is the individual who out of fear is forced to steal. Blackmail is a theme that we usually think belongs only to the realm of fiction and fantasy. How often have you read a newspaper account, for example, of someone involved in actual blackmail? Yet blackmail does occur, especially in white collar crime. In general the white collar worker is more sensitive than others to the mores of his environment. Constricted by the greatest sense of propriety, he is least immune to the shame that would follow, if, for example, he should become involved in an occasional dishonest act and those thefts should become public knowledge. As I mentioned in Chapter 3 he may even be framed by a so-called friend who starts by asking the innocent employee to do him an occasional favor and ends by threatening him with exposure if he refuses to continue to make up fake invoices or doctor the books. There are times when he may even be strong-armed into thievery.

Consider the plight of a man I'll call Joe. Joe belonged to the world of Paddy Chayefsky. Soft-spoken, shy, his hair creeping towards baldness, Joe, a bachelor, was still living at home with his parents at the age of thirty-seven. Then one night an event took place in Joe's life that would fill the next three years with terror.

As he frequently did, Joe attended a social at the neighborhood church. There he met a girl whom he had never seen before. In Joe's eyes she was lovely, exciting, different. He began dating her and for the first time in many years he was truly happy. Unknown to Joe the girl was leading two lives. Until she had met him her amorous adventures had been restricted to the underworld. Friendship with a man had meant something that was coarse and crude. The love she had known came in a bottle of whiskey at a hoodlum brawl. Yet there was desire and longing within her that could not be spoiled. She wanted kindness and respectability, someone who would treat her like a lady. So she decided to attend a church social where she met Joe. She had, at last, found a gentleman.

Her happiness didn't last long though. Her ex-boyfriend and a couple of his pals learned about her desertion. They came to Joe one night and they beat him until his body was broken. Joe spent the next three and a half months in the hospital. The doctors and time finally mended his wounds. But Joe could not forget that night of terror. No doctor could do that for him.

Shortly after he was released from the hospital, the hoodlums paid Joe a second visit. They had learned where he worked and they knew that he could accomplish for them what they couldn't do for themselves.

Joe was the head cashier in the main dining room of a large hotel. Business was very good so that Joe had an assistant. The two cashiers worked together five nights a week. One night a week Joe or his assistant worked alone. The hoodlums who had learned how the operation functioned told Joe that on the night he was alone he should close out the cash register an hour and a half before quitting time. That last hour and a half was to be devoted to the profits of the gang. Joe would give them one half the proceeds. He could keep what was left. They felt that by sharing the take with Joe he would have a stake in the scheme and would be less likely to object. Joe, remembering the nightmare of their violence, agreed. He was still too frightened to report them to the authorities.

The first night Joe tried the blackmailers' plan he was sure that it wouldn't be long before his thefts would be discovered. Most waiters' checks are numbered in sequence. Those checks are eventually arranged according to the numbered sequence, totaled and then the balance is compared to the amount of money in the cash register. Rearranging the waiters' checks in a consecutive order is a simple way of insuring that no check has been destroyed. Thus, no employee can pocket the cash the customer paid for the check without the loss eventually been detected. This is a standard control procedure and is used in almost every restaurant in the country.

An ironic set of circumstances, though, made it possible for Joe to steal money from the cash register one night a week for three years without having the shortage discovered. Joe would total the cash receipts an hour and a half before closing. He would also set aside the register tape that showed the amounts rung up. He would then destroy all subsequent incoming waiters' checks, as well as the register tape on which the cash from the discarded checks were recorded. Finally, he would pocket the cash. Joe's thievery was unwittingly aided by management. One of the girls in the hotel's bookkeeping department had quit and management had asked the five remaining employees if they could handle her work. The other girls said that they thought they could. And, after a fashion, they did. But in the process they cut a few corners. One of the shortcuts consisted of neglecting to arrange the waiters' checks in sequence. They would simply total the amounts on the ones that had been received and then balance the final figure against the final sum on the cash register. The balance, of course, always came out perfectly. As the result of its penny pinching, management, which was saving $60 a week by not hiring a bookkeeper, actually was losing $300 a week as the result of Joe's thefts. Over a three year period the total loss came to $45,000.

The thefts probably would have gone on as long as Joe worked as a cashier except that the Internal Revenue Department decided to do a full tax check on the hotel. It was one of those routine investigations. One of the hotel's clerks began assembling the records. No sooner had he tried to place the waiters' checks in sequence than he quickly realized that a number of checks were missing. Management was perplexed. The Internal Revenue agents were equally troubled. They suspected that the hotel had been merrily fleecing the government out of several thousand dollars.

A further check on management's part showed that six days of each week everything was in order. But on the seventh day there were always some waiters' checks missing. And the day that their records were in disorder invariably turned out to be the day when Joe was on duty alone. The hotel management accused Joe of the thefts. When faced with the evidence, he asked them to accompany him to his home. There he went into his bedroom, opened a bureau drawer and took out about $22,000 in cash. It was the exact amount that the hoodlums had allowed Joe to keep as his share. Joe felt that some day he would be caught. Since the money didn't belong to him, he wanted to be able to return it.

The hotel management, though, wasn't satisfied. A complete audit showed that an additional $22,000 was missing. Joe, they felt, was only being half-honest, that he knew where the remainder of the money had gone. After lengthy questioning, Joe finally admitted the whole story including the original beating. He also identified the men who had forced him to steal. The men were soon caught, tried, convicted and sent to jail. Joe lost his job and was given a suspended sentence.

The cases of Waldo, Jenny and Joe have in common the fact that external circumstances over which they had no control forced them to commit dishonest acts. There is another type of white collar worker who becomes an accomplice in a crime in that he is aware that thievery is taking place, yet is unable to prevent the crime or expose the criminal. In a sense his guilt is as great as the person who steals. Yet there is often a mitigating circumstance, for the individual he is protecting usually is a close relative, friend or loved one. To ask a husband to turn in a wife, an aunt a niece, or a girl her boyfriend is to expect too much of human nature. Many companies protect themselves by not hiring a close relative or friend of a white collar worker already on their payroll. Otherwise, they may find themselves in unexpected difficulty.

Here is a story of a young woman whom we shall call Edna. She worked at a woman's specialty store. At the age of twenty-eight after five years with the organization she was made a store manager. The store, which had four outlets, employed more than seventy workers. Edna was constantly faced with the patronage problem—friends and relatives constantly badgering her for part or full time jobs. Although it was against management's policy to hire the employees' close friends or relatives, Edna flouted the rule and gave jobs to a number of acquaintances and several relatives including a sister whom I'll call Jean.

Jean worked only during the Christmas and Easter vacations and the summertime when she was home from college. Jean had been at the store only a few days when Edna discovered that she had been stealing the store's merchandise. Edna found herself in a dilemma. If she fired Jean she would have to face the wrath not only of her sister but other relatives. So she began covering Jean's thefts. Edna began manipulating inventory figures and donating to the store several hundred dollars' worth of merchandise gifts and samples that she had solicited from the manufacturers. If it had been up to Edna, she would have allowed Jean to indulge herself as long as she had the strength to carry out the merchandise. In fact for two and a half years, during which Jean worked a total of eight months, Edna managed to hide over $10,000 worth of her sister's pilferage.

Jean, however, wasn't satisfied with just taking the store's goods. After a while she began rifling her fellow workers' pocketbooks. The other employees were not sure that it was Jean. However, the first day she began work during her Easter vacation two employees in Jean's department found that cash had been stolen from their handbags. From then on, the girl's co-workers would always hide their money when Jean worked in the store. Two years passed, the tension mounting each time Jean returned from college and reported for work. Finally, several employees could no longer stand the strain and wrote a letter to top management explaining the situation. Jean, no longer able to find her fellow employees' money, had begun to pilfer handkerchiefs, lipsticks, mirrors, combs and compacts. Edna's sister couldn't help herself. She was a kleptomaniac.

Chapter 6

"Mr. Jones, Meet Mr. Jones"

WHEN MRS. LYDIA BURTON and her seventeen-year-old daughter, Sheila Joy, arrived in Decatur, Georgia, in November, 1954, their earthly riches consisted of $1,000, a used car and the clothes on their backs. When they hurriedly departed three years later with the law at their heels, the very same Mrs. Burton could easily have been mistaken for the eccentric widow of an oil tycoon. Her retinue stretched a city block and included a pink, air-conditioned Lincoln, a Mercury station wagon, a Pontiac sedan, three vans crammed with household goods, three traveling companions and forty-five cocker spaniels including a trio of prize winners known to the haut monde of the dog world as Piccolo Pete, Capital Gain and Rise and Shine, the country's top show dog in 1954. Mrs. Burton's arrival and departure climaxed one of the most amazing adventures of any white collar thief who has been driven by the dream of outdoing Croesus, the Rockefeller of the ancients.

Mrs. Lydia Burton's background sounds as improbable as her subsequent career. Her maiden name was Margaret Lydia McGlashan. The daughter of an English couple, she was born in Tientsin, China, in 1906 and spent her early years in England. By the age of twenty-eight her itch to travel became a veritable rash and she loped around the globe arriving finally in the Canal Zone where she got a job in the offices of the Chinese Rug Company of Tientsin. In 1935 at the age of twenty-nine she married a man named Jasper W. Burton. Three years later the rug company transferred Mrs. Burton to Honolulu. With her went her two-year-old daughter, Sheila Joy. Her husband, though, stayed behind and the couple were eventually divorced. Mrs. Burton was on her own. The first thing she did was to swindle the Chinese rug merchants of several thousand dollars and with her youngster in tow skip to California. A short time later she was indicted by a grand jury in Honolulu for embezzling from her former employers. But the state of California, in an unexpected display of chivalry, refused to extradite her. During the succeeding eighteen years, Mrs. Burton blazed a trail of thievery, chicanery and confusion that included fraud and embezzlement in four states and British Columbia. Always a step ahead of the law, she escaped one bad check charge when the only witness died. Yet during all these peregrinations she was never detained long enough to spend so much as an hour in jail. By the time she had arrived in Decatur she had used twenty-two aliases, and her daughter had employed nine.

Shortly after Mrs. Lydia Burton, now Mrs. Janet Gray, came to Decatur she applied for a job as general office manager of a successful private clinic. The staff included a dozen physicians, half of whom worked full time. Since Mrs. Gray would be handling large amounts of cash, one of the doctors decided to check her references personally. He placed a long distance call to Baltimore where Mrs. Burton (Gray) claimed she had previously worked for another physician. The voice at the other end of the line not only verified that she had indeed worked in Baltimore but assured the doctor that she was the best kind of employee to have, reliable, responsible and experienced. And experienced she certainly was. An F.B.I. check later showed no such physician or address in Baltimore. The doctors, of course, were unaware that Mrs. Gray was a fraud and hired her. She immediately set her sights on the life of luxury and southern comfort. This time, though, she wasn't interested in just keeping up with the Joneses. She would, if her powers hadn't failed her, be Jones incarnate, the one whom everybody else wants to be.

Her first step was to find a suitable community in which she could endow the charade of her past with reality. It wasn't long before she and her daughter, now seventeen, located in the fashionable suburb of Doraville, ten miles from Decatur. There she made a down payment on a $26,000 home, built a $14,000 swimming pool and started on a three-year shopping spree that included several hundred dresses, a kennel of prize-winning dogs and that delirious-looking pink Lincoln. As far as her neighbors were concerned, the nice middle-aged lady in the big house was the daughter of a general and the widow of a millionaire, for that is what she told them. Her own daughter, meanwhile, had been given the improbable alias of Candace Victoria Lane, and sent off to the exclusive Westminster Private School for Girls in Atlanta's fashionable northside. Candace, who was posing as her mother's niece, had presented no credentials from other schools to the authorities at Westminster. She gave a simple explanation. Since her aunt's business affairs had required an excess of traveling, she had received private instruction from tutors. Candace, a school spokesman said later, was considered a "bright" student.

Where did Mrs. Burton get the money to support a daughter in an exclusive southern finishing school, an expensive home, a swimming pool and a menagerie of prize cocker spaniels? This larcenous Auntie Mame had found an almost inexhaustible source of ready cash at the physician's clinic. She would simply dip into the fees paid to the physicians, keeping several hundred dollars a week for herself while neglecting to mark down the missing amounts in the clinic's accounts. Since the doctors were taking in hundreds daily, Mrs. Burton figured that the shortage would go undetected. And it did for nearly three years until Mrs. Burton became somewhat greedy and increased her take. The physicians finally came to the conclusion that they would do well to apply their stethoscopes to their pocketbooks. For some inexplicable reason they felt they were experiencing a decided income drop. So they called in a New

Orleans accountant named John C. Walsh. Walsh began checking the clinic's books and on the third day noticed a decided discrepancy. "When I got to March," said Walsh, "it suddenly struck me that there were no deposits of currency." When Mrs. Burton was asked to come to the office with an explanation, she did the thing she had been doing for nearly half her life, she disappeared.

Lydia Burton's flight through the South was almost as prominent as Sherman's march through Georgia. Yet, she managed to avoid capture for three weeks, despite the efforts of southern law enforcement officials and the F.B.I. which had been called in on the case. Apparently all that the police could learn was that Mrs. Burton was traveling in a somewhat northerly direction. And it was Lydia herself who left the clues including the abandonment of the pink Lincoln in Greenville, South Carolina, and a meeting with a dog trainer at Greensboro, North Carolina, who brought twenty of the cocker spaniels to a kennel at Rocky Hill, Connecticut. It was obvious that Mrs. Burton, in the interests of speed, was stripping her caravan of all essentials.

No sooner had the galloping Mrs. Burton disappeared into the heartlands of anonymity, than the local merchants who ran the swank shops of Decatur and Atlanta discovered that the millionaire's widow had left them holding a hefty bagfull of unpaid bills. The bills ranged from $59.50 in one fashionable millinery shop to a $1,600 clothing account in another store. In addition she had a $2,121 mortgage on the pink Lincoln and owed $14,000 on her swimming-pool-equipped home. A photographer who took pictures at a party for her dog-loving friends said the general's daughter had failed to pay some $30 for her services. M. M. Armistead, named custodian of the property she left behind, assembled a list of her possessions in an attempt to satisfy some of her creditors. The list ran eight pages and included a car, 113 dresses, 334 books, numerous cockers and dog show trophies. Mrs. Burton had finally achieved her goal of breaking bread with the upper crust. Apparently her hasty departure had left them with only half a loaf, and the moldy half at that.

Although Mrs. Burton was undoubtedly a Houdini at disappearing, there was one thing she couldn't hide, her freckles, and this led to her detection and apprehension. She decided to make her new home in Tulsa, Oklahoma, the oil capital of the world. Returning to her favorite dodge, she applied for an office position with a doctor there. And on August 15, 1957, two weeks and three days after she left Decatur, she was back at work. It wasn't long before she told one of her co-workers that she could save her new employer money by taking over the monthly auditing of books. However, Mrs. Juanita Hettwer, the physician's receptionist, became suspicious. She had read a newspaper account of Mrs. Burton and her Georgia fling. The news story reported the significant detail that the wanted woman's face was peppered with freckles. "I guess the first thing that really caught my eye," said Mrs. Hettwer, "was the business about the freckles. Then there was the fact that she had worked in Decatur for some doctors. She had told us that she was forty-two, but she looked older. [Actually she was fifty-one and her hair had turned gray.] And then she had talked some about having pet dogs at home." The doctor's receptionist informed the F.B.I. and Mrs. Burton along with her daughter were arrested. In checking the modest Tulsa home the two had rented, officers found only three cocker spaniels including Mrs. Burton's favorite Rise and Shine. The dogs were about all that remained from Lydia's venture into the nether world of southern aristocracy.

Shortly after Mrs. Burton was taken to jail, she received a telegram that must have seemed like a final note of irony which no doubt left her with the feeling that her past had inexorably caught up with her. The telegram was signed, Jasper Burton, Lydia's ex-husband. He, too, had read newspaper accounts of his former wife's escapades. They included her description as well as the fact that her real name was Mrs. Margaret Burton. Burton himself had taken a job as a hotel manager in Athens, Georgia, just sixty miles from Decatur, in March, 1955. Unknown to all he had been living within a two-hour drive from his ex-wife and daughter for two years and four months. Neither Burton nor his former wife and daughter were aware of the other's whereabouts. In fact they hadn't been for the last eighteen years. At first Mrs. Burton refused to acknowledge any relationship to her ex-husband. Burton telegraphed Lydia after trying unsuccessfully to phone Sheila Joy at the Tulsa jail. Mrs. Burton responded, "Who is that? I don't know him. No, I don't want to reply to the telegram." Eventually, though, she softened and accepted a phone call from the man she hadn't seen in nearly two decades. She told him: "I've raised Sheila Joy into a very fine girl—just as honest and true as she can be. It is the one thing I've done well."

Six days later Sheila Joy and her mother were brought to Atlanta where Jasper Burton saw his daughter for the first time since she was two. Charges against Sheila Joy were dropped and she departed from the United States marshal's office the next day with her father and her uncle, Ian McGlashan, a Los Angeles theatrical producer. Ian hadn't seen his sister in nearly seven years since she and Sheila Joy had spent about four months in her brother's California home. Ian apparently had expected that some day his sister would come to an unhappy end. "My sister," he explained, "is a very sweet, kind, gentle person. She is the sort of person who faints at the sight of blood. I understand she almost fainted at the jail Friday morning when they were trying to take a blood test." Then somewhat wistfully he added, "But she seems to have a penchant for getting in jams." Lydia apparently called her brother rarely, only when she was in trouble. When she phoned him from a Tulsa jail, it was he who advised her to give herself up to Georgia extradition. "I knew it was bound to come," he said afterwards. "I'd been waiting seven years for it."

As was to be expected Margaret Lydia McGlashan Burton's day in court had its madcap moments. In the first place she didn't have one trial but two, and all because of a minister's offhand remark. During the first trial there had been a great deal of testimony about the one million dollars the doctors had earned at the clinic during the thirty-one months Mrs. Burton had worked there as bookkeeper and business manager. Mrs. Burton herself had been charged with stealing $186,757. One Sunday, while the first trial was in progress, the Reverend

R. Frank Crawley of the First Methodist Church in Decatur had commented from the pulpit that instead of Mrs. Burton being on trial for taking the money, it appeared that the doctors might be on trial for making that much money. The remark resulted in a good laugh for the congregation and the minister himself, who apparently afforded himself an occasional jest. Unfortunately for the state, one of his parishioners was a member of the jury. The remark was also heard by Frank Thomas, a grand jury foreman, who did his civic duty and reported the preacher's comment to the court. Judge Frank Guess promptly declared a mistrial on a defense counsel motion.

Mrs. Burton, meanwhile, who had spent nearly five months in jail, was beginning to feel the strain. While awaiting her second trial she suffered a series of fainting spells, which she had experienced intermittently over the past fifteen years. In the last six months they had occurred with increasing frequency. By the end of her second trial, which lasted four days, she was in a semiconscious stupor. While the all-male jury was out deliberating her fate, Mrs. Burton blacked out in a room less than one hundred feet from the jury room. Her own doctor could not be found. The court, however, had no trouble finding a physician, calling on one of the doctors whom Mrs. Burton had fleeced. True to his Hippocratic oath, he quickly went to her aid and restored her to consciousness so that she could be wheeled into the courtroom where the jury returned moments later with its verdict.

When Judge Clarence Vaughn asked the jury if it had reached a decision, her eyes momentarily flickered, only to close again as the solicitor general read the verdict in a loud voice, guilty on two counts of larceny after trust. The jury, which is allowed to do so under Georgia law, fixed her sentence at five years on each count and recommended that they be served concurrently. The judge followed the jury's recommendation. Mrs. Burton was released from jail after serving only eighteen months.

Although Mrs. Burton is an extreme example of the status-seeking white collar thief, she dramatically illustrates how such needs serve as the basic cause or motivation for much white collar crime. Our society has often been described as being so material conscious that an individual's success and importance are rated not by what he knows, but by what he owns. A family, for example, may purchase a second car or a house with rooms it doesn't need to show off its wealth and importance. Such purchases are called "conspicuous consumption," the expenditure made not for comfort or use, but for purely display purposes. The phrase incidentally was coined and explored by that pioneering thinker Thorstein Veblen in his classic *The Theory of the Leisure Class.* Written in 1899, the Veblen thesis is even more applicable today.

Mrs. Burton, in her own eccentric way, had turned to crime in order to support her irrational hunger for "conspicuous consumption." Her purchase of more dresses than she could wear in a year, a house too big for her needs, three cars, and a kennel of expensive show dogs—her favorite Rise and Shine cost $10,000—had no useful purpose except to give her the status of a woman of means and importance. Although her peculiar needs put her, if only temporarily, in the world of the very rich, she was driven by the same senseless desire that has consumed so many of us, the all-encompassing need to keep up with the Joneses.

The striving for status and acceptance through the ownership and display of material possessions operates on all levels of white collar crime, from the clerk to the executive. In one instance a twenty-five-year-old stock clerk working in a department store took as many as a dozen dresses a week as well as a varied assortment of costume jewelry. Her thefts over a two-year period totaled $15,000. Her explanation: "I have no excuse other than I needed the money to go out with a bunch of girls who are well dressed and I couldn't help myself." In another instance five divisional heads of a large electrical-supply company decided to move up the Joneses' ladder and improve their status in the community by owning bigger and larger homes. In three years they stole enough lumber and electrical equipment from their own company to build themselves homes valued at $30,000 each. They also had enough material left over to sell the surplus for an extra $100,000 profit. The five divisional heads, all model members of their community, never got a chance to enjoy their new found status. For soon after their homes were completed their thefts were detected and they were taken into custody.

Although the cases of the stock clerk and the department heads are widely disparate in the material objects of their thefts, they are similar in the basic motive involved, the need and desire to improve their status among friends or neighbors and thus win new or added respect. Their joint failure is obvious. They believed, and tragically this is too often true, that they would gain prestige because they could display the newest or most expensive material possessions.

This need to keep up with or surpass the Joneses occurs most frequently among individuals whose early years were spent amidst poor surroundings. Place such a person in an environment of conspicuous consumption, give him the opportunity to steal, and he may find the temptation overwhelming.

Take the case of Roscoe David Coon. Coon was born in 1908, in the little town of Atlanta, Texas. It was not an easy time for young Roscoe who never completed high school but worked instead. When his parents moved to Pasadena, California, Roscoe, an only child, kept himself busy. He married at the age of sixteen, and soon became the father of two daughters and one son. An ambitious lad, he attended night school and college and business college in Pasadena. Roscoe had the makings of another Horatio Alger. But somehow the legend became twisted.

In 1929 at the age of twenty-one, Roscoe obtained a position at a Los Angeles bank. He worked there two years, but the depression began taking its toll and Roscoe found himself with the U.S. Forestry Service, where he remained for three more years. Roscoe was determined to make himself a career in banking and once again got a job with another bank, this one back in Pasadena. His starting salary was $21.50 a week, not much with which to support a family. In order to meet current expenses, Roscoe began borrowing, $50 from one bank, $100 or $150 from another. Between October 1938, and August, 1948, he made five personal loans from one institution, eleven from a second. Roscoe, though, had a hard time meeting the payments. Finally be became ineligible to borrow so much as $50 within the Pasadena area. Life looked bleak for Roscoe, that is until May, 1949, when a rich new world was dangled before him, a world Roscoe couldn't resist.

Roscoe's new world was known as Twentynine Palms, a fast-growing, rich desert community located 150 miles east of Los Angeles. The Joshua Monument National Bank had just been chartered at Twentynine Palms and its president wanted a bright, young executive to take over the bank's day-to-day affairs. He asked a personal acquaintance to take the position. The friend declined the offer, but recommended Roscoe David Coon for the job. Just at the point where life had seemed to fail for Coon, he was offered a partnership in paradise. At the age of forty-one, he was made vice-president and cashier of the Joshua Monument National Bank. More important than his annual salary of $4,800, Roscoe was in complete charge.

During the next six years Roscoe's social and financial status improved considerably. When he came to Twentynine Palms his earthly riches consisted of two twelve-year-old cars, equity in a small house, its furnishings and his personal effects. By the summer of 1955, Coon had done the following: built at least seven houses in the community, engaged in turkey ranching, gold mining, had made investments in a night club and bar, a lumber company, a finance company, plus other investments totaling $100,000. In addition Roscoe bought thirty-six thoroughbred race horses including one he purchased in New Jersey for $60,000 and another he got in Kentucky for $53,500. Over the years Coon had paid one trainer $112,000 to care and train the horses. The former bank clerk's horses could be seen at one time or another at six tracks in California, the Las Vegas track and at Agua Caliente, Mexico. Roscoe, who only a few years back had been barred from borrowing so much as $50, had become the Aga Kahn of Twentynine Palms.

Perhaps most amazing of all was the trust the bank's superiors had in their vice-president. Not only did Coon personally loan money to customers who had been refused credit at the bank, but he also numbered among his borrowers at least two members of the board of directors and the president of the bank. Yet nobody ever even suspected let alone questioned Roscoe's financial affluence. When investigators finally made a delayed bank examination, they learned that Roscoe David Coon had embezzled $678,000 from the Joshua Monument National Bank. Coon is now serving a twenty-year sentence for bank fund manipulations. Ironically, the day the bank's doors were permanently closed, the titan of Twentynine Palms was arrested at the Del Mar track, the favorite racing site for his own thoroughbreds and the place where as a former bank clerk he used to come with the hope of winning enough money to pay back $150 bank loans.

Roscoe's early years had been a long, sapping period of continual financial strain. His drive to make good, to gain affluence and status through honest means invariably foundered. Thus, the moment easy wealth was placed within reach of his eager fingertips, Roscoe could not resist, he began stealing. Until he was forty-one he had never experienced the pride of true ownership. In essence Roscoe was building a world of prestige that he had never known in his youth.

A dramatic contrast to Roscoe Coon is the following story from our files. It is the case of a man who attempted to recapture the easy living and material status of his childhood.

Egbert's father was a well-to-do businessman who gave his family a fine substantial home with all the upper-middle-class advantages. Many of Egbert's leisure childhood hours were spent riding a pony, just one of the toys his father had given him. While Egbert was only a youngster, his older brother was able to attend an exclusive college. Then, when Egbert was fourteen, his father died. His brother, who had a head start on life, no longer needed his father's help. At the same time his sister made a successful marriage while Egbert was still young. Egbert, though, was not so fortunate. He had to hunt success unaided and alone, for the money that his father had left the family was soon exhausted.

At the age of twenty-five, Egbert who was already the father of two with the third on its way, got a job as an auditor with an electrical appliances distributing company. Although his take-home salary never topped $95 a week, he eventually owned an $11,500 home, three saddle horses and a new car that cost him $4,578. Egbert explained to anybody who was curious that his mother had died and that he had inherited three small apartment houses which gave him a substantial secondary income. Everybody believed Egbert, even his wife. At night he would remain at home, play with his children, watch television, help his wife with the dishes. Only on occasional weekends would he disappear on what he would explain as a business trip or a jaunt with the horses. Those who knew him thought Egbert a little drab perhaps, but a good family man. Certainly no one would entertain the slightest suspicion that Egbert was a thief. He simply didn't have the imagination.

The office where Egbert worked consisted of a reliable, conscientious manager who had been with the firm thirty-five years, two clerks, a bookkeeping staff and Egbert, the company's auditor. The people in the office were responsible for the paperwork involved in the receiving and shipping of appliances like toasters, mixers, electric blankets, and so on to and from a nearby warehouse. The office would receive the merchandise from a number of major manufacturers, store them in the warehouse and then ship them out to retailers. The whole operation was only one branch of a large electrical appliance distributing company which had other branches throughout the country.

Although Egbert's office was doing a large volume of business, they somehow seemed to be losing money. Our firm was called on to locate the difficulty. We soon discovered that there was considerable dishonesty among the truck drivers in the shipping department. However, this discovery did not explain the branch's total losses. We began a check on the employees in the bookkeeping department and immediately became suspicious of Egbert when we discovered his relatively expensive tastes. The explanation as to how he was able to pay for all these possessions was only partly true. He did own the three small apartment houses. But he had not inherited them from his mother. He bought them outright. The clinching clue that Egbert was a thief came when one of our industrial engineers discovered the torn tissue between a carbon and a bill which Egbert had voided. Besides pocketing money from cash sales and then destroying the records of the sales, Egbert would ship merchandise to a friend's house. The friend, in turn, would sell it to individual customers including a number of employees who had actually worked in the plants that manufactured the goods.

When Egbert was confronted with the evidence, he not only admitted that he had been stealing $15,000 to $20,000 a year for the past five years, but that on the weekends he was supposed to be away on business or playing with his horses, he would travel to New York City, a distance of some 250 miles, with a secretary who worked for a neighboring company. Egbert and his paramour would retire to a plush hotel after spending the earlier hours of the evening night club hopping. The auditor, known to his friends as shy and retiring, would drop as much as $500 during a weekend fling. Egbert had reached the point where he could afford the ultimate in a rich man's possessions, a mistress.

Chapter 7

The Insecure Executive

THE FOLLOWING took place in Indiana. But it could have happened anywhere. Not long ago the three-year-old daughter of a supermarket manager picked up the telephone. Recognizing the somewhat familiar voice at the other end, she asked, "Daddy, are you coming to our house tonight?" The little girl's father worked such long hours that his own child had almost become a stranger to him.

This incident, reported in *Supermarket News*, illustrates the plight of the American executive. Sometimes overworked, often laden with responsibilities that would give a marine general an ulcer, the typical executive may well be the twentieth century's most benighted and harassed worker.

Many middle and top management personnel work between forty-eight and sixty hours a week, seeing little of their children and making business widows of their wives. While the overwhelming majority of chief executives of America's top 606 companies earn $55,000 a year and above, there is a whole legion of middle management personnel who earn from $6,500 to $18,000 annually. And there is an even larger number of first line supervisors whose annual take-home pay ranges between $4,000 and $6,500. The picture of the typical successful executive who lives in a $150,000 home with a maid, a butler and three cars is an over-simplification. There are, of course, some who do, but they are comparatively few. The mountain of executive success probably has the smallest of all plateaus.

Besides working long hours, the average executive frequently must live with on-the-job pressures that are to say the least harrowing. For example, *Fortune* reports this situation in an article entitled "How Executives Crack Up." A certain oil company determines its promotion-demotion policy by making up a dossier for each management decision, detailing who supported it and who opposed it, and then checking back at the end of the year when some of the results of the decision are apparent. Although the above example is somewhat extreme, many executives find themselves without jobs because the profit goals given to them were not reached. And once out on the street the branch director, department head or vice-president may find that after thirty years of experience he is sometimes not wanted because he is too old or that his knowledge is too specialized for the job openings that do occur.

In addition to external pressures, the successful executive is frequently in a state of tension as the result of his own basic insecurities which war within him. Robert N. McMurry, writing in the *Harvard Business Review*, gives this picture of the human dynamo, the man who epitomizes the split-level mind and the gray flannel heart.

"Superficially," writes McMurry, "such men appear to be ideal employees. They have no distractions from their concentration on work. They are extremely ambitious and unusually competitive. They are frequently the best producers, especially from the standpoint of quantity. Their single-minded devotion to the job tends to attract the attention of management. (In fact, such individuals are usually careful to see that they do attract attention.) They are the contest winners, the quota breakers, the contributors to suggestion plans. They are the ones to whom hours mean nothing and who are willing to travel and spend nights and week-ends on the job. Often, too, they are intelligent, well qualified technically, and excellent personal salesmen. They can make brilliant analyses; they can compile complete, comprehensive, and carefully reasoned reports. In consequence, they are earmarked early as 'comers' and rise rapidly in the organization. Management quickly spots them as potential material for top jobs in the company.

"Many men showing these qualifications *do* have genuine potential, of course. But some have basic limitations for *top-management* responsibilities which their brilliance, competence, energy, and obvious devotion to the job tend to obscure. For instance, they are frequently, despite their seeming dynamism and self-confidence, persons with inner feelings of insecurity and frustration who have a strong need to deny these characteristics and often possess a surprising capacity for hatred, rivalry and resentment. These aggressive characteristics stimulate them to great activity. Moreover, when they are promoted to positions which are too demanding, the threat of their deficiencies being exposed creates pressures which further accentuate their limitations and weaken their self-control. As a result, such men attempt to get out of the morass in the only way they know how—by working harder. They become tense and anxiety ridden, with occasional temper flareups when the pressure becomes unbearable. They are driven more and more to overwork in an attempt to 'work off' their hostilities, compensate for their shortcomings, and conceal their inadequacies."

McMurry sums up by saying that this spiral of anxiety-hostility-activity reaches a tension point where something must give. For some, he adds, it is a heart attack. For others it may be a nervous breakdown, excessive drinking, or "indulgence" in vices of one kind or another. And I might add a further consequence that may result from the combination of external pressures and "executive neurosis" is white collar crime on a grand scale. Of the more than 400 million dollars in losses uncovered by my firm in just the last ten years, about sixty per cent can be traced to employees on the supervisory or executive level.

The most important cause of executive thievery is what I would call top management myopia, the near-sighted board of directors or president who shortchanges the firm's high echelon personnel. On the one hand the executive is expected to answer and be responsible for an operation that not only may run into millions of dollars but is vital to the company's very existence. Regardless of how he may have worked to build the firm, should he make just one wrong decision it could mean the loss of his job and even the end of his career. Yet in numerous instances the financial rewards he receives are not commensurate with the value of the work that he does. He is a little like the prize-fighter who cannot afford to lose a match if he wishes to remain in the ring. At the same time his contract may give him only a fraction of the purse while his manager and promoter take the rest.

Consider the case of John Russell Cooney who rose from office boy to a titan in the insurance industry. When Cooney went to jail after pleading no defense he had embezzled $668,-942 from the organization he had singlehandedly built into one of the most successful insurance companies in the country. Why did this man dishonor himself by cheating the firm to which he had given so much of his life's blood? The cause of his thefts was the promise of a salary raise that was fulfilled too late.

The life of John Russell Cooney began as it ended, with tragedy. The son of a Wabash Railroad conductor, Cooney was born in 1891 in Butler, Indiana. It was a large and happy family. John had six brothers and sisters to play with. Although the elder Cooney's income was comparatively humble, his brood was never in want. Then tragedy struck. When John was six, his mother died. Two years later his father passed away. The children scattered, little John going to live in a Detroit orphanage. At fourteen John left the orphanage for Chicago and the warmth of his sister's home. The struggle for existence had already begun.

While attending Chicago's Hyde Park High School, John took his first job as handy boy with the western department of the Firemen's Insurance Company. After leaving school, he joined Firemen's as an office boy. The insurance firm began to expand. A shy but popular, hard-working fellow, Cooney shifted from one department to another, always adding to his knowledge of the insurance business. His big chance came in 1928 at the age of thirty-seven. In that year Cooney was appointed assistant manager of the Pacific office in San Francisco. He wrote so much insurance on the coast that he was returned to the firm's headquarters, in 1931, with a new title, executive vice-president. Three years later at the age of forty-three he was appointed president. But John Russell Cooney's struggle was far from over.

Cooney had taken over the direction of a company which like thousands of others was barely bobbing over the tides of the depression. Firemen's along with a number of other firms had amalgamated to form the Loyalty Insurance Group. It was Cooney who was in large part responsible for the formation of the Loyalty Group affiliates. In order to keep the Group from sinking, Cooney, as president, worked night and day, week after week and month after month. When Cooney began his reign as head of the Loyalty Group, the association's stock sold at $2 a share. When he left the stock had risen to nearly $45 a share. During the same period the Group's assets had climbed from $56 million to $300 million. Banking executives eventually recognized this son of a railroad conductor as a financial wizard. Indeed, in his later years he became one of the most respected and revered men in the industry. He numbered among his friends the nation's great businessmen. And John Russell Cooney deserved the acclaim.

How did Cooney manage this financial miracle? A short, burly man with a gravel voice, Cooney dominated all who worked under him. The Loyalty Insurance Group was almost like a marionette in Cooney's hands. When Cooney barked a command someone always jumped to do his bidding. Perhaps most important of all, Cooney's generalship was masterful. He would sniff out an important financial objective—he traveled more than any other insurance company president in the country—and then like Napoleon marshal and deploy his forces with unerring skill.

But there was another facet of Cooney's personality. It was born in the mortar of his youth, those years of privation and tragedy which he never forgot. Cooney gave to almost every charity imaginable. As one friend put it, "It was nothing for Cooney to write out a four figure check for any one whom he thought needed help." Said another friend, "John not only was free with his money when it came to charity, but he would throw himself wholeheartedly into any worthwhile campaign. It wasn't just a matter of giving money, the man gave himself." Although one of the nation's hardest working insurance company presidents, Cooney found time to participate actively in the Community Chest, the Red Cross, the Salvation Army, the YMCA and the Boy Scouts. In keeping with his good works, Conney shunned all publicity. There was one time, though, when he watched thousands march, his heart high for the special honor given him that day. It was 1951 and the honor guard of the Newark St. Patrick's Day parade had named him Irishman of the Year.

The thing that led to Cooney's destruction, according to his lawyer, John Clancy, has an ironic twist. Two members of the board of directors had suggested to Cooney that he purchase an expensive 256-acre Blairstown, New Jersey, dairy farm where he could escape from the tension of running the multimillion-dollar insurance company. The directors, now dead, had assured him that the company would compensate him in salary. Cooney, meanwhile, discovered that the dairy farm which was to give him peace and rest proved an impossible burden. During the succeeding years Cooney sunk between $200,000 and $300,000 in a losing venture. The insurance genius was failing in his one attempt to go into business for himself.

Cooney, who was earning about $30,000 a year when he began his farming venture, did not receive the relief that had been promised him until too late. When years later his annual salary was finally raised to $81,000, Cooney was already in financial difficulty. Obsessed by his own burden and the wrong he felt had been done him, Cooney began to make up his losses by embezzling money from his own firm.

The main source of his thefts, of all places, was the company's petty cash account. Cooney would simply write out a voucher every few days for anywhere from $2,000 to $9,000, charge it to advertising, sign it, send it downstairs to the cashier's cage, receive the money and put it in his bank account. The money would come from the petty cash account which usually contained no more than $30,000. It had to be replenished frequently to keep up with Cooney's withdrawals.

How did Cooney manage to fool twenty-three prominent bankers, lawyers and other big businessmen who comprised the insurance company's board of directors? It was simple. Cooney's success had been so great that he dominated the huge company to the point where no one ever doubted either his judgment or his probity. Not once had they seen or asked to see the auditor's annual report, each of which since 1940 questioned Cooney's lavish use of company funds. In fact it wasn't until 1954 that any serious attempt was made to investigate Cooney's activities. The secret probe, at first unknown to the board of directors, was carried out by the New Jersey and New York State insurance examiners. The investigation resulted in Cooney's forced retirement. In 1956, Cooney was stricken by personal tragedy. For about the same time the state insurance investigators began to look into his affairs, his wife, Loretta, died. A year later Cooney himself developed a blood clot and had his left leg amputated.

When the case finally made the headlines in the summer of 1957, John Russell Cooney was already a broken man. A cause célèbre during that summer's New Jersey gubernatorial campaign, Cooney's name was coated with an additional layer of mud. On January 22, 1958, the sixty-six-year-old executive was wheeled into court where he was sentenced to one to two years in prison and fined $5,000. According to Clancy, all that he had left was $1,200. He had sold his property including his Blairstown farm and had turned over $330,942 to the company to which he had given and from which he had taken so much. On his arrival at the state prison, the man who had ruled a multimillion-dollar empire, turned to Warden Alvin Wangner with this request. "I would like," he said, "to have the waiter get me a glass of milk."

Twenty-two days later Cooney was given a suspended sentence. Said Judge Alexander P. Waugh, "The court did not intend that he die in prison and I am sure that no one in this community thinks that would be justice." Cooney was critically ill. Fourteen hours after his prison sentence was canceled, he died in St. Mary's Hospital in Orange, New Jersey. At his side were two of his three sons. John Russell Cooney's heart had given out.

A situation similar to Cooney's tragic predicament is the executive who is expected to cut an impressive figure in his community on a salary that is far from adequate. One of the most dramatic illustrations of this all too common occurrence is the story of Richard Crowe, the assistant manager of the 195 Broadway branch of the National City Bank of New York. The forty-one-year-old banker earned $7,250 a year. But in one day he enriched himself by $883,660, the sum that he stole from the bank's vaults. Until he was caught nine days later Richard Crowe had become the F.B.I.'s most wanted man.

Crowe lived on Staten Island in a fourteen-room house with his pretty blue-eyed wife, Honora, and their three children. The Island had been Crowe's home for many years. In 1932 National City Bank had bought another bank, which had a branch there. Since Richard Crowe was well acquainted with Staten Island he was assigned to work at the branch. Crowe who had started out as a clearance clerk with the National City had risen to teller, then note teller, loan teller and finally to chief clerk. Although his starting salary as chief clerk in Staten Island was about $1,800 a year—Crowe had made more working for the Miami *Herald* before he went to college— it looked as though this young, ambitious lad would go far. In fact he definitely appeared to all as "a comer." Crowe himself in a singularly revealing article in *Cosmopolitan* explained what brought him to committing one of the largest bank thefts on record:

When war came, a prominent lady on Staten Island began a drive to raise funds for the USO. Her husband called the president of the National City and asked him to recommend someone out on Staten Island to help her. The bank recommended me; then they called me to New York and told me of the importance of the job I was to do, and how it would help both the country and the bank. I readily agreed to help— after all, the only hobby I'd ever had was people. The lady managed to get an office in Borough Hall, and we launched the campaign. It was a great success.

Prior to this time, I'd like to emphasize, I'd been living a fairly modest life. The newspapers have made me sound as though I were living like a millionaire. They made much of my fourteen-room house, my speedboat, my two cars. The truth was that the house cost $20,000—and I'm still paying off the mortgage. It just happened to be a good, sound buy, and I got the down payment by selling a small house my aunt had given my wife and me as a wedding present. I'd turned the power boat over to the government during the war, and I later sold it at a modest price. The two automobiles I bought on time payments, like any other man with a modest income.

But once the USO campaign was over, the deluge began. Next thing I knew, I was mixed up in every conceivable kind of local cause and activity. I ran the War Bonds drive for Staten Island for the duration of the war. I was a director of the Community Chest, treasurer of the Red Cross, director of the Chamber of Commerce, co-chairman of the Salvation Army, Boy Scout committeeman, member of the Police Athletic League, director of the U.S. Volunteer Lifesaving Corps, president of the Richmond County Bankers Association, and president of Group seven of the New York State Bankers Association. I also founded and was president of the Stapleton Board of Trade. I organized the Staten Island Servicemen's Center and attended it once a week. I helped raise funds for the Catholic Youth Organization and the Jewish Youth Center. Hon (Crowe's wife) helped me in all these things by the way. She kept as busy as I did—busier, in fact, considering that she was running the house and taking care of two small children (the third hadn't arrived yet).

I never took on any of these outside jobs without consulting the bank. They always told me to go ahead; encouraged me, in fact. After all, every time my name got in the paper, the bank's did, too. But sometimes, in connection with these volunteer jobs, which were supposed to help build the bank's good name, I had to take a party to lunch or dinner. The

check would be, say, forty dollars. Sometimes I got the full
amount back from the bank; sometimes I didn't. And many
times I took a customer to an eight-dollar lunch and presented
the bank with an expense item of about three-fifty—which,
I knew well, was about all they would allow.

Don't misunderstand me. I was living high and enjoying it
to the hilt. I guess I got cocky and big-headed; the public
servant business went to my head. But I was never home at
night—I had too many places to go—and when I was home,
I was irritable with my wife and children. I suppose the out-of-
pocket expenses were worrying me. They were terrific. Some
nights, going to a formal dinner, I had to spend twenty-five
dollars or more for flowers for the hostess, getting my tails and
white tie in shape, cab fares, tips, etc. Before long, I had to begin
borrowing (don't forget, during the war I was only making
around a hundred dollars a week). At that time, too, I was
trying to pay off the mortgage on my house. All told, when I
ran off to Florida, I owed about $35,000, including the mort-
gage. If I had been sensible, Hon and I could have sat down
and figured out a way of liquidating these debts. But I wasn't
sensible; I was caught up in a maze of what I thought were
important activities, and I was most concerned with keeping
up that big front.

When the war ended, I felt as though I'd burned myself
out. And I had—but, again, the reaction didn't set in until
later.

The bank was evidently well satisfied with the job I'd done
during the war. They called me in and asked how I would
feel about transfering to a bigger branch in the city. The salary
would be better, they said, but I would have to take a reduction in title. The plan was for me to go in as assistant manager,
with the understanding that I would be made manager at some
not-too-distant date. I agreed immediately. It seemed that I
was getting somewhere at last.

After a year and a half at 195 Broadway, however, things
didn't look so rosy. I'd got my raise, all right, but I found that
it wasn't enough to keep my head out of the financial swamp
I'd fallen into. The manager there, moreover, was just about

my own age. There seemed to be no chance of my replacing him, and it seemed unlikely I would be transferred to some other branch. Shortly after I'd gone to the Broadway branch, I'd begun to have spells of what my doctor called "bad nerves." I couldn't sleep nights—oh, I could get to sleep, all right, but I always awakened a few hours later. Some nights I went down and wandered the beach aimlessly. And all this time I was trying to keep up the front I'd established during the war. Hon and I had been asked to join the country club, and we were going around with people who had a lot more money than we did. (I resigned from the club after I ran off to Florida, to keep from embarrassing the members.)

So you can see what a mess I was in. And, after months of keeping everything bottled up inside me, I found out I couldn't do it anymore. One day—that Wednesday in March, as I stood there in Lawler's (a favorite bar)—everything exploded. I suddenly got disgusted with myself for leading such a phony life, trying to keep up with the Joneses. And I transferred the blame from myself to the bank—I somehow held the bank responsible for the situation I was in.

I thought, What am I going to do?

And then I thought, I'll fix their wagon, good.

And that was how I decided to take the money.

It was Friday, March 25, 1949, when Richard Crowe silently finished stuffing a brand new leather suitcase with nearly one million dollars in cash and government bonds from four tellers' vaults. Since everyone who worked at the bank had already gone home, Crowe had only one fear, that he would be spotted by the cleaning women who regularly came at about that time. As he raced to leave the bank one lock on the suitcase popped open and tens of thousands of dollars scattered down a flight of stairs. Crowe had forgotten to fasten the straps. For a moment he was tempted to flee, but he had gone too far. Scooping up the money, he shoved it back into the suitcase. Just as he walked out of the lobby, he saw the cleaning women checking in.

Crowe, suitcase in hand, took the ferry to Staten Island,

where he remained over the weekend. Not once did he hint to his wife what he had done. But Crowe had plenty to keep him busy. Of the $883,660 he had taken, he hid nearly $700,-000 in his attic. Another $50,000 was stashed away in the family cemetery plot. And an additional $15,000 was secreted in his parents' home. He also sent some $60,000 to friends and creditors. That Sunday night he flew to Jacksonville, Florida. He had told Honora that he was going away on a business trip. By Monday afternoon bank officials were able to open the vault that Crowe had jammed and their discovery started one of the year's most extensive F.B.I. hunts. Six days later Crowe was arrested in the washroom of a small Daytona Beach night-club. A stranger had spotted his picture in the local newspaper.

Crowe was brought back to New York, tried and sentenced to three years in jail. A model prisoner, he served only thirteen months. When he returned home he was not only warmly greeted by his family but his neighbors as well. The only people who no longer spoke to Richard Crowe were those he had worked with for some twenty years. Officials at the bank had told their employees, including the best man at his wedding, never to see Richard Crowe again. Every one of them obeyed.

Although Cooney and Crowe had dared to storm their respective industries' Fort Knox, their dishonesty was, if not entirely, at least partially excusable. In Cooney's case, the two directors had acted at least thoughtlessly and perhaps dishonorably. One may say that Cooney should have brought his case to the rest of the directors of the company. But he had done too much and had risen too high to bend a rightfully proud knee. On the other hand Crowe, through his own admission "was living high and enjoying it to the hilt." Love of luxury is an explanation but, of course, no excuse for crime. At the same time though the bank for which he labored so industriously was well aware of Crowe's extracurricular activities, which not only benefited him but his employers as well.

While all businessmen, whether large or small, should never neglect the human element in dealing with their employees, it does not follow that being a good fellow is either their prime duty or responsibility. The chief purpose of business is to make a profit. To believe otherwise is to border on madness for an obvious reason. Any concern operating in the red will soon cease to function. Sometimes, for example, it is necessary for a concern to shift the duties of one or more of its executive personnel in order to operate at maximum efficiency. Such a shift may even result in a demotion or a loss of responsibility. Indeed, a downward status change for an entrenched executive may turn him into a vengeful employee who aims his vendetta at the point where his employer's heart beats fastest, his boss's pocketbook.

Consider the case of a man I'll call Evan, who was born and raised in a southern harbor town. At the age of thirteen, Evan went to work as a clerk for the local hardware store. While other boys spent their youth smacking fungos in the neighboring sandlots, little Evan had already begun a lifelong romance among his employer's nuts and bolts. Except for weekends, all the sunny days of his childhood were spent helping out in the store. Fortunately for him his employer was eventually able to reward Evan's devotion.

Over the years fishing boats from the Caribbean islands and South America began docking at the town's harbor. It wasn't long before the little hardware store took on marine supplies. As more and more boats chugged into port to sell their catch or buy the equipment needed for their next trip, traffic at the marine and hardware store boomed until it became a million-dollar-a-year business. And as the store began to grow so did Evan's knowledge of the ship chandler's trade. It wasn't long before he knew the thousands of kinds of supplies used by the ships' captains for their fishing ventures. He also made it his business to know personally all the boat captains who came to the town's harbor. By learning their idiosyncrasies as well as their needs, he soon built up for his employer a thriving business. His employer, in turn, did the only sensible thing he could. He promoted Evan to manager of the whole organization. His salary of $150 a week was considered unusually substantial for the community. Evan was in his glory.

For the next two decades this happy relationship between

employer and his second-in-command continued unabated. Although Evan no longer would drum up business with the same exuberance he displayed in his youth, the marine and hardware establishment remained a gold mine, for it was the only one of its kind in the town. The only thing that Evan felt that he lacked, for him the ultimate satisfaction, was a partnership in the firm which he had helped to build. But his employer had promised it to him and he knew that some day he would receive his final reward. But Evan's expectations, indeed his entire life and career, were to be smashed by a chain of circumstances which began with a force over which no man has control, a heart beat.

One day his employer suffered a heart attack. His doctor warned him that if he wanted to live he would have to take life easy, and that the first thing he would have to do would be to give up his business. Although it was like selling his own child, the owner of the store had no other choice. When the new owners took over, they immediately took stock. Included in the inventory was Evan. The new employers noted among other things that Evan was getting on in years—he was in his late fifties—and that his management lacked the aggressive blood of youth. So Evan who had believed he would soon reach the summit of his glory was demoted from general manager to head of the wholesale department, still an important post. After the initial shock, Evan's resentment burgeoned. He looked upon the new employers as "foreigners" who had stolen property that rightfully belonged to him. Finally, after two years of increasing bitterness, Evan decided on a plan that would not only compensate him for the wrong he felt had been done, but would result in a sweet vengeance.

When the original owner headed the firm, Evan would take care of all the firm's printing needs including the forms for invoices and bills. The new management changed the forms for the invoices and bills. Each new invoice or bill was given a serial number so that the accounting office could keep a check on each purchase and receipt. Evan, meanwhile, found several cartons of the old invoices or bills in his garage. With the old forms at his disposal, he systematically began to loot the new employers of nearly $91,000. This is how he did it.

Whenever a large shipment was made to one of the boat captains, Evan would personally go down to the docks to insure safe delivery and collect the money. He would also take along an extra supply of food, tools and equipment, often selling the additional goods to the ship captains. Since the captains usually demanded receipts for the merchandise they purchased, Evan would hand them one of the old invoices—the firm had kept its original name—and then pocket the money. During the next two years he managed to amass a small fortune. Despite the change in employers and his demotion, Evan had achieved the ultimate reward he had dreamed about. For all practical purposes, he had become a silent partner.

The partnership, unknown, of course, to his new employers came to light when the captain of a fishing fleet decided to exchange some of the merchandise he had purchased through Evan. When he sent one of the clerks back to the store with the request, the new manager asked to see the captain's receipt to check when the goods were bought in the store and the amount involved. When the old form bill reached the accounting department, an alert bookkeeper was puzzled by the rather antiquated, yellow-looking invoice. The problem was brought to the attention of management which called us in to analyze the firm's operation. The bank and board of directors had felt that the company's profit and expenses did not compare favorably with the firm's performance under the old management. It wasn't long before we learned where the profits had gone. Indeed, Evan when presented with the evidence, readily admitted his guilt.

"I gave my life to build this business," he said. "I started here when I was thirteen. This is the only job I ever had. My lifetime friend, my old boss left me nothing. Every penny that I took rightfully belongs to me."

That same afternoon Evan visited the firm's attorney and produced $91,000 including $50,000 in stocks and cash from five bank accounts. It was the total amount he had taken. A meticulous man, he had kept a little black book listing all the money he had stolen. If his thefts had gone undetected for about two more months, he would have reached the $100,000 mark, the point when he felt that he would have received his fair share of the profits. It was at that point that Evan planned to quit the ship chandler's business.

Evan was the victim of the Darwinian rule under which only the fittest survive. His demotion came about because someone else could pull a stronger and faster oar. And such was the case. However, Evan, though he lost prestige, still had a position that he could both live with and live on. Although life may have seemed harsh to him, it was not cruel. Even though Evan didn't realize it, he was comparatively lucky. He had survived for forty-one years.

Not long ago the *Wall Street Journal* ran a roundup on what a primitive people would call cannibalism but what a more civilized world prefers to describe as "throat cutting." Throat cutting is a rite being practiced by thousands of executives in hundreds of businesses. The result is a jungle that would prematurely gray even the financial Machiavellis of the nineteenth century. The purpose of throat cutting is just what its name implies, to get ahead no matter what. The *Journal* which interviewed fifty executives in twelve cities on the subject came up with a number of typical cases. In one instance, a vice-president of an Eastern corporation plugged the carburetor in the auto of a new rival to make him late for the first executive meeting. In another instance an elevator company executive waited for his rival's special project to flop, then submitted to the boss a series of memos, carefully backdated, to show that he had opposed the project all along. Perhaps one executive of a big Southwest oil company unconsciously summed up the situation by first denying that there was any throat cutting in his business. But after thinking it over, he added somewhat ruefully, "Of course, some people in this company will do just anything to get ahead."

This atmosphere forms a natural breeding ground for white collar crime. Its chief elements consist of trickery, a venomous subtlety and complete lack of ethics. One of the best examples of this form of knavery involves an assistant to the head of the purchasing department who was out to get his superior's job by proving that his boss had been stealing from the firm. The assistant's complaint was valid. His superior had been dishonest. But, as you shall see, the assistant himself had told management only a half-truth.

The two men involved in this case began their lives more than three thousand miles apart. In the end both men not only shared a joint office but a mutual guilt. I'll begin with a man I'll call Charles, vice-president in charge of the purchasing department of a ready-to-wear manufacturer with a chain of 180 stores. Charles, who had been working for the firm for some thirteen years, had risen from an $18 a week clerk to a position that brought him an annual salary of $12,000 a year plus company stock and an annual bonus. To give you an idea of his responsibilities, his department purchased for the Christmas season alone $500,000 worth of special gift packages. As far as the top management was concerned Charles deserved every penny he received. He was constantly coming up with new ideas and gimmicks on how to save the firm money. It wasn't long before the president of the firm invited Charles to join his entourage on the links. Charles was not only a member of the top management team but the golf team as well. His colleagues soon agreed that the vice-president in charge of purchasing was shooting more than his share of birdies. What they didn't know was that he was stealing everything but the president's golf balls.

One day Charles found himself in need of an assistant. He decided to go outside his department of fourteen people and hired a man we shall call Hans, a World War II refugee who in his earlier days had served as the general manager of a multimillion-dollar firm in the land of his birth. About fifty, Hans was a tall, thin nervous fellow who despite his somewhat nondescript appearance would display when necessary a whiplash mind. Hans not only had experience but brains and as far as Charles was concerned he had made an excellent choice, or so he thought.

For the next three years Charles and Hans worked in perfect harmony. Although the purchasing department was not expected to show a profit, the top management team was pleased as ever with Charles's money saving schemes. Indeed, they were firmly convinced that he could do no wrong. Hans, however, thought differently. He began planting insidious little seeds of suspicion whenever he happened to have a routine meeting with the firm's treasurer. He would call on the treasurer to sign a document or obtain an authorization. There would always be a few minutes discussion, just enough time for Hans to drop an almost invisible but lethal germ. "I don't think," he would say, "the weight of this paper we are ordering is consistent. But the mill is probably having problems with production." Another gambit would be: "I think we rushed in placing this order. But my boss feels the market is going up and we should order in large quantities. Of course, he knows better than I."

After about six months of carefully plotted innuendo, Charles's assistant decided to drop the bomb. So one day he entered the treasurer's office, his voice a little firmer, his step more assured. After the passing of a few pleasantries, Hans got down to business.

"I'm very much upset," he said. "And as much as I need the job, I've talked it over with my wife and I'm afraid I will have to resign."

"Have you discussed this with Charley?" asked the treasurer.

"No," said Hans, "I haven't."

"Why not?"

Hans looked appropriately confused. "I don't know what to tell him."

"What do you mean, you don't know what to tell him?" the treasurer retorted. The whole thing was beginning to sound a bit strange. And Hans was not offering any easy explanations.

"I want to tell you the truth," said Hans. "I'm applying for my citizenship papers and I don't want anything to interfere with my getting them."

"What's that got to do with it?" the treasurer said, more puzzled than ever.

"There are an awful lot of bad things going on in my department," said Hans. "And I'm afraid that some day it is going to break and I'm going to get in trouble. I know the business well. I could run that department with my eyes closed. Why, I ran a multimillion-dollar business like this one in my own country. So I have a pretty good idea how these things work. But to be more specific. The person from whom we buy a quarter of a million dollars' worth of stationery and supplies each year drives a milk truck. Every Friday afternoon he comes to our office dressed in a business suit as the representative of an established printing and supply firm. His quotes and figures and timely knowledge of what we want are remarkable. It was as though he knew exactly what is on our minds. The truth of the matter, he is Charley's brother-in-law. My boss through his brother-in-law is operating a phony stationery supply company. He gets the exact quotes from the best competitors in the field and then tells his brother-in-law what to quote when he comes around. The brother-in-law then buys the stationery supplies from one of the legitimate companies at the going market price and sells them to us, after having them shipped to his home. The hitch is that our firm is getting a short count. Where the receiving ticket says that the vice-president's brother-in-law gave us one hundred reams, we get only ninety."

The treasurer shook his head. The whole thing sounded preposterous. Yet whenever he had checked Charles's department his purchasing prices always matched the competitive prices. When the treasurer thought about it Charles's performance was just a little too good.

"I've been aware that this has been going on for several months now," Hans continued. "It took me some time to become suspicious. After all who would ever think that such a thing could be happening. But those stationery prices. They were always just right. I did a little investigating of my own. I had a friend draw up a Dun and Bradstreet report. And who do you think owned the business? It was registered under Charles's wife's maiden name. I also went to the address of the phony company's office. It turned out to be a two-family house. And the brother-in-law lived on the first floor. That and a little checking in the office proved the whole thing is a fraud."

When Hans had finished, the treasurer had recovered sufficiently to thank him for his sincerity and honesty and promised that whatever would be done he would not be involved. As soon as Hans left, the treasurer called on the president of the company. Together with the firm's lawyer the three men held the most painful conference in the company's history. They finally decided to get answers to the following three questions: 1. How true was Hans's story? Even though the treasurer had been impressed, it was still hard to believe. 2. If the story was true, what were the losses involved? 3. How to handle the case without creating a public scandal.

Since the situation was beyond the experience of the president and his chief lieutenants, they asked us for our advice. It was obvious from the start that the problem had to be handled with extreme delicacy. The most immediate question that we wanted to answer: Was the vice-president a thief or was the story simply a fantasy of his assistant's imagination?

As it turned out, the story Hans had told the treasurer was essentially true. Besides shortshipping merchandise, Charles was gathering additional coin through kickbacks from manufacturers who supplied the firm. Each year he bought a new car. He was living in a completely air-conditioned home, costing $35,000. Although he had frequently complained about excessive mortgage payments, his house was free and clear.

But we didn't stop our investigation with Charles. We also probed into Hans's affairs. And Hans we discovered was an even bigger thief than his boss. Six months, not three years, after he had joined the firm, Hans had learned through a vendor that Charles had set up a dummy company with his brother-in-law. The Dun and Bradstreet report never existed. In addition, Hans followed in his superior's footsteps, taking kickbacks without his knowledge and shortcounting merchandise, shipping the loot to his own business, which like Charles he ran under his wife's name. Hans had felt that the corruption in the purchasing department had reached a scale too large to hide. Since exposure, he believed, was inevitable, he decided to betray his boss, who was unaware of Hans's defalcations. He firmly expected that the forthcoming investigation would concentrate on his superior's dishonesty and that no effort would be made to check on the activities of his assistant. Besides there was the possibility that Hans would end up with his boss's job.

When confronted with the evidence, Hans had no choice but to admit the whole scheme, even repeating his conversation with the treasurer. As far as Hans was concerned he was only imitating the customs that he had learned in the New World. Could he be condemned, he asked, because his scheme had a continental touch?

Whatever the circumstances, all the top echelon thieves described so far benefited financially from their dishonest acts. There is a large group of executives, however, who doctor books and manipulate funds but who never personally gain a cent from their wrongdoing. Their fraudulent acts are the result of an impossible profit or work goal set by their superiors or an attempt to cover up their own poor business judgment. Their failing is not so much a lack of ethical candor but courage to say they cannot do the impossible or admit that they had made a mistake.

The case that follows is a typical example of what an executive will sometimes do when he finds that he has made a vital error in judgment. The man involved was the executive head of a major department store, one of several owned by a corporation. I might add that I, who had seen my share of white collar crime, was as surprised by the store executive's dishonesty as was the head of the corporation. For I had once worked with him and found his probity beyond question.

It all began when the president of the company came to my office. Over the years we had handled several projects for the corporation and had just completed one that involved the executive's store. We had remodeled both the warehouses and the entire store, designing a new layout and establishing new receiving and marking controls. The head of the corporation asked us to check on an employee in the central buying office whom, he believed, had built himself a sizable bank account through kickbacks and falsification of inventory.

"You know," he continued, "we would really like to use your firm more often. But your fees are too high."

It was obvious the head of the corporation wasn't joking.

"If any other engineering firm," I said, "could do that last job for less than $25,000 and do it right, you can have my services gratis."

"Then why did you charge us $50,000?"

"Impossible," I protested. "There must be a mistake somewhere."

I immediately had my secretary bring me the file on the project in question. The job which had involved three members of my staff over several months cost about $25,000. I took out the bills and showed them to the head of the corporation. He was aghast.

He then returned to his own office where he hastily made a check of his firm's files. What he discovered resulted in an investigation that a few hours before he never imagined would take place. For the head of the chain discovered a number of fictitious entries made in the records presented by the store executive to the corporation's headquarters. The head of the corporation was sure that the store executive was somehow cheating the firm. He asked us to look into the matter. It took us two weeks to get the answer.

The branch president had been one of the main promoters of his store's extensive renovation program. He even had to overcome the resistance of some members of the top management team. But the job, which cost three million dollars, was done nevertheless. During the next year he made the agonizing discovery that the costly renovation project simply wasn't paying off, that sales and profits were way below the figures he had projected. He was afraid that if he didn't falsify the figures he would soon feel the blade of the executives' guillotine. So he inflated sales figures by $1,000,000 and then did the same with expenditures involving construction costs, a comparatively easy matter. The fact that he inflated our fee was the coincidence that led to his undoing. As far as the central office was concerned, the high expenditures were balanced out by the booming sales which justified the costly renovation program. If costs could be kept down, the store would eventually show an excellent profit.

The branch store executive was fired from his $65,000-a-year job. The man who was once driven about in a chauffeured car paid for by his own firm is now running a small wholesale jobbing business. Although he never stole a cent himself, the firm for which he worked had paid thousands of dollars in taxes on money it never actually made. He had committed the one dishonest act besides thievery which no executive can ever hope to get away with. He had conned his own colleagues.

Although an element of greed often enters into white collar crime, it rarely occurs as the sole cause for dishonesty. In the chapter that follows you will meet the exception, a man whose lust for money and power destroyed giant corporations and caused a financial crisis in at least two countries. If an award should ever be given for the meanest thief in the world he would assuredly have no challengers. In fact, it would be the only contest he would ever win honestly.

Chapter 8

The Complete Scoundrel

THIS is the story of the late but not lamented Serge Rubinstein, the last of the truly great financial swindlers. Although other scoundrels have built richer empires, no one has ever done so with Rubinstein's consummate wizardry and chicanery. For Rubinstein not only manipulated the finances of two rich and powerful nations, but defrauded at last half a dozen multi-million-dollar corporations as well as some of the shrewdest businessmen who ever sold short in the bourses of Europe, Asia and America.

Serge Rubinstein's life began and ended in mansions. He was born on May 31, 1908, on the fabulously rich St. Petersburg estate of his father, Dmitri. Papa Rubinstein was a financial genius in his own right. A leading executive of the Junkers Bank in Moscow and the Franco-Russian Bank at St. Petersburg, Dmitri Rubinstein served as an advisor to Rasputin the mad Monk and lent vast sums to the Czar himself. The elder Rubin-stein's power was so great and his position so secure, that it would have taken a national upheaval to make Dmitri and his brood leave Russia. And that is just what happened.

With the 1917 revolution raging around him, he prudently slipped across the frozen Gulf of Finland in a horse-drawn sleigh. Shortly after Dmitri reached Sweden he had some exit papers forged and sent them to St. Petersburg. These enabled his family which consisted of his wife, Stella; a sixteen-year-old son, Andre; and Serge, then ten, to follow Papa into permanent exile. Although Dmitri had to leave the bulk of his personal fortune behind, the family's predicament afforded young Serge his first opportunity to participate in an international financial venture. For pinned to his underwear were some of Mama Rubinstein's precious jewels.

During the next eight years Serge and his family wandered over most of the Continent. The Rubinsteins, though rootless, lived well during this grand tour residing in most of the famous capitals of Europe at one time or another. Although young Serge's education was often interrupted, he picked up one useful set of tools, languages, which were to help him later in his dealings with a polyglot business world. By the time he was eighteen, he spoke Russian, English, French, German and Swedish fluently. Once his tongue had been amply trained, Serge's next step was to hone his mind. For the next three years he studied at Cambridge under John Maynard Keynes, England's greatest economic thinker of the twentieth century. Serge Rubinstein proved himself a brilliant student, one whom the master prophesied would go far. Unfortunately Keynes was unable to point out the direction.

Serge, then twenty-one, lacked one other tool necessary for financial venture, working capital. His first attempt at making money was, like almost all his other dealings, predicated on fraud. Since, however, it was only his first, it is understandable that the game he went hunting was comparatively small. His aim was to snare as many Russian heirs as he could.

Serge knew that the banks of Europe were crammed with the fortunes of numerous Russian capitalists who had been liquidated by the Bolsheviks. So he decided to track down the accounts, find the heirs who had escaped, and collect his reward. Posing as a student making surveys of dormant accounts, Rubinstein, armed with a letter from a Cambridge professor, found a banker in Lausanne, Switzerland, willing to open his ledgers. It didn't take Serge long to pluck out the name of an unfortunate, Nichola Chakhoff, who had been liquidated by the Russians. He then proceeded to track down eleven heirs, who rewarded his efforts with $17,000. The Swiss banks soon realized

Serge's economic survey had nothing to do with scholarship and quickly closed their vaults, books and doors to the young "student." But Serge Rubinstein no longer cared. He had obtained the one thing he needed most, sufficient capital to make his first investment.

Returning to Paris, he joined with Alfred Massenet, nephew of the composer, and together they formed the Banque Franco-Asiatique. Serge's next step would set the pattern of many of his future operations. He himself put it simply and baldly: "I figure out how much a company is worth dead—not living. I'm most interested in finding out if the liquidation price of the company's assets is more than the price of the stock."

His first victim was a chain of Parisian restaurants. Serge discovered that he could buy control of the restaurants for $60,000. He also learned that the chain's cash assets totaled the equivalent of $450,000 in francs. The rest was easy. He bought the chain, and then used the restaurants' liquid assets to speculate on the money market. His working capital had grown from $17,000 to $450,000. As a result of selling the French franc short he made himself an additional $210,000. Premier Pierre Laval, later executed as a traitor, claimed that Serge had depressed the French franc, and kicked him out of the country. Serge, though, couldn't have cared less. In the space of three years he had bankrolled at least one lie and two swindles into more than $600,000. At twenty-five he was on his way to making his first million. Moreover, the young financier already had another deal in the works, one that would take him halfway around the world and net him an even larger fortune.

His first stop was London. Residing in the English capital at the time was a man named Martin Coles Harman, an eccentric promoter who had already come to the attention of the Crown when he purchased Lundy Island and declared that its ancient charter made him a feudal lord with the right to coin his own currency. When the first Harman pennies bearing the profile of the promoter appeared, the British Government stepped in. That was in 1933. One year later the government again found it necessary to halt the promoter's activities, which this time were more bald than ribald. Harman had gained control of Chosen

Corporation, which owned three gold mining subsidiaries in Korea. In 1932 several other Harman companies had run into financial difficulty. To rescue them, Harman had them buy Chosen Corporation shares on the open market. He then ordered the three Korean subsidiaries to repurchase the Chosen stock from the other Harman companies at a much higher price. This way the promoter took money from Chosen's subsidiaries, money which didn't belong to him, and put it in the till of his own companies which needed to have their assets bolstered. It would have been a slick deal, except that the Crown found out about it and indicted Harman.

Harman decided to sell out to Serge. Serge, in turn, was more than happy to oblige. He bought up Harman's 100,000 shares, gobbled up 50,000 more on the open market, and then with Chosen under his control he had the mining company issue and sell him another 150,000 one pound par value shares for which he made little more than a token payment. While Harman was trundled off to jail, Serge completed his coup by gaining control of 173,029 more Chosen shares which as the result of Harman's manipulations were owned by the three Korean subsidiaries. The shares were then worth about $776,000. Rubinstein simply had the subsidiaries exchange their shares for stock in two other companies which he controlled. The swap was a pure fraud. For the two companies which received the 173,000-odd Chosen shares had no assets. Serge had just swindled Chosen, its subsidiaries and seven thousand stockholders out of $776,000.

Rubinstein, though, wasn't satisfied. He added insult to injury by selling some of his Chosen stock on the open market during the ensuing boom in gold securities. The sensational advance in Chosen stock allowed Serge to make an additional profit of 150,000 pounds. Rubinstein, who had not yet turned thirty, was not only the talk of the world's financial circles but a multimillionaire. While others may have drowned in the process, Serge hadn't even got his feet wet. His next move was to produce international headlines. As Serge himself later described it: "It was a financial Pearl Harbor in reverse."

The year was 1937 and the distant rumble of mankind's most terrifying war could be heard in the bushland of Africa, the hills of Europe and the rice paddies of China. Benito Mussolini and his black shirts had already raped Ethiopia, General Francisco Franco had captured Madrid, and the island of Japan was preparing to swallow the colossus of China. Imperialism was on the march and it seemed at the time that no nation, let alone individual, could withstand the march of the hobnailed boot. The rulers of the Land of the Rising Sun, however, had not reckoned with a slightly stocky young man who just measured five-foot-seven in his bare feet and issued his battle commands in a strident, high-pitched voice. And like the general who had become his idol, the Napoleon of international financial swindlers was to turn what seemed like an assured defeat into an amazing victory.

The spark that set off the war between the government of Japan and Serge Rubinstein was the threat by the Japanese government to expropriate all foreign-owned mines. This meant that unless Serge did something drastic the three Korean gold mines owned by Chosen would become an integral part of the Imperial treasury since Korea was under Japanese rule. Since Serge had no shares in the treasury, the loss would be irreparable. The young financier acted swiftly. He packed his Trojan Horse and headed for the heart of the enemy's country, Tokyo.

Upon his arrival he set out to woo the foe. One of the first things he did was grease the palm of the Korean governor with 140,000 yen. This was followed by a statement praising "the valor" of the Japanese soldier. In the process of seasoning the fatted calf, he made contact with a number of influential Japanese, among them Prince Ito and Viscount Inoyue. Together they organized a holding company which took over Chosen's three Korean subsidiaries. This removed the gold mines from the curse of foreign ownership.

So far Serge had only accomplished a bit of fast paper work. The gold mines were still at the mercy of the Japanese. His next step was simplicity itself. The Nippon Mining Company, a Japanese firm, had already expressed interest in buying the Korean gold mines. Serge quickly negotiated the sale which was completed in May, 1937, a few days short of his twenty-ninth birthday. Chosen's shares totaled nearly fifteen million yen or more than $3,500,000. Some 4,000,000 yen were lost as the result of taxes and expenses.

Serge's next problem, and the toughest of all, was getting the remaining yen out of Japan. The Japanese government frowned on allowing its currency to leave the country. Although it was then illegal to send out more than 100 yen or $28 a month without express permission of the Finance Ministry, Rubinstein did manage to persuade the government to allow him to take out a little more than half of the yen in British pounds sterling. This left some 5,000,000 yen blocked in Japanese banks. Of that sum, 3,000,000 yen were locked in the vaults of the Yokohama Specie Bank.

Rubinstein, who had already returned to Europe, called upon an old associate and pal, and asked him to try his hand at removing as much of the remaining yen as possible. This associate, a wily promotor himself who knew nearly all there was to know about the inner workings of high finance, readily took on the assignment. Together they worked out a scheme that was to shake the very economic foundation of Imperial Japan.

As soon as Rubinstein's partner took up residence at the Imperial Hotel in Tokyo he began purchasing cartons of obis, a garment which Japanese women wear around their waists. Each obis consisted of seven yards of silk wrapped around a cardboard tube. After he had collected a sufficient number of obis, he dropped in at the Yokohoma Specie Bank where he bribed one of its officers with 300,000 yen or ten per cent of the Chosen assets locked in its vaults. In turn, the bank official obligingly permitted him to withdraw the remaining 2,700,000 yen or about $1,000,000.

He took the money in 100-yen notes, brought the cash to the hotel and then proceeded to stuff the obis with the Japanese bills. He then loaded the yen-laden obis on board the *Empress of Japan,* which was docked in Kobe, sailed away to Hawaii where he landed in September, 1938, doubtless the most successful obi exporter in history. It wasn't until he began exchanging some of the yen for dollars that the Finance Ministry discovered the loss. Almost every bank in Honolulu has some Japanese employees and someone reported the sudden mysterious dumping of the homeland's currency. While the Japanese government choked with impotent rage, the obi dealer moved on to San Francisco where he was eagerly greeted by Rubinstein, who proceeded to unload the remaining yen in banks throughout the United States.

As a result, Japanese currency dropped in value to a point from which it never recovered until the beginning of World War II. The Japanese government, of course, wasn't the only victim of Serge's tricky maneuvers. Over the years he had personally acquired more than $5,900,000 that rightfully belonged to Chosen Corporation. Years later he was forced to make an out-of-court settlement and return some $2,000,000 to Chosen's minority stockholders.

Serge, meanwhile, decided to set up shop in the United States. As unscrupulous as ever, his very act of crossing the border from Canada on April 2, 1938, was based on fraud. During his Asian journeys he had picked up a Portuguese passport in Macao. To get the passport, Serge blithely swore that he was the illegitimate offspring of a Portuguese woman and her Russian lover. The name that he penned on the passport was Serge Manuel Rubinstein de Rovello. He was later to admit that despite his worldwide travels he had never actually set foot in Portugal, and he claimed his father had "arranged" the passport for him for the picayune payment of $2,000 in legal fees. Later, his elder brother, André, who was to devote a good part of his life to suing Serge, charged him with defaming his mother's character. As usual André lost the suit.

Serge's first step was to open offices at 63 Wall Street where he set up the British American Equities, Inc., nominally a Chosen subsidiary, but actually controlled by Rubinstein himself. Next he began siphoning Chosen money, using British American equities as his funnel. During the next four years Serge proceeded to gather about him a group of former European associates who had immigrated to New York's financial district. He also started wooing friends among influential figures in political and financial circles in both Washington and New York. Soon he could count among his acquaintances Senators Claude Pepper and Robert F. Wagner, "Happy" Chandler,

Bronx Democratic boss Ed Flynn and others. He was even invited by Mrs. Eleanor Roosevelt for dinner at the White House.

His first sensational American coup involved the Brooklyn Manhattan Transport Company, better known to New York City's subway riders as the BMT. Serge learned that the BMT was about to merge with other New York subways. According to a suit later dismissed, several directors of the BMT gave Rubinstein some very valuable information which allowed him to profit handsomely on the proposed merger. As part of the merger plan the Brooklyn Manhattan Transport Company began buying up its own outstanding bonds and preferred stock. While other stockholders were depositing their securities in exchange for city bonds or cash, Serge proceeded to buy as much BMT stock as he could lay his hands on. He waited until the merger was consummated, before turning in his securities. Apparently Rubinstein knew that by sitting on his BMT securities he would receive the full call price while other stockholders who had already turned in their shares received lesser sums. As a result while others were given $65 for each preferred share, Serge was handed the full call price of $116.50. For each surrendered bond he netted $1,050 instead of the pre-merger price of $950. Rubinstein's profit in this deal was over $800,000. Although nobody could prove it in a court of law, Serge had just taken the old BMT for its most expensive ride.

By 1941 Serge had Wall Street standing on its financial ear —he had just made another million out of the merger of Western Union and Postal Telegraph. The glib swindler who could be charming when it suited his purposes had become one of New York's most eligible bachelors. He lived in a plush thirty-room, five-story house at 814 Fifth Avenue. Characteristically, he had picked the mansion up for a song. It was once the home of the late Jules Bache who had decorated its walls with a $15,000,000 art collection. Since he didn't get Bache's paintings, Serge did some collecting of his own including Rembrandt's "The Notary," valued at $75,000, and a magnificent tapestry which once draped a wall in the British Embassy in Washington. As Serge strutted over the tesselated marble floors, climbed the broad and noble staircases and gazed into the thousand-year-old French fireplace in the foyer, he must have been touched and pleased at his own handiwork. For almost singlehandedly he had recreated the splendor and glory of his father's mansion.

Despite his wealth and success, Serge remained dissatisfied. As he himself once put it: "I ask only one thing of life. That every day be a perfect adventure. I'm deathly afraid of boredom." He might have added that the nights had to blaze with excitement too. And usually they did. Every fortnight he would fill his home with as many as one hundred frolicking guests who had their choice of four bars, each located on a different floor. On the nights when he wasn't giving parties, he could be seen at some of New York's most expensive night clubs escorting a statuesque blonde invariably two to three inches taller than himself. As Serge, the Continental, was fond of saying: "Treat them with a little sincerity and compassion and they will respond in kind. A woman is like a flower. It needs to be watered and cultivated." And Serge must have known the secret, for he had a bigger collection of female friends than Carter had liver pills.

Yet despite the hurly burly of his life, Serge at thirty-three suffered from moments of intense loneliness. The financial genius decided it was time to make an investment in love. The object of his affections was a beautiful nineteen-year-old blond model, Laurette Kilbourne. They eloped by plane to Alexandria, Virginia, on March 19, 1941, and then returned to Washington for a gala wedding reception where they were toasted by an impressive list of political bigwigs as well as a number of ambassadors and ministers including nine from South America, where Serge incidentally was doing business.

Rubinstein, who up to now had only been dabbling, decided it was time to do something momentous like building a financial empire that some day might rival the House of Morgan. Serge, however, had already built up a reputation as a sharp and shady trader, a man who could steal the shirt off your back without removing your jacket. Although he could not cover his activities completely, he managed to camouflage them with a series of phony flags. He did this by setting up a number of dummy corporations which had few if any assets of their own, but which did form interlocking links. Like an anchor chain, most of the links were submerged and hence invisible. For example, Serge owned all the stock of Chosen Corporation, now a mere shell of the original concern. In turn Chosen held all of British American Equities, Inc., which owned all of Norfolk Equities, which in turn held all of Norfolk International, a Panamanian firm. Norfolk International controlled all the preferred stock of Victory Oil Corporation and Victory Oil owned all of Midway Victory Oil Company. And it was with Midway Victory Oil Company that Serge launched his greatest onslaught on those still gullible enough to do business with him.

Rubinstein's first object was to gain control of a firm with sufficient capital which could then be used to buy up the stock in other companies. A ready-made solution presented itself to Rubinstein in July, 1942. At that time Oscar Gruss, a "deal finder" and a former European acquaintance of Rubinstein's, introduced a man named Romeo Muller to Serge. Muller, a former stockbroker, was serving as a director of Panhandle Producing & Refining Company. Panhandle's main interests were in Texas where it produced crude oil which was piped and sold to several major oil companies. It also refined and marketed gasoline and lubricating oils. Muller knew that a controlling block of stock, owned by the estate of the late William Rhodes Davis, was going to be sold by the government for back income tax purposes. Muller had been searching for a "friendly" party to purchase the stock. When he informed Rubinstein about the situation, Serge immediately saw the possibilities and acted with the speed of a greased fox.

Using Midway Victory Oil Company as a front, Serge put in a bid for the 147,844 Panhandle shares owned by the Davis estate. Midway Victory Oil Company, which in reality was controlled by Rubinstein, got the block of stock at $1.25 per share, the top bid. Serge then proceeded to move. In fact, six days before the stock was actually transferred to Rubinstein's control, Serge had Panhandle's board of directors call a meeting at the Savoy Plaza Hotel in New York. Shortly after the meeting began, three directors handed in their resignations and Serge and two of his associates were elected to take their places. Rubinstein, who had been hovering in a nearby room, joined the meeting and suggested that what Panhandle needed was a good oil production engineer. And whose name do you think he offered? Why, the versatile associate last heard of as an obi exporter.

Within the next three days there were two more board meetings during which two more directors and the board chairman bowed out. Two more Rubinstein men took the directors' places and Serge wound up as chairman of the board. As board chairman, Serge's first act was to name the obi dealer as assistant to the president of Panhandle as well as assistant general manager. Finally, to insure total control of Panhandle's operations, he had the board of directors set up an executive committee, with his ever faithful henchman acting in an advisory capacity.

Between July 18 and July 21, 1942, he had accomplished the following: gained control of five out of nine directors and three out of four members of the executive committee, and become chairman of the board. And he did all this without actually owning one share of Panhandle stock, title not being transferred to Midway Victory Oil Company until July 24. Serge had neatly and effectively taken over. By the time Panhandle's stockholders held their annual meeting in Wilmington, Delaware, some six months later, they faced a *fait accompli*. Serge was not only chairman of the board of directors but president of Panhandle as well. He also had increased his control from five to seven of the nine-member board of directors and had another of his dummy corporations purchase an additional 50,000 shares of common at $1.25 a share.

Serge's next step was to change Panhandle's charter. As the charter then read, Panhandle was not allowed to make investments or speculate in outside enterprises. So on October 8, 1943, Serge called a special stockholders meeting where the charter was amended to permit Panhandle's officers and directors to funnel its liquid assets into the coffers of other corporations. In effect Panhandle had been turned into a holding company and the man who was holding the holding company in the palm of his hand was one Serge Rubinstein.

During the next year the inveterate swindler began looking for deals, schemes and propositions in which he could invest Panhandle's money. They ranged from the wax business to the contemplated purchase of controlling stock in the Flushing National Bank on Long Island. Although most of the plans fell through, Panhandle did make several buys, including an option on a large block of Taylorcraft Aviation Company stock, which Serge later claimed, at his draft-dodging trial, made him essential to the war effort.

By the summer of 1944 Serge finally found the firm that he decided would serve as the foundation for the Rubinstein financial empire. The firm was the old and highly respected James Stewart and Company, Incorporated, one of the world's leading construction concerns. The buildings to James Stewart's credit included the New York Central Building, Madison Square Garden, the Chamber of Commerce Building in Washington, Tokyo's Mitsui Bank, the Revere Copper & Brass plant and the Savoy Hotel in London.

Rubinstein had learned through an associate and Panhandle director, one Hamilton Pell, the Stewart's majority stockholders were interested in selling out. Pell, a socialite and ardent golfer, had over the years become quite friendly with Harry D. Watts, then president of Stewart. This friendship, nurtured on the greens of a Long Island golf course, resulted in the Stewart plum falling into Rubinstein's lap. For it was Watts who told Pell who in turn told Serge that the construction company could be bought.

During the next two months Rubinstein, Watts and a Stewart attorney worked out a contract. It was quite a document. Under it the majority stockholders who owned 50.5 per cent of Stewart's common shares would receive $2,000,000. Those who owned the remaining 49.5 per cent of the shares would get a miserly $400,000. Naturally, the minority stock-holders objected and an internal hassle exploded, which de-layed consummation of the agreement.

Rubinstein meanwhile brought up a problem to his own board of directors. Under the contract worked out with Stewart's majority stockholders, Panhandle would have to make a down payment of some $700,000 to Stewart. Since Panhandle didn't have that much in liquid assets on hand, Serge magnanimously offered to open his own reservoir—for a price, of course. Rubinstein's suggestion: he or Midway Victory Oil Company would purchase 120,000 shares of Panhandle stock for $3.50 a share, which, incidentally was then selling on the New York Stock Exchange for $4 per share. The $420,000 of Rubinstein's money would be added to Pan-handle's own funds then on hand. The total sum would be sufficient to make the down payment.

The executive committe pointed out to Rubinstein that the issuance of 120,000 shares of stock would have to be ap-proved by Panhandle's stockholders. Otherwise, Serge might find himself in trouble with the law. Serge simply met this probability by having the executive committee agree to the scheme in strictest confidence. To protect himself Serge took an option on the stock instead of receiving the shares outright. Rubinstein had no intention of letting the cat out of the bag until it had been thoroughly skinned.

Finally a settlement was worked out between the majority and minority stockholders at Stewart and the deal between Stewart and Panhandle was consummated with the down pay-ment made on December 20, 1945.

Serge's plans for Stewart were impressive. Three months be-fore the down payment on the Stewart stock was actually made, Rubinstein entered into negotiations with represent-atives of the Philippine government. Serge's plan—to have James Stewart and Company become responsible for the com-plete rehabilitation of the country. This stupendous undertak-ing would cost the Philippines in the neighborhood of one billion dollars, with Stewart's profit coming to $37,500,000. Since Panhandle would soon control Stewart this meant that the Philippine scheme alone would have amounted to over $37 per share on the then outstanding Panhandle stock. It would have been nice work if Serge could have got it. But the Philippine president who favored the plan didn't remain in office long enough to put it into effect. Rubinstein, of course, never let on that negotiations had been dropped.

Although the financial experts of Wall Street didn't know it at the time, Serge was aware that Stewart was rapidly reaching a point where it needed some kind of enormously profitable deal to save it from bankruptcy. This is what happened. In April, 1945, seven months before Panhandle made its $700,000 down payment for control of Stewart, the construction company entered into a $7,000,000 contract to build a naval hospital in Houston, Texas. The board of directors at Stewart—Serge had yet to enter the picture—agreed to a fixed fee or lump sum contract instead of an agreement that would have given Stewart a 5 per cent fee based on final construction costs. The fixed fee contract made no provisions for unexpected increases in labor and material costs. Under this contract Stewart expected to make a net profit of $275,000.

By the time mid-August, 1945, had rolled around James Stewart found itself indirectly hit by the two atomic bombs dropped respectively on Hiroshima and Nagasaki. For with the sudden and unexpected end of World War II, the government lifted a number of controls on wages, materials and priorities, causing Stewart's expenses to skyrocket. Since they were bound by a fixed price contract, Stewart could do nothing to overcome the mounting loss. By the time Panhandle made its down payment in December, 1945, Stewart's loss at Houston was $568,000. Four months later, when the naval hospital contract was completed the total loss to Stewart came to a whopping $1,350,000. Indeed, Stewart's entire working capital had been dissipated. The great Serge Rubinstein had gone to the orchard and plucked himself a lemon, or so it seemed. Actually Rubinstein had already worked out a swindle that was to leave Panhandle in the lurch and net him a $3,500,000 profit.

In the summer of 1945, a certain highly respected securities analyst was poking among the ticker tapes and stock charts in search of a company that would make a good investment. He was, at the time, employed by a well-known member of the New York Stock Exchange. He was also a member of an organization consisting of analysts, statisticians and other brokerage firm members. At their meetings and luncheons held several times a week the members of this organization would discuss appraisals and analyses of different companies and their stock potential. The wide distribution of this information passed on to the brokers' clients would in many instances create a tremendous buying demand for certain securities. This could result in a spectacular increase in the value of a company's stocks. Unwittingly, both the analyst and the society would help Rubinstein make a killing.

In the summer of 1945, the securities expert's interest in Rubinstein was aroused when he learned that Serge had taken over control of Panhandle. He had already heard of Serge's ability to make money. He also knew that the financier's reputation for honesty left much to be desired. So around July, 1945, he called Rubinstein and made an appointment to see him. Realizing what such an expert's recommendation of Panhandle stock could mean, Serge prepared with great care for their first meeting. During the two-hour confab, Rubinstein told the analyst that he was the first person who had given him the benefit of the doubt. He then proceeded to unroll the story of his life starting with his childhood days in Russia. He even prepared a written autobiography, a memorandum which told just how Rubinstein had been "persecuted," and a chart called "The Panhandle Group" detailing the financier's holdings. By the time Serge had finished his dance of the seven veils, the gullible broker was to characterize those nasty stories about Rubinstein as the product of small and jealous minds.

Nevertheless he did some further checking and found nothing that would upset his favorable opinion of Rubinstein. He then returned to his office and told his immediate superior that Panhandle's possibilities were favorable and a recommendation to the firm's customers to purchase Panhandle stock might be made. During subsequent meetings Rubinstein continued to build up a picture of a company that was going places. Included in this glowing portrait were such morsels as the projected purchase of Stewart, that fine old construction company, and some inflated figures showing that Panhandle's assets from its oil reserves alone were equivalent to $7 or $8 a share. Panhandle at the time was selling at about $5 a share on the New York Stock Exchange.

On August 7, 1945, the analyst's firm came out with a bulletin recommending the purchase of Panhandle stock. On the very same day the bulletin was issued the firm's customers started to purchase shares in Rubinstein's company. By September 27, a month and a half after the bulletin came out, the brokerage house's clients had purchased 40,000 shares of Panhandle stock. During the same period the price per share had risen from $6.12 a share to $8.75.

But this was just the beginning. On September 27, the analyst handed his superior a confidential report which practically touted Panhandle as the greatest discovery since Columbus stumbled onto the New World. Among other things the report stated that Stewart was already a Panhandle subsidiary, a slight inaccuracy since Panhandle had yet to make its down payment for the Stewart stock. It went on to say that Stewart would probably average $50,000,000 profit. These Stewart earnings alone would be worth a $1.25 per share for Panhandle. Actually this was all pie in the sky. For at the time the report was written, Stewart's estimated loss on its Houston Naval Hospital project came to $500,000. Rubinstein, who knew all about the Stewart losses, had never bothered to pass this information on to his new-found friend. Instead, Serge continued to supply the security analyst with sweetened lies and half-truths.

The latter, meanwhile, started talking up Panhandle at his society's luncheons. As a result, numerous brokers along Wall Street began purchasing Panhandle stock. Word was getting around that if you wanted to speculate, Panhandle was the stock to buy. On October 9, Panhandle was selling at $10.36 a share and for the first time in its history had risen above $10.00. To put it another way, within a period of only nine weeks, the price of Panhandle stock had increased by seventy per cent. Rubinstein, who by now owned nearly 300,000 shares of Panhandle stock, had just made himself a paper profit of nearly $2,500,000. He was soon to tack on another $500,000 and turn the whole sum into cash.

The financier's next victim was William F. Edwards, a partner in the investment counseling firm of Naess & Cummings. The firm's clients represented an investment potential between 75 and 100 million. Edwards' appetite had been whetted by glowing reports of Panhandle and on October 19 he was introduced to Rubinstein. As soon as Edwards told Rubinstein that he was thinking of recommending Panhandle stock to his firm's clients, Serge glittered with golden promises. One nugget involved a newly discovered oil field in Texas. Rubinstein confidently claimed that the field contained a reserve of 15,000,000 barrels of oil. Actually it had less than one million barrels. Another nugget concerned an enormously valuable Bolivian oil concession which was about to fall into Panhandle's possession. The concession itself would not only have been worthless but the Bolivian government would have had to pass special laws before it could be put into effect, laws which Bolivia had no intention of promulgating. Serge topped it all off with the abortive one billion dollar Philippine contract which he claimed would net Panhandle $37 a share, and then wound up by saying that Panhandle's net earnings for 1945 would come to $1.75 a share, when actually they amounted to seventy-seven cents.

Edwards was transfixed but posed one key question. Did Serge have any intention of selling his stock in Panhandle? Because if he did all of Rubinstein's claims would smack of fraud, since he personally would stand to benefit handsomely from any rise in Panhandle stock. Serge swore on his honor that he would never, never do anything like that. So Edwards returned to Naess & Cummings and wrote a long memorandum in which he declared that Panhandle would make an extraordinary purchase. Needless to say Naess & Cummings clients began buying Panhandle stock with abandon.

At this point, Rubinstein decided it was time to make his

killing. He would sell out his nearly 300,000 shares of Panhandle stock, most of which he had bought for $1.25 a share,
at a fantastic profit. There was one problem: how to dump
nearly one-third of Panhandle's outstanding shares without
depressing the market and at the same time keep Rubinstein's
activities secret. Serge solved his problem by calling on Frank
E. Bliss, known as the Silver Fox of Wall Street. According to
Arthur M. Wickwire in his book, *The Weeds of Wall Street*,
the Silver Fox ". . . has bought and sold more stock than any
floor trader in history, and has handled larger blocks at a
time. Billions of dollars have flowed through his hands, fortunes
affecting the basic industrial fabric of the land . . . His first
spectacular achievement was in American Sumatra Tobacco
in 1918. A pool employed him to take charge of the stock.
He did. He took it when it was below 50 and shoved it to 145.
He made millions for his clients." And he was to do the same
for Serge.

On October 18, a day before Rubinstein swore to Edwards
that he would not sell his controlling share of Panhandle
stock, Serge ordered the Silver Fox to sell between 200,000
and 250,000 shares, nearly all his Panhandle holdings. Bliss
spent the next day, a Friday, looking over the market and on
the following day he began working out arrangements for the
dumping of Serge's holdings. By the end of April, 1946, the
Silver Fox had disposed of all of Serge's stock, which was
eagerly gobbled up in large part by the clients of the two
firms Rubinstein had bilked. The stock had soared from $1.25
when Serge had purchased it four years back, to a high of $14
a share. His profit came to $3,000,000 on a $600,000 investment.
Not bad if you can get away with it, and Serge did.

On April 15, 1946, Rubinstein informed Panhandle's board
of directors that he and his various dummy corporations had
completely divested themselves of all their Panhandle shares
and that the time had come for him to resign. Serge had
been indicted two and a half months earlier on a draft-dodging
charge. His retirement from Panhandle, he said, was motivated
by a "desire not in any way to embarrass the company."

As soon as he had severed his ties with the company he

had so handsomely swindled, he proceeded to bilk the stock-buying public of an additional $78,262. This is how he managed it. Rubinstein was well aware that Panhandle's stock would crash just as soon as the true facts became public knowledge. The lies he had told about the Bolivian concession, the Philippine contract, the overrated Texas oil reserves—as well as the huge Stewart losses—would deflate the Panhandle balloon like a fistful of darts. So Serge decided to sell Panhandle short.

Short selling in the securities market is selling shares you don't own and borrowing the same number of shares in order to make delivery to the purchaser. For example, right this minute you decide you want to sell 100 shares of Typical stock, which is now selling at $50 a share. However, you do not own this stock. So you call your broker and he borrows 100 shares of Typical stock and sells it at $50 a share. Let's say in three weeks the stock drops to $40 a share. You then tell your broker to buy up 100 shares at $40 a share and then return the 100 shares he had originally borrowed. By selling short, for that is what it is called, you have just made a profit of $10 a share or a total profit of $1,000. If, however, the stock instead of dropping to $40 a share should rise in value say to $60 a share, you can either replace the borrowed shares at a loss or wait until it falls.

Rubinstein, however, knew that Panhandle stock had been inflated way beyond its actual worth and that it could only go in one direction, down. Serge was also aware that selling Panhandle short under such circumstances was illegal, since it is against the law to manipulate the market. To hide his activities the financier called on another long-time Rubinstein associate, who was then residing in Europe. At Serge's request this worthy gentleman came to the United States to act as Rubinstein's agent. The financier's cover for him was simple. According to the minutes of the board of directors of Midway Victory Oil Company, Serge's chief dummy corporation, the purpose of this new expert's trip was to set up an export and import business for Midway, who, in turn, paid him $10,295 for his traveling and hotel expenses. Serge, as usual, was working all the angles.

Twenty-four hours after he had resigned from Panhandle, Rubinstein, with his new-found export-import authority acting as his chief agent, began selling Panhandle short. As Rubinstein's lies and misrepresentations were revealed to the stock-buying public, Panhandle's market value steadily declined. Between April 29, 1946, and December, 1946, a period of six months, Panhandle dropped from a high of $13.60 a share to a low of $4.75. Rubinstein's profit—$78,000.

Serge, then thirty-eight, could look back on an unparalleled series of successful financial swindles which had netted him a fortune which many estimated at around $10,000,000. His future, though, was not to glow as brightly as his past. Over the war years Rubinstein had successfully managed to avoid military service by claiming that his interests in Panhandle and Taylorcraft Aviation Company made him essential to national defense. Although he was worth millions, he blithely announced that he had insufficient funds to support his wife, mother-in-law, two sisters-in-law, his mother, his aunt and an old family friend. If drafted, he said, at least seven people would be forced to live in poverty. And finally, he declared, that as a Portuguese citizen the government had no claim on his services.

Despite his pleas, Rubinstein was classified 1A eight times and served with four induction notices. Serge's answer was to bellow. "I'm being persecuted for my assets." The government, though, looked askance at Rubinstein's claims and finally caught up with him on April 23, 1947, when he was convicted and sentenced to two and a half years in prison for filing false statements with his draft board. Paradoxically, it was the first and last time Rubinstein was convicted of disobeying the law, although he had committed almost every business crime imaginable. The man who had walked hand in hand with lawyers during most of his adult life insisted that if his high-priced attorneys had put him on the stand he would never have been found guilty.

During his two and a half years residence in the federal penitentiary at Lewisburg, Pennsylvania, Rubinstein had little opportunity for chicanery, except for an abortive attempt to swindle his wife. Laurette Rubinstein had decided to get a divorce from Serge, who had told her she was "a dampening influence on him" because she objected to his affairs with other women. When Serge heard about his wife's divorce plans, he bleated, "If the roof of the prison had fallen in on me at that moment, I could not have been more stunned." Rubinstein's fear was that Mrs. Rubinstein would take over his assets if the divorce was granted. To avoid this possibility, Serge did his best to delay the divorce proceedings while he tried to remove his financial reserves outside of New York. Meanwhile, he told Laurette, "If you do not write to me and say kind things, I will hang myself in my cell and it will be on your conscience for the rest of your life." So Laurette wrote a series of wifely letters which Serge carefully kept and then used to show that her charges of cruelty were unfounded. Serge finally gave up the battle when a New York court appointed the former blond model as the receiver of all his assets. The ex-Mrs. Rubinstein, who finally obtained her divorce in Las Vegas, won custody of their two daughters and $1,500 a month alimony.

As soon as he got out of prison in April, 1949, Serge found himself involved in another legal battle. Three months prior to his release, a federal grand jury had indicted him for stock fraud, mail fraud and violation of the Securities Acts. In reality he was being accused of swindling Panhandle, its stockholders, and the general public. The legal battle lasted two years with Rubinstein finally going to trial on June 22, 1951. A jury consisting of a civil engineer, an actuarial clerk, a secretary, a general credit manager, three housewives, two insurance brokers and three executives acquitted him, apparently believing Serge's claim that he had sold most of his Panhandle holdings to meet pressing financial commitments. In his one hour and forty minute summation Rubinstein's attorney added the clincher with the pronouncement: "You talk about this man [Rubinstein] being a clever man. I think he is the worst fool I ever met." Needless to say others have caviled at this characterization. But the jury didn't. And that was all that mattered to Serge.

Rubinstein spent the next four years giving gala masquerade

parties at his Fifth Avenue mansion, fighting a government deportation order, and working out a characteristically complex swindle that would have given him control of Stanwell Oil & Gas, Ltd., a rich Canadian oil company. Serge Rubinstein's numerous activities, however, were abruptly interrupted in the early hours of January 27, 1955. For around 5:00 A.M. of that chill winter morning, a killer entered his richly furnished third floor bedroom, tied his hands and feet, closed his mouth with adhesive tape and strangled the life out of his silk-pajama-clad body. Just a few feet away stood a photograph of Rubinstein dressed up as his favorite character and model, Napoleon. When Serge's butler discovered his master's corpse at 8:30 A.M. and called the police, New Yorkers found themselves titillated by the most sensational murder since the public shooting of architect Stanford White by millionaire-socialite Harry K. Thaw.

To this day the police have been unable to solve one of the century's most famous killings. And they probably never will. For when they inspected the murder scene they discovered six loose-leaf notebooks crammed with the phone numbers and names of nearly two thousand people, including chorus girls, bankers, sportsmen, headwaiters and blackmailers. Some of them were Serge's associates, others his underlings or playmates, and still others his enemies. It was and still is a case of too many suspects.

Perhaps the most incisive descriptions of those ever made concerning Serge Rubinstein came from two people whose lives and interests never touched, yet who both became involved with a man who, inordinately afraid of violence, violated others all his adult life and whose death at forty-six was brutal and savage.

Except for his murderer, the last person to see Rubinstein alive was a lovely brunette model and showgirl, Estelle Gardner. Serge had taken Estelle dining and dancing at Nino's La Rue, a plush supper club on New York's Upper East Side. At 1:40 A.M. they returned to Rubinstein's mansion where Estelle remained for about fifteen minutes. After Serge's body was found a reporter asked Miss Gardner to describe that last visit to

Rubinstein's mansion. Estelle, perhaps unwittingly, summed up Rubinstein's essential evil: "When we got to his town house we went up to his study and Serge walked over to a chess board he always kept out and made a move. He would always do that. He loved chess and sometimes I had the feeling he played with people that way too."

When Serge's body was finally placed in a $6,000 seamless copper casket, Rabbi Julius Mark of Temple Emanu-el was asked to deliver the funeral oration. It stands out as one of the frankest ever made, for it explained simply and vividly Serge Rubinstein's failures. This is what Rabbi Mark told the bereaved and the curious:

"There is little to be said on this tragic occasion except to voice our horror over a murder committed in cold blood and with premeditation and to express the deep-felt pity in our hearts over brilliant talents wasted and a life that might have been useful blasted. 'Oh, the wasted hours of life that have drifted by! Oh, the good that might have been.'

"It is not my intention to defend or in any manner condone the actions of Serge Rubinstein during his lifetime. Others are in a better position to judge him and even they must not usurp the prerogative of God, to whom belongs the final judgment. The man is dead and therefore in the hands of God.

"The word 'paradox' best describes the strangely complex, ambiguous and unquestioned psychopathic personality of Serge Rubinstein.

"He possessed a brilliant mind, but was utterly lacking in wisdom.

"He had a genius for acquiring wealth, yet never learned the simple lesson that money is a good servant, but a harsh master.

"He was a frustrated man because he wanted friends and never had them, since he never seemed to realize that to have friends one must be a friend.

"He wanted love, but never knew that love must be earned and cannot be bought.

"He declared that America was the finest of all countries in the world, yet stubbornly scorned the counsel of those nearest to him who pleaded with him to answer America's call to service.

"He wanted to be accepted, but on his own terms.

"He wanted security, a natural desire, but lacked what is more important—inner security!

"He feared death, because in his heart there was no faith. And the irony of his life was that death should have come to him in so brutal a guise.

"And yet standing here before his lifeless form, there is no condemnation in my heart—nor should there be in yours—but only pity for a man who was his own worst enemy, a man whose intellectual endowments promised so much, but whose deficiency in moral fiber proved his undoing. 'Is not their tent-cord plucked up within them? They die, and that without wisdom.'

"There was a side to Serge Rubinstein's character that is known only to his family and a favored few. It was Serge, the devoted son, the doting father, who cheerfully assumed responsibility for the support of all the members of his family when times became difficult, who regularly assisted family, servants and retainers as well as old friends who were refugees from his native Russia. There are many beneficiaries of his generosity who speak of him as kind and good.

"Our hearts go out in understanding sympathy to his beloved and adoring mother. We pray that she may find comfort in the thought that her gifted, impetuous son now rests in peace."

On March 26, 1958, the lawyers for the executors of Serge's estate filed in Surrogate Court an intermediate accounting of their administration. Their report showed that Rubinstein's assets came to nearly $2,000,000. But against that sum were claims of more than $10,000,000.

All that Serge Rubinstein had left in the world, his entire legacy, was a huge debt of unsatisfied claims which no one could or would ever fulfill.

Chapter 9

Horses, Losses and the Big Gamble

DESPITE HIS flamboyance and penchant for doing things differently, Serge Rubinstein at heart was a conservative. When it came to investing his own assets or those he had swindled from others, he rarely if ever took any risks. As Serge once put it: "I never speculate unless the elements of speculation have been removed, and I turn the wheels, or the man who turns them is on my payroll." Not so, however, in the case of a strikingly large number of white collar thieves. They deliberately risk not only their own money and the funds they have embezzled but their careers as well in the most hazardous speculation of all, gambling. The result is that horses, cards and dice have become the largest single causative factor in white collar crime.

Virgil W. Peterson, writing in the *Journal of Criminal Law and Criminology* on "Why Honest People Steal," has this to say:

"Based on the experience of over twenty of the largest surety companies, it would appear that the two principal factors contributing to employee dishonesty are gambling and extravagant living standards. Some companies estimated that gambling on the part of employees has been responsible for 30% of the losses of those companies. Other companies blamed gambling for as high as 75% of their total losses. The manager of the bonding department of one company wrote, 'Gambling is one of the greatest evils sureties must contend with under their fidelity bonds.' Another manager stated that 'Gambling appears in more embezzlements than any of the other causes . . .' "

Gambling can be either the cause or the effect of white collar dishonesty. For some people gambling is a disease. The causes of this illness are numerous, a drive for self-destruction or rebellion, or an abnormal sublimation of the mock struggle for fear of the real one. The bacillus of this disease, of course, feasts on a ready supply of cash. To support it many an otherwise honest white collar worker will turn into a thief. He steals in order to meet his debts or to be able to continue to gamble.

Such was the case of a highly respected forty-four-year-old New York lawyer, Arthur Nash, who stole $148,000 from his clients over a nine-year period to support his mania, dice. When Nash surrendered himself to the authorities because his conscience was troubling him, all that he had left from the money he embezzled was fifty cents.

The other side of the coin is the employee who, having already embezzled funds, gambles with the hope of replacing them. Though such cases are invariably tragic, the following has a seriocomic note. Pietro Gudenzi, a twenty-eight-year-old former paratrooper, took over his father's security business while the elder Gudenzi was visiting Europe. During his father's absence, Pietro decided to do some investing on his own and helped himself to about $150,000, the money belonging to his father's clients. Pietro promptly lost the money by speculating in Italian lira. In order to recoup the loss, he went to the race track and bet another $25,000. Again he lost. And again he returned to the till for more money. This time, though, instead of playing the horses, he bought one. The horse was named Support, something which Pietro needed in the worst way. Support, though, did not live up to its name. In the only race that Pietro's horse entered, he came in ninth. Pietro finally did get support. It came from the state. It was six to twelve years with free room and board.

Both Arthur Nash and Pietro Gudenzi had caught different

strains of the gambling bacillus. More typical, perhaps, is the white collar employee who turns to gambling as a way of ending his day-to-day frustrations, the endless and always mounting bills, the job that holds little promise of advancement, the bleak future already laden with the weariness and boredom of tomorrow's routine existence. Sometimes all these elements permeate a white collar worker's whole being until in desperation he bucks the percentages that few have ever licked, staking his grocery money on the 20 to 1 shot, or the two horse parley. Rarely, ever so rarely, he hits the jackpot. But most of the time he loses.

John Siemer was a young teller at the West Brighton Branch of the Staten Island National Bank and Trust Company. John became a bank employee at eighteen, starting as a clerk in a Brooklyn savings bank and then at twenty moving on to the Staten Island bank, where he became a teller. Despite his small earnings—he never earned more than $68 a week—John decided to marry his high school sweetheart, Henrietta, and raise a family. By the time he was twenty-three John was already supporting his wife, their three children, and his seventeen-year-old sister. They lived in a modest four-room flat in a three-story house on Staten Island. Later, John Siemer was to explain some of his frustrations:

"It was the little things that got me started, I suppose. I was only twenty when I went to work for the bank. And they promised me $60 a week. But they gave me only $55. Now, that may seem like nothing to you. But it was a terrible disaster to me. I was married to a wonderful girl, honest and kind, and we had one child and we were expecting another. My God, at a time like that every penny counts. But we didn't even get much when we worked overtime. Other people would get time and a half, but we only got half time. Besides, we were general flunkeys—we even had to clean the cellar. When we had our third child, I was supposed to get Monday off. But I didn't get it. Somebody else got it. By then I owed the bank $400. All the clerks were in hock to the bank."

John Siemer began dreaming about the illusive pot of gold that looms so invitingly at the finish line of every race track.

Starting in March, 1954, John began playing the horses. His first bets were modest, one or two dollars. Soon John found himself cracking the $50 and $100 windows.

"It got like a disease," he said. "I bet everywhere. In Brooklyn, Manhattan and Staten Island. And I started dipping into the till. In May I won $750. That was my first big flyer. But then I started to lose.

"I don't know how it happened but in July I owed $7,000 to the bank. I had to manipulate to keep the bank from finding out. All the time I was trying to get even. Once in August I had it down to $2,000. But the following week it was up to $12,000. Finally in September it got to be $30,000 and I was so scared I didn't know what to do. Finally, I knew I was going to have to go to jail. So I decided to run. The day before I took off, I took $35,000 and I went home and told my wife."

At first his wife refused to flee with John, telling him that it was wrong to run away. In his desperation Siemer used the one threat that would force his wife to accompany him. Early Tuesday morning, he gathered their two eldest children, went into town and called his wife.

"I told her she'd never see the kids again unless she came with me," John later said. "So she came, bringing the baby. We went to Philadelphia carrying the $35,000 in a suitcase. Then I bought a car, a '52 Ford, even though I had never driven before and we drove to Ohio. I passed my driver's test in Canton and got a license."

At 9:15 A.M. the bank received a call purportedly from the young teller's wife. The message was brief, "I just want to tell you that John overslept. The alarm didn't go off," was all the voice said. Several minutes later a substitute clerk went to the vault to get Siemer's cash drawer. All he found was a few dollars in change. Bank officials then rushed to John's home to discover that except for his sister the entire family had disappeared. In their haste they forgot to inform the local police that one of their tellers was missing. They did, however, call the U.S. Attorney's office which in turn brought the F.B.I. into the case. The bank official's haste, however, was not as costly as John Siemer's. The night he and his family disappeared his sister raided the refrigerator. While rummaging around for a snack she pulled out the vegetable bin and discovered $5,500 of the bank's cash. In his excitement, the young teller had forgotten to take the money.

John Siemer's disappearence was an amazing feat. An amateur thief, Siemer managed to upset police predictions that he would be caught within twenty-four hours. Indeed, for ten months he was able to hide not only himself but his wife and three kids. Never before had so conspicuous a fugitive managed to avoid detection for so long a time.

After taking a bus to Philadelphia, Siemer bought a second-hand car for $1,300. That was as far as the police were able to trace him. He then piled his family into the Ford and drove his brood along the less traveled back roads. Overnight he would find lodgings in second-rate motels. His main object was to get far away from New York and at the same time avoid any area where the police would expect him to go. Quickly passing up Florida and California, destinations that were too obvious, Siemer headed for the Midwest, where he hoped that no one had ever heard of the absconding Staten Island teller and his missing family. Finally after about a week of leisurely driving, he decided to settle in South Amherst, Ohio. Although some thirty miles from Cleveland, South Amherst was an insular community where people were neighborly without being too nosy. For Siemer's purpose it was ideal.

The teller's next step was to find a place where he could house his family without danger of the children becoming too talkative with other youngsters. For at this point Siemer had dyed his light brown hair a dark brown and was raising a bushy mustache. His wife, a brunette, had suddenly become a redhead. To those who were mildly curious, John would impart the sad tale that he and his wife were Californians and that both their parents had passed away within a year. Oh yes, he would add, they had inherited some money, too. They had decided to try and make a go of it in Ohio. The name, of course, was no longer John Siemer, but Charles Mac-Tavish. But there was still the problem posed by the children.

The bank teller couldn't very well disguise them. They would ask too many questions.

The only solution was to find a house sufficiently isolated so that the teller's youngsters would be forced to play by themselves. Of course, it couldn't be a fancy house because people would start wondering about these young rich strangers. Siemer's dilemma was unwittingly solved by a middle-aged real estate man, who showed the young couple a partly finished one-room cinderblock home located near a rural road. The house itself was surrounded by dense woods and the nearest neighbor lived 100 yards away. The price was $3,500 cash. John Siemer bought it with 175 of the Staten Island bank's twenty-dollar bills. The agent wasn't even mildly suspicious, for later he asked Charles MacTavish to help him sell real estate. It was too risky and the young bank teller never actually worked at the job, although he did obtain an Ohio real estate license.

For nearly a year the Siemers hid in their one-room cinderblock house. It was a hard year, harder than all those drudging weary months that John had worked as a teller. The young couple had decided they would save as much of the stolen money as possible. There was always the chance that they would be discovered and if they were they at least would be able to return some of the cash that John had embezzled. So they took the suitcase stuffed with about $31,000 and hoisted it among the rafters. Occasionally they would open it up to spend a few hundred dollars on a TV set or refrigerator. Most of the time, though, the money remained untouched. They would somehow make a go of it on their own. But how?

John couldn't go out and get a job without the risk of detection. For he was in constant fear that somebody would recognize him. So John stayed home with the children while his wife worked in a five and dime store in nearby Lorain. To keep himself busy, the young fugitive puttered around the house, putting up a few shelves and minding the youngsters.

Then one day the young mother took some clothes to a dry cleaner in South Amherst. A customer who had read a follow-up story in a Sunday newspaper supplement recognized her despite her attempted disguise and called the F.B.I. That night eight agents called on the Siemers, who readily admitted their identity. The agents themselves were not surprised by the young couple's relief at finally being caught. For what the F.B.I. men saw was sordid poverty. Crowded into the one room were the three children, their parents, six dogs and two chinchillas which John eventually hoped to sell. On the floor of the one room, separated by a curtain into two compartments, were five springless mattresses on cast iron legs. The walls were bare to the rafters and the furniture consisted of a couple of lawn chairs. A one burner hot plate served as a stove. Water came from an open well and the toilet was an outhouse some thirty feet away. The young bank teller who had defied all the odds had had enough.

Waiving extradition, the Siemers were taken back to New York where John was tried and sentenced to eight years in jail. The $31,072 the F.B.I. agents found in the suitcase hoisted among the rafters hadn't helped.

Shortly after the young teller was arrested, the F.B.I. discovered a winning $300 Yonkers Raceway ticket in his pocket. The stub was dated September 27, the date John Siemer had walked out of his teller's cage never to return. It was also the last time he played the horses. Although he had won, he never had the opportunity to claim the winner's purse.

The cases described so far show gambling as an individual illness. Actually, it is more than that. Indeed one may go so far as to say it is a national disease. The yearly attendance at the nation's tracks runs nearly 40,000,000, and is increasing. The amount bet legally is more than two and one-half billion dollars. Another two and one-half billion are expended on dog races, cards, dice, roulette. But the five billion squandered legally is only a fraction of that amount gambled illegally, the total sum being estimated as high as thirty billion dollars annually. When you consider that one-third that amount is spent for the education of the entire nation's elementary and high school population, the comparative figures are in themselves a sad commentary on our mores and values. I might add that the crippling effects that gambling has had on the business world is inestimable. Indeed on occasion it has reached the point where a customer would find it easier to place a bet than an order for merchandise. The following case from our files involved an actual gambling ring which netted three million dollars a year and cost the company some six million annually. Perhaps most amazing of all was that top management, although forewarned, started its investigation when it was nearly too late.

This story starts over 100 years ago when the company's founder turned his harness and carriage accessories shop into a foundry. A century later the foundry had grown into one of the nation's fifty largest durable goods manufacturers with a working force of more than 30,000 and ten booming plants throughout the United States. The firm manufactured 40,000 different products, one third of which were custom made. The company's items, distributed throughout the world, can be found in houses, sewers, battleships, almost any place where man happens to be. Not long ago, management decided that this mammoth operation had reached the point where its unwieldiness prevented it from operating at maximum efficiency and profit.

We began our investigation at the company's main manufacturing plant which management felt was the source of the trouble. As our industrial engineers checked over the plant, a sprawling complex of thirty buildings that employed some 5,000 people, they became intrigued by an underground vault, which stretched for nearly a city block. The vault contained the most important components in the production process. Called patterns, these components serve as the prototype or the mother mold from which the progeny or numerous secondary molds are made. The progeny, in turn, serve as the sires of a particular item that is being manufactured. The amazing thing about the vault was the fantastic number of different patterns stored there. The vault contained literally tens of thousands of different patterns, each the mother mold of a specific product. Over the years management, like an eccentric antique collector, had kept nearly every pattern the company had ever made. In fact, for the last twenty-five years it had never thrown away a single mother mold although many thousands had not been used for the last two decades. (Eventually management was to dispose of enough outmoded patterns to fill some eighty dump trucks.)

Here it appeared was the company's bottleneck. When a customer placed an order, the production department would check the item's specifications against its list of patterns. Almost invariably it would find in its files a pattern that perfectly fitted the order. The item would then be scheduled for production while a memo was sent to the underground vault requesting the appropriate pattern. One of the vault's thirty-five employees would be delegated to look for it. And that's when the hitch developed. The underground vault had a selector system or card index file listing the whereabouts of the mother molds. The molds either were in the wrong bin—the pattern finders having previously failed to note a mold's new location on the card file—or the congestion was so great that the patterns simply could not be found. Indeed, there were so many unassorted man-sized mounds of mother molds that nearly fifty per cent of the time the employee was unable to locate the desired pattern.

Since it usually takes at least two weeks to make a pattern, incidentally one of the most highly skilled jobs in industry, the result was at least a fortnight's delay in production. This complication, in turn, further upset the actual production schedule, because the item that had been scheduled was often replaced by another item which might take four to five weeks to manufacture. Thus, the final delay in production of the original item might be at least six to seven weeks. Multiply this situation several thousandfold and you can imagine the chaos that resulted. Promised delivery dates were rarely kept. The consequence—scores of new as well as old customers began canceling their orders. The loss to the company— $4,000,000 a year.

But that wasn't the only damage. For the mess in the pattern vault was just a symptom of a much more serious problem, a kind of communal disease destroying the values of the plant's working force of 5,000.

This is what had happened over the years. The plant, once a model of efficiency and employee morale, had become a huge gambling warren. A worker who wished to place a bet on a horse simply waited until one of 150 runners, all company employees, passed his bench. Generally, the runners, selected for their mobility, worked as fork truck operators or members of the maintenance crew. The runners, in turn, had ample opportunity to pass on the bets to a host of eager bookies. For the plant was surrounded by newspaper stands, bars and grills, service stations, pool halls and barber shops, all of them drop-off points for bets.

The business of playing the horses had become so lucrative that the underworld decided it was a fertile field for its own operations. One day the head of the personnel department received an anonymous letter identifying about fifty employees as bookies and runners. Management acted swiftly. All those identified in the letter were questioned and then given the choice of ending their bookmaking activities or losing their jobs. Most of those called on the carpet had twenty to twenty-five years service. They preferred to keep their jobs. The organized underworld was overjoyed. For it was the syndicate that had sent the letter and it was the syndicate which then proceded to fill the vacuum and replace the runners who had quit with employees loyal to their own criminally run organization.

Indeed when we arrived on the scene three years later, we found the fantastic situation in which the underworld was a ruling authority in the main plant of one of the nation's most respected manufacturers.

The situation, I might add, was filled with incidents that belong in some madcap Alec Guinness escapade. Once two runners learned that a certain horse had been doped with speed pills. They scrounged up $30,000 for the killing. But on the day of the race word had got around that the race had been fixed. It was getting close to track time and the two runners not only had what every horse player dreams about, a sure thing, but the cash to bet as well. Yet no bookie would take their money. After a couple of frenetic phone calls they solved their problem. Chartering a plane, they flew to the track over a hundred miles away and arrived just in time to place their bets. The horse won and the runners cleaned up.

Horses were not the only mania. Crap shooting and poker games were rampant. And the ideal site, of course, was the huge pattern vault, a maze of aisles and corridors that could have hidden an elephant. The man who organized and ran the games there had been with the company for over fifteen years. His case was perhaps the most tragic. For as a result of his gambling activities he was to be crippled for life.

I'll call him Johnny. Johnny's job was to find the patterns which the production department requested. In his early forties, he was earning about $90 a week and owned a $12,000 home. Johnny, though, was never in need of cash. For he had more rackets going than he had fingers. As a runner for the syndicate he collected over $100,000 a year on bets alone. In turn the underworld paid him a ten per cent commission on the cash he took in. Like other bookies Johnny netted an additional profit as loan shark. If one of his betters needed financing, and most of them did, Johnny would oblige at the usurious interest rate of $1.25 a week for each $5 loaned. Since every horse player sooner or later pyramided his bets—losing $5, he'd bet $10, losing $10, he'd bet $15—he would invariably either ask Johnny to carry his losses or loan him more money so he could place more bets. Indeed many would find they had to pay Johnny three or four times as much interest as the actual loan. And it wasn't unusual for a horse player to lose several hundred dollars in a desperate attempt to recoup a $5 bet.

A hearty bluff fellow, Johnny was a natural-born hustler. The racket that gave him most pleasure were the daily card games which he organized and set up in the pattern vault. If any of the workers there wanted to join in the card game, they would simply volunteer to make a fruitless search for a pattern. For the next three hours, they would lose themselves in the vast labyrinth where Johnny had set up a table and chairs. And they got service too. If someone wanted a barber, one of the workers who had learned how to cut hair would drop his other duties and scurry over to "The Casino." Sometimes the card players would become hungry. So Johnny worked out an arrangement with the men at the foundry. Whenever a big game was scheduled he would send word to the foundry workers, who kept a supply of eggs, bacon, ham and coffee. One of the "chefs," using the heated surfaces of the foundry as a grill, would whip up hot sandwiches, omelets and coffee, which were brought to the gaming table in "The Casino" and sold to the players.

By the time we had finished our report on Johnny's underground Las Vegas and the activities of other loan sharks, runners and bookies, management was reaching for a bromide. Besides the breakdown in employee morale, the company was losing as much as a million dollars annually as the result of overstaffing and an additional millon dollars a year through unnecessary overtime. Many of the plant's supervisors, who were in debt to the syndicate, would schedule the overtime so that the horse players could make up their losses.

In desperation, management began cleaning house. One of those fired was Johnny, the hustler who would shepherd his fellow workers to neighborhood bars for beer parties, parties which he readily paid for because he wanted to keep his clients happy. But Johnny, the man who everybody looked up to, no longer was boss of "The Casino." By losing his job he had lost the source of his power, his contacts and his prestige. At first Johnny tried to find another job. But a recession had come and nobody could figure out just what could be done with a forty-year-old man whose only qualifications were selecting patterns and collecting bets. As the months passed Johnny became despondent and began drinking. One night they found him lying along a railroad track, his legs cut off. In his drunkenness, Johnny the runner, had stumbled onto a trestle and had fallen into the path of a passing freight train. The underworld turned Johnny's tragedy to its own advantage. Word was spread that Johnny had been pushed because he had stepped out of line. It was warning to others, they said, who might be inclined to expose the syndicate.

The sorrow inherent in lives like these is not just the harm they did to others but the greater hurt they inflicted upon themselves. Even more tragic is the case of the white collar thief who seeks his own destruction.

Chapter 10

The Outcasts

ANY REPORT on white collar crime must take into account an alarming problem involving millions of Americans, many of whom resort to stealing because of a sickness which allows them no other recourse. They are the outcasts, the nation's alcoholics, homosexuals and drug addicts. Their very number is in itself deeply disturbing, for they make up at least one-tenth of our total working population. According to a recent Yale University study there are approximately 5,015,000 alcoholics in the United States. To put it another way, out of every 100,000 adults in the population, 4,760 drink compulsively and habitually. Add to that an almost equal number of homosexuals plus some 60,000 narcotic addicts and the problem begins to take on frightening proportions. For whatever their emotional disturbance may be, all outcasts are of necessity potential thieves. Like the compulsive gambler, they need a constant supply of money. The result so often is another white collar employee turned thief.

How a man becomes twice cursed, first as an alcoholic and then as a thief, is tragically illustrated in this case from our files. The setting was a mammoth drug and sundries company, many of whose retail outlets cover half a city block. The drugstores, and there are hundreds of them, are operated just like supermarkets. In fact if a supermarket should open near one of the firm's cavernous self-service drugstores, the drug and sundries company would meet the competition (the supermarket would sell drugs and cosmetics) by offering its customers hams, steaks and poultry along with its assortment of pills and triple dip sundaes. In addition, the drug company not only manufactured chemicals, vitamins, drugs and sundries but prepared, bottled and packed pickles, cherries, ice cream and other fountain items. These products were sold over the counter at its own retail outlets and to other drugstores throughout the country. In an age of bigness, this company marched with the giants.

As successful as the firm's business ventures had become, its relations with its own employees were equally impressive. It not only supported an excellent pension plan, but voluntarily offered numerous fringe benefits. If an employee's youngster had the qualifications, the firm would pay his tuition to pharmacy school and then hire him when he graduated. As a result the employees swore by the firm and it wasn't unusual to find both a father and son working in the same store, plant or office. On occasion top management would gaze down upon its handiwork and glow with deserved satisfaction. Then a terrible thing was to happen. For the company which prided itself in its employee relations was to find a gang of thieves in its midst. The story of how and why this came about begins over a quarter of a century ago.

The story actually starts and ends with one white collar employee, a man whom I'll call Ralph. When Ralph joined the company as a clerk, he was twenty-two and eager. Ralph decided that hard work would bring him the promotions and awards that come to those who persevere. It wasn't long before he received his first award. A young secretary who labored in the firm's main office had caught his eye. The secretary, whom I'll call Belle, found the young clerk ambitious, attractive and persuasive. Three years after Ralph had joined the firm, they were married.

At first Ralph and Belle were like any other newly married couple. They were very much in love and very happy. But as the years passed their marriage was bruised by the differences in their careers. Ralph eventually became a supervisor in charge of the valuables' room in the company's main warehouse, not far from the firm's executive offices. As head of the valuables' department, Ralph was responsible for the handling of millions of dollars' worth of goods ranging from $50 watches and cameras to transistor radios and expensive drugs and narcotics. Because of the vastness of the firm's operation, the valuables' department alone employed forty clerks, all of whom worked under Ralph.

As impressive as Ralph's position appeared, his wife had advanced even further. For Belle, who was childless, had been promoted to private secretary in the executive vice-president's office. She would sit in on policy-making conferences and go on trips. She even had a key to an executive washroom while her husband had to share one with the forty other employees in his department. As the executive vice-president's Gal Friday, Belle was pampered and catered to. For the Belles are the Madame Pompadours of the business world. Their power, though indirect, is immense. Belle herself spent more waking hours with her boss than his wife did.

Ralph, in turn, bore the brunt of a thousand complaints. While Belle as a rule quit promptly at five, Ralph was often forced to remain at the warehouse until seven or eight in the evening filling orders. Although he did his job well, there were rumors that if it hadn't been for Belle's influence, Ralph would never have become head of the valuables' department. Eventually the seeds of frustration and inadequacy began to ripen within Ralph.

At first he had only one drink with his lunch. But one somehow wasn't enough and it wasn't long before he was subsisting on a liquid diet. Although his wife had her scheduled coffee breaks, Ralph had to sneak out for his afternoon shot. It didn't take Belle long to realize what Ralph was up to. At the end of the week his paycheck had all but disappeared. Some nights he would come home in a stupor. Then one day when Ralph called on Belle at the executive offices, he was forced to wait for her, something he always resented. He had been drinking and became abusive. And Belle's embarrassment was so great that she decided to do a drastic thing. Using her influence with the accounting department, Belle had all of Ralph's paychecks turned over to her. She then put her husband on a strict budget, handing him three dollars each day, with which he could buy his lunch, cigarettes and the gas for his car. Belle figured he would even have some change left over for an occasional beer. By cutting off his supply of money, Belle thought that she could force Ralph to stop his constant drinking. The day that Ralph started living off an allowance came only a few months after he and Belle celebrated their twentieth anniversary. For Ralph it was one more indignity.

Ralph, of course, continued to drink. For the first month he managed by running up credits at the neighborhood bars. Then he began borrowing from his fellow employees, a dollar from one, three from another, five from a third, whatever he could get. Eventually his credit with the local bartenders and his co-workers was no longer honored. Ralph simply didn't have the money to pay them back. Then one day a bartender asked Ralph for a favor. The bartender wondered if Ralph could purchase a camera for him at the company's store and pass on the fifteen per cent employee discount. Ralph, who was in debt to the bartender, readily agreed. But instead of purchasing the camera at the employee discount store, Ralph helped himself to the item in the valuables' room. He then sold it to the bartender for $50 —it retailed for $59.50—and Ralph kept the cash. The bartender, grateful for the $9.50 savings again treated Ralph with respect. Ralph soon paid off many of his debts and once more found himself back among his many drinking companions. In fact his prestige burgeoned as it never could have before. For Ralph had become a man of many favors. If one companion desired a watch for his daughter's graduation or another needed an expensive medicine, they just called on Ralph who would supply it at a marked discount. Soon he had customers scattered throughout half a dozen bars and grills. They would hand the bartenders lists with as many as ten items on them, lists which Ralph easily filled. Ralph, the alcoholic, was not only able to buy all the liquor he craved, but he was making a profit as well.

During the next year Ralph stole over $20,000 worth of merchandise, smuggling all of it past the plant's guards. How did he manage? It was simple. As supervisor he was in complete charge of the valuables' department. He could help himself to whatever he wanted without having to report to any of the employees in the department since all of them were his subordinates. The plant guards, who watched the gates were inefficient and bored. Some of them had once done other work for the company but because of an injury, failing health or job disqualification, they were shifted to the guard force. Several others were supplementing their police or civil service pensions.

But most important none of them really cared, for as so often happens, the company had found the job for the man instead of the man for the job. Over the years Ralph had gotten to know the guard force well. He had met their wives and children. With some he had gone bowling and had passed more than one companionable evening drinking beer at the nearby bars. And many times Ralph would give the guards breaks in slightly damaged merchandise. So it was easy for him to walk out with a package without a guard stopping him and checking its contents. Indeed, it reached the point where his friends on the force would bring his car around to the receiving dock when Ralph was ready to leave, and unwittingly help him load it with the merchandise he had stolen.

Ralph, though, did have a problem. The employees in his department soon became aware that he was filling his pockets and arms with the company's goods. And it wasn't long before they too began to steal. The outlet for their thefts—three gas stations on the edge of the city. The service stations would offer each customer $5 worth of free merchandise for every $25 worth of repairs or purchases of gas and oil. The service station customers had their choice of watches, vitamins, fountain pens, electric shavers, wallets, perfumes and cameras.

Two years had passed since Belle first collected Ralph's paycheck. Although Ralph occasionally came home in a stupor, he was careful not to consume so much liquor that his wife would question him. And those few times when he tottered over the threshold he would mumble something about the boys treating him. Belle became convinced that her plan had worked. After all their bank account was growing.

Management, meanwhile, had continued to expand, opening new stores and enlarging its wholesale and manufacturing departments. Somewhere along the way they felt that they had lost control of the operations of their main warehouse. Although records showed the merchandise on hand, they had difficulty locating it. So they called on us to work out a new inventory control plan as well as a complete new layout of the warehouse itself. Management was convinced that the reason the books didn't reflect the stock on hand was due to the pressure of new business which resulted in merchandise being lost in the warehouse. But when we checked for the missing items we soon learned that the goods had literally vanished. After a further investigation we discovered what had actually happened. Out of the forty employees in the valuables' department, thirty-one were involved in stealing the merchandise. They either kept it for themselves, gave it to family or friends, or sold it to outside sources including the service stations. In just a two-year period they had bilked the company out of $180,000 worth of goods.

Fortunately for Ralph his wife was able to intercede in his behalf and the company refrained from prosecuting him. In two years he had stolen $45,000 in merchandise. Belle took their life savings including money due them under the pension plan, government bonds which they had bought on the payroll plan and the money she received by selling their house and turned it over to the bonding company which made up her husband's losses.

For Belle the disgrace of what her husband had done had been too much. Although they separated several times Belle always allowed her husband to return to her because she felt he needed her. As for Ralph, his is the final indignity. A confirmed alcoholic, he is unable to keep a job for more than a few months. For the rest of his days Ralph's survival depends upon the charity of his wife's earnings.

The part that the alcoholic plays in the rising incidence of white collar crime, is probably surpassed only by the homosexual. Until Alfred C. Kinsey and his associates came out with their momentous *Sexual Behavior in the Human Male* in 1948, the incidence of homosexuality in the United States had been generally underestimated. Kinsey, however, reported a series of startlingly high figures. According to Kinsey thirty-seven per cent of the total male population has at least some overt homosexual experience between adolescence and old age. This is equivalent to more than one out of every three males that you might happen to meet on a city street. He adds: "Among the males who remain unmarried until the age of 35, almost exactly 50 per cent have homosexual experience between the beginning of adolescence and that age. Some of those persons have but a single experience, and some of them have much more or even a lifetime of experience; but all of them have at least some experience to the point of orgasm."

In a further breakdown, Kinsey notes that eight per cent of males are exclusively homosexual for at least three years between the ages of sixteen and fifty-five and that four per cent of the white males are exclusively homosexual throughout their lives, after the onset of adolescence. This means that out of every 100,000 of the white male population, 4,000 are confirmed homosexuals. To put it another way, there are almost as many white male homosexuals per 100,000 as there are adult alcoholics. Indeed, from my own experience I would hazard the statement that homosexuality is responsible for more white collar crime than alcoholism. The problem is compounded by the fact that an alcoholic is often easier to detect than a confirmed homosexual.

A case that dramatically illustrates this point concerns one of Chicago's most exclusive stores. Located within walking distance of a reknowned North Side hotel, this store numbered among its clientele some of the city's richest residents. To service his customers, the manager of the store kept a mental dossier not only of his clientele's family histories (some of whom traced their heritage to the Mayflower and others to Al Capone) but was equally acquainted with their needs and idiosyncrasies. When he received an assortment of diamond-studded dog collars, the store manager had no difficulty selecting those customers who would be interested.

One customer, a dowager worth millions, had the habit of running her monthly charge account to as high as $3,000.

Knowing that the dowager was affllicted with a chronic case of superstition, the manager spent at least two hours each month going over her bills, making sure that none contained the figure 13. The store, as you can imagine, had quite a fine reputation not only because of the quality of its merchandise but for the personalized service that the store manager had given over the years. The manager, in turn, expected his subordinates to offer the same courtesy in dealing with the store's clientele. So when the store opened a men's wear department, the manager felt he was singularly lucky in obtaining the services of a man we shall call Vaughn to head the department.

In his sixties, Vaughn was as distinguished-looking as his name sounded. Tall, slim, graying, he dressed and acted impeccably. The store for which he had previously worked had a reputation equal to that of his new employer. When Vaughn applied for his new position, he arrived laden with the finest references. As far as the store manager was concerned he had made the right choice in naming Vaughn as head of the new men's department. The manager, though, was to experience a rather severe shock.

A year after he started on his new job, the store took an inventory in Vaughn's department and found a shortage equivalent to five per cent of sales. Management attributed the shortage to bookkeeping errors and the newness of the department. The shortage, they were convinced, would correct itself by the end of the second year. Instead, it rose to seven per cent. In dollars and cents the loss for the two-year period came to $100,000.

Indeed, the store's executives found themselves strapped with a king-sized financial headache. To build the extension for the men's wear department, the store had borrowed from the bank. In turn they had anticipated an annual volume of a million dollars in the men's wear department and an expected profit of two and a half per cent. The volume they got. But instead of a profit, they had ended up with a seven per cent shortage. It would take the store three years just to make back the loss. The store president would have to divulge the shortage to the board of directors. The directors, in turn, would have to explain the loss to the bank and the store's stockholders. Management could no longer rationalize the problem as a simple bookkeeping error. The president called on us and this is what we discovered.

Often when a well-to-do customer came to the men's wear department, the department head himself would wait on him, instead of allowing his salesmen to take the orders. In fact Vaughn not only noted the type, size and style of the garments to be purchased, but even delivered them during his lunch hour. It was personal service with a capital P and the store manager considered Vaughn the prize find of the year. And that is exactly what he turned out to be.

For the head of the men's wear department was actually stealing the merchandise he was supposed to be selling. He had a large following who selected their wardrobes at the store. Vaughn would simply remove their selections from the racks. Then, on his lunch hour, he would drop off the clothes to his own clientele, pocketing the money. To cover the fact that he was taking packages out of the store, he would also deliver a legitimate order to a paying customer, for which he was frequently praised by management.

Who was this man who came with excellent references and who seemed to know his customers so well? A bachelor, he rented an expensive apartment in one of Chicago's fanciest hotels. A big spender, he tipped the doorman $10 a week just to walk his dog. Vaughn, though, didn't live alone. His companion was a retired admiral who, like Vaughn, was a homosexual. The admiral, however, did not fulfill Vaughn's needs. Sometimes late at night Vaughn would wander off to the park where he would wait impatiently until a Cadillac pulled up with his date for the evening. A confirmed homosexual, the head of the men's wear department had found that his salary far from covered his expenses. For Vaughn, living had become a lavish affair.

As soon as he was arrested management began receiving phone calls, almost all in his behalf, from some of Chicago's most prominent residents. One of the many who phoned, however, had called for another reason. He was Vaughn's previous employer and he wanted to apologize. He had read about the

$100,000 loss and Vaughn's arrest in the newspapers. "During the four years that Vaughn was with us," his former employer said, "we suffered a loss of over $150,000. When you called us up for a reference we were suspicious but we couldn't prove a thing. We figured this was our chance to get rid of him. You see, we didn't want to offend him because he seemed to know so many influential people." After a short pause he added. "We were just wondering. Now that he's been arrested, maybe you can help us collect our $150,000."

Vaughn's two former employers apparently were not the only ones to have suffered losses. He had previously worked seven years for a company that had been in business for a quarter of a century. When Vaughn departed, the company was forced into bankruptcy.

Unlike the employer who was unaware of Vaughn's illness, many companies willingly hire confirmed homosexuals and give them responsible positions. Management, in such cases, often feels that the employee's talents far outweigh the problems their illness poses. In fact in numerous instances, homosexuality is viewed as a harmless idiosyncrasy, something to gossip about and laugh over. Almost invariably the employer learns that this "harmless idiosyncrasy" is more than a backstairs joke. But then it is too late.

Here is a case from our files involving one of the nation's most exclusive dress manufacturers and their chief dress designer. The story begins in Paris. Several times a year the heads of the company would travel to the women's fashion mecca to select the dresses and styles for the coming season. Much depended on the choices made there. In fact, an error in judgment could cost many thousands of dollars. Besides the expense of the trips, the livelihood of several hundred workers employed by the contractor and the jobs of at least a dozen salesmen, models, cutters, bookkeepers and shipping clerks were dependent upon the heads of the firm making the right selection. To avoid mistakes in judgment, several members of the firm usually made the trip together. Even so, the act of selection was a pretty nerve-racking business.

As the result of one voyage to Paris, the heads of the company were convinced they had picked an exceptionally successful collection. They had gone to a showing held exclusively for them and had purchased a line of new dresses whose style and cut had never before draped the American female figure. The model dresses themselves cost $1,000 to $2,000 apiece and the company had the exclusive right to reproduce them. Eventually the dresses would retail for $100 to $400. But before they were put on the market, the manufacturer had to make a heavy investment in material and labor. To begin with the piece goods buyer had to select and purchase the material that would go into the dresses. He had to make sure that he chose the right fabrics and the most appropriate color schemes and patterns. While the company did its own cutting, it hired a contractor to do the sewing. The contractor, in turn, had to make up samples of the dresses so that the manufacturer could estimate the total costs of production. Finally the chief designer had to work out just the right refinements so that the dresses still exuded the aura of Paris chicness while at the same time finding acceptance on the American market. As the weeks progressed the company continued to expend its capital in getting the line ready for its own exclusive showing for buyers from the high-priced retail stores and salons around the country. But a few days before the big showing, the company was shocked to discover its new finds appearing in the highly promotional stores like Orhbach's and Macy's. Except for modifications that permitted cheap mass production, the dresses were identical to those the company had brought back from Paris.

Now it is not unusual for an expensive and exclusive line to appear in the high-fashion stores and then for that same line to be copied and then reproduced at much lower prices. The garment industry, I might add, is one of the most competitive businesses and there is no copyright on the items produced. However, because of the production problems involved, there usually is a time lag between the appearance of the original dress and its inexpensive imitation. In this case, though, the high-priced dresses had not even gone into full production when they were already being sold on the floors of low-priced, high-volume department stores. The original company which had expended so much time and money discovered its season had been ruined. The loss from projected sales totaled over a million dollars. How did it happen?

The chief dress designer, whom I'll call Mark, was a homosexual, though on first glance it wasn't apparent. About thirty-eight, he was soft-spoken, genteel and meticulously dressed. Indeed with his boyish crew cut and tailor-made suits he could easily be mistaken for a successful advertising executive. His somewhat masculine appearance, however, was not surprising, since he usually played the part of the male in his relationships. Continually searching for new companions to add to his harem, Mark was quick to let it be known in the trade that he preferred to spend his two-hour lunches with other males who would give him the intrigue and excitement he feasted on.

The dress designer's latest romance was a young man fifteen years his junior. A designer himself, he had gone to Hollywood where he had gotten several commissions to create costumes for the movies. The young designer, though, wasn't too successful. So when Mark heard of his plight, he suggested that the youth return to New York. In fact Mark was even willing to pay his transportation. He also assured him of a place to live, Mark's place, of course. The offer was tempting enough. For Mark's place was a chic $350 a month apartment in the exclusive East Fifties. Mark not only boasted a superb library and an expensive collection of paintings, but plush furnishings including a hi-fi set and a bear rug. The young designer couldn't refuse, especially when Mark tossed in the promise that he would also get him a job. As soon as Mark's young acquaintance arrived, the phone began ringing, new friends calling up for dates, invitations to lunch, concerts, parties. Mark quickly became jealous. To keep his young friend from wandering, he decided to make a freelance designer out of him, converting one of the rooms in his sumptuous apartment into a studio.

There was only one problem. His young friend was almost completely lacking in talent. So Mark stole the designs of the dresses his company had brought back from Paris. He then helped his friend redesign the collection so that the exclusive

French imports could be inexpensively mass produced. Mark and his young companion then sold the designs to a manufacturer who soon began flooding the market. His coup, of course, turned out to be the original company's loss. But that's the dress business.

When the company that had first bought the dresses learned about Mark's handiwork, they immediately fired him. Another firm, though, quickly hired him again. His reputation for dress designing had not been damaged. The new employer felt that despite Mark's idiosyncrasies, the dress designer's golden talents were too valuable to waste.

Neither Vaughn, the head of the men's wear department, nor Mark, the dress designer, displayed any signs of remorse or guilt when their thefts were exposed. Whatever ethical values they might have had were blunted by their own unnatural needs. This, however, is not always the case.

I remember the Princeton graduate, a fine-looking lad of twenty-four, who had landed a promising job as executive trainee in a well-known department store. Heavy shortages were discovered four months after he had joined the firm. When he was questioned, he readily admitted stealing some fifteen suits worth $150 apiece, several dozen expensive shirts and an assortment of ties, each retailing at a minimum of $10. In addition he had helped himself to an average of $50 to $75 in cash each day. His total haul for four months came to $5,000. The young man was charged with embezzlement and at his arraignment he not only refused a lawyer but bail as well. In fact he seemed eager to plead guilty. The judge was puzzled, troubled. The young man seemed clean-cut, honest, not the kind of person who would violate a position of trust. The judge wanted to reason with this young defendant, and give him some old-fashioned fatherly advice. But the young man needed more than advice. He needed help. He pleaded with the judge to jail him for life if need be because he could no longer control himself. He told the judge that perhaps in prison somebody would be found who could make him well. For the young Princeton graduate was a homosexual who stole in order to support his various affairs. The pity is that his plea for help so far has gone unanswered. For neither science nor psychiatry has yet found a cure for homosexuality.

The problem of the outcasts in our society raises an important and, at times, insoluble dilemma. The millions who make up society's outcasts generally must work to live. Yet because of their insatiable craving, most are potentially dishonest, if they haven't already turned to thievery. The obvious question is should an employer hire a person he knows is an alcoholic, a homosexual or a drug addict. If he does, I can only suggest that the employer should take the obvious precaution of not putting such an employee in a position of trust. It would be foolhardy, for example, to make an alcoholic the treasurer of the firm. I would also add that the employer must be aware of the special problem on his hands and that he must continually watch and check the employees on the job operations. The final decision as to whether such an individual should be hired rests with the individual employer's conscience and good judgment.

I hope that at least some of the cases so far described in this chapter have evoked a feeling of compassion. No matter how unseemly a person's mental or physical illness may appear, he is still a human being and must be treated as such. The mentally ill should be understood, not condemned or shunned.

There is, however, an exception, the individual whose mind is so twisted that he purposefully destroys others to enrich himself. Such is the case of a man whom we shall call Frank. Frank had thought he had concocted the almost perfect embezzler's plot, a scheme, I might add, unmatched for its fiendishness. A hardy, portly man in his early forties, Frank's gregariousness and jovial appearance was the perfect mask for the evil that germinated within him. On the job he seemed to be especially successful in his efforts at increasing the number of his acquaintances among his fellow workers. As the responsible employee of a major parcel and freight truck carrier at a department store, Frank commanded an important position. As routing supervisor, Frank was in charge of some twenty-five truck drivers who hauled nearly 100 million dollars' worth of merchandise a year. His salary was $6,000 and he had a home, a wife, and three bank accounts. He had never been arrested and had no known vices. Frank was a solid citizen. Ask anybody. The trouble was nobody ever did.

Three or four nights a week Frank used to play host to his co-workers, most of whom were in their late teens or early twenties. The gang would be invited to Frank's home for a friendly card game where there would be plenty of beer, jokes and easy companionship. There was something, though, which made Frank's friendly card games somewhat different for the newcomer. He would usually find several of his companions avid smokers, which is not unusual, except that the cigarettes happened to be filled with marijuana. The newcomer meanwhile, would invariably start off with a winning streak. And as his winnings increased so did the stakes. After a couple of weeks of Frank's hospitality, the initiate would be invited to take a puff or two on one of the marijuana-laden cigarettes. "Just for kicks," Frank would say. "You can always stop." But usually the newcomer didn't stop. It wasn't long before marijuana seemed too tame and he would switch to heroin. Frank, still playing the role of the genial host, would gladly supply the narcotics. The newcomer was hooked.

And then things began to change. He would suddenly find himself losing at cards. The stakes by this time were more than he could afford. He would turn to Frank for more heroin. Frank would supply it, but this time for a price. Since his latest victim was now losing heavily at cards, he knew that he would be unable to pay for the drugs. Frank, though, would magnanimously offer a solution.

"You need some extra money," he would say. "Well, I've got a sideline that's very profitable. In fact, it's so profitable I could afford to buy a new car every year. But I don't because I wouldn't want people to ask me where I got the money. Anyhow, I'm a pretty fair guy. I might have a spot for a smart fellow like you. Get me all the lingerie, men's clothing, jewelry, housewares—anything you get your hands on. And I'll see to it that you're well taken care of."

Over the years Frank was to repeat variants of this little speech some twenty times. For that was the number of department store employees he turned into drug addicts and thieves, all of them stealing goods for Frank. Frank himself picked his victims carefully. One was a salesman in the small electrical appliances' department, another a marker in the ready-to-wear department, a third a stock boy in the receiving department. Each would supply Frank with different kinds of merchandise. Eventually Frank was robbing almost every department in the store.

This is how Frank worked it. The stolen goods were delivered to the loading platform. Since Frank was the chief dispatcher, he would simply load the merchandise on the trucks driven by his confederates. Three of the drivers who were in Frank's employ would detour on their way to the central reclassification point and drop off the stolen merchandise at a garage belonging to Frank. Next to the garage was a variety store, also owned by Frank. He simply transferred the stolen goods from the garage to the variety store where the items were sold with Frank pocketing the money. Frank found an item like a $1,000 fur coat too hot to handle at the variety store. So he turned it over to a member of his gang who would take a weekend trip of 150 to 200 miles from the city in a car he supplied. The coat would then be sold to one of several fences whom Frank knew.

During a three-year period Frank and his network of drug addicts had pilfered over $200,000 worth of goods.

Ironically, Frank, who had perfected the almost perfect embezzling plot, was caught when management asked us to investigate an inventory shortage caused by another group of thieves, a gang which not only operated independently but completely unknown to Frank himself.

Chapter 11

The Underhanded Kickback

OF ALL the elements that make up white collar crime, the most costly in terms of both ethics and money is the ubiquitous kickback. The variety of kickbacks or bribes that have been offered prove, if nothing else, man's infinite ingenuity. To mention just a few that I have encountered: payment of call girl and gambling charge accounts, financing stock market flings, contributions to favorite charities, loans which are not repaid, granting an interest in a business, distributing expensive gift certificates, lavish entertainment, placing buyers or relatives on the payroll. The item that makes the biggest hit, of course, is money. Some five billion dollars probably changed hands in kickbacks, payoffs and bribes in this past year alone. An astounding amount of grease just to help keep the wheels of commerce turning.

The extent to which an employee on the take will go was dramatically illustrated several years ago with the case of one Stanley Sternberg, a wholesale buyer of women's dresses and coats for one of the world's largest mail order firms. According to New York District Attorney Frank Hogan, Stanley, who measured slightly more than five feet, "was known as a tyrant and was hated and feared throughout the trade." Sternberg exacted his levies by threatening manufacturers with a sudden and disastrous curtailment in orders. Between 1945 and 1952, when the firm severed Stanley from the payroll, the five-foot "tyrant" bought $6,000,000 in dresses and coats for the mail order firm and personally pocketed at least $250,000 in kickbacks. The quarter of a million dollars Sternberg received in cash and gifts is only a minimal estimate. While earning only $12,000 a year plus a $5500 bonus, Stanley paid out $185,000 in back taxes in 1951. The tax lien covered just a three-year period. To satisfy the government's claim Sternberg dipped into his reserves, selling 307 United States Saving Bonds valued at $80,000 and withdrawing the remaining $105,000 from thirty different bank accounts.

Not only Sternberg, but his family lived off the tribute he received. When he bought a plush home in Long Island, for which he paid $42,000 in cash, manufacturers practically fell all over each other supplying the forty-eight-year-old buyer with housewarming presents. One gave him a custom-built TV set, another a $475 dryer, a third a deluxe gas range and refrigerator. In addition Stanley and his family bought their entire wardrobes through different vendors' charge accounts. He also chiseled a year's supply of pharmaceuticals from a clothing manufacturer whose relative owned a drugstore. Indeed nothing was too small or too mean for Stanley. Once he found himself shopping alongside a manufacturer in a delicatessen store. When Stanley walked out a few minutes later he was carrying two pounds of sturgeon which cost the manufacturer $5.25 a pound. He even enlisted the services of another manufacturer to care for his aged parents while he was courting his wife. If Stanley desired a home-cooked turkey dinner, the wife of a vendor was called upon to supply it. If he needed a tuxedo, theater tickets, even cigarettes, stamps and stationery, almost any item at all, it would be supplied, compliments of the donor.

Occasionally a manufacturer or vendor would attempt to throw off the Sternberg yoke. But as soon as there was the slightest decrease in the flow of gifts, Stanley would retaliate by cutting off the manufacturer's sales to little more than a dribble. Once Stanley and the son-in-law of a manufacturer got into an argument. The manufacturer, who had sold $286,000 worth of merchandise to the firm, stopped paying Sternberg his tribute of Saving Bonds. Stanley, of course, took his business elsewhere.

His firm eventually learned about the dress buyer's activities and turned the information over to the district attorney. Stanley was charged with accepting gratuities in order to influence his employer's business, a violation of Section 439 of the penal law, tried, convicted and sentenced to six months in the workhouse and fined $1,000. This time Stanley Sternberg couldn't kick back.

This case explains in part why business graft is able to flourish. When District Attorney Frank Hogan was asked if he would prosecute the manufacturers who bribed Sternberg, he replied: "No. We have to find out who the villian is and proceed against the villian. Generally, law enforcement officials fail to prosecute the real villian, the giver. Section 439 of The New York State penal law, for example, explicitly states it is unlawful for any one 'to give, offer or promise' to 'an agent, servant or employee of another, any gift or gratuity whatever, without the knowledge and consent of the principal employer or master of such agent, employee or servant, with intent to influence such agent, employee's or servant's action in relation to his principal's, employer's or master's business . . .'" Most other states have similar statutes. Yet they are rarely if ever invoked.

The problem is identical to the policeman who accepts a bribe. In most instances, the real culprit is the so-called honest citizen who offers the bribe in the first place. For it is his private act of dishonesty that is responsible for most of the public corruption he will be so quick to fulminate against.

Here is a case from our files that may shock you, but one which strikingly points up the heart of the problem. One day, the head of a restaurant that did a multimillion-dollar-a-year business was called in by his landlord, a huge corporation, and warned that if his sales and profits didn't increase the restaurant's lease, which had three years to run, would not be renewed. The rent the restaurant was paying was based on a minimum guarantee plus a percentage of sales, hence the landlord's concern.

The head of the restaurant asked us to analyze his operations and work out a controls system that would eliminate both inefficiency and malpractices. We soon discovered an astounding amount of corruption. Payroll records were being padded. The restaurant was not only overstaffed but its employees were collecting thousands of dollars in unnecessary overtime. Waiters, cashiers and hostesses were taking home turkeys, steaks, and lobster thermidor, prepared to order by the chef, who in turn was receiving kickbacks from the meat wholesalers. The bartender, who purchased supplies for his department, also was in on the take. The manager of the restaurant was lavishly entertaining friends and business acquaintances in return for favors they did for him. The restaurant of course, footed the bills. In addition, the manager allowed the landlord's agent to place his female acquaintances, some of whom were prostitutes, as hatcheck girls. Although they were paid good wages, they pocketed the tips they were supposed to turn over to the restaurant. It was a miracle the whole operation showed any profit.

By restaffing and reassigning some employees' functions, management was able to clean out most of the dishonesty that had been uncovered. In order to solve the kickback problem, all purchases were concentrated in a single steward, instead of spreading the buying among the chef and head bartender. But in the space of one year, management had to fire seven different stewards, all of whom were unable to resist the under-the-table offers made by nearly every company representative with whom they did business. Management decided that no steward, no matter how honest at first, would be able to withstand the constant temptation. To end kickbacks the climate of corruption would have to be changed. But how?

After much thought, management hit on this plan. An executive not known to the salesmen would pose as the new steward. For six weeks he would keep a record of all the kickbacks, bribes and payoffs offered to him. When the six weeks had passed, the firms who found their way into the dossier would be contacted and warned that if they didn't stop offering kickbacks the information would be turned over to the district attorney for prosecution. Here are some typical entries:

1. The vice president of X meat corporation offered to take me and my wife to a show and extended an invitation to

us to spend a week-end at his summer home on Long Island. The vice president suggested that I accompany him, as his guest, to a few baseball games. I refused all these offers, claiming that I was too busy assuming new responsibilities to find time for these invitations.

2. On April 17, the representative of Y liquor company approached me on the premises. He is supplementing his gratuities (liquor and entertainment offers) with cash payments. In making this offer, he stated, "The company doesn't overpay any of you fellows, but this will kind of make up a little for you. That's why we like to give it to the fellow instead of the company." The specific offer follows: One dollar on every case of vermouth purchased, three dollars on every case of champagne purchased, two dollars on every case of bourbon purchased, one dollar on all wines purchased. The liquor representative said that he would send the money over to my home in an unsigned envelope, but that I would know what it was for. I ordered 20 cases of vermouth, one case of champagne, one case of bourbon, and five cases of assorted wines. This purchase would have entitled me to $30.

On May 6, a letter was delivered to my home which contained $30 wrapped in plain yellow paper. No name appeared on the envelope other than my address, and there was no note attached to the money. The representative of the Y liquor company visited the premises on May 6 and asked if I had received the "note" he had sent me. I answered affirmatively and thanked him for the $30.

While sitting in the bar, I placed an order of three cases of bourbon and a case of gin, with the representative of Y liquor company. The salesman handed me a $5 bill and said that it was for the bourbon order. It may be noted that I was short changed on this occasion as I had originally been promised a gratuity of $2 on every case of bourbon, which should have resulted in a $6 gratuity. From his manner, it appeared that the Y liquor company representative felt I was obligated to him and that it was not necessary for him to live up to the letter of his offer. This was somewhat borne out later that afternoon when he called me up and remarked, "You know, you only gave me a four-case order. Let's make it an even five by ordering a case of (brand) Whisky." When I hesitated, replying that I did not believe that this liquor was included in the restaurant's liquor purchasing policy, he replied: "Look, I've been doing business there for years and I know that liquor policy backwards. (Brand) Whisky is on your liquor policy. I wouldn't steer you wrong." I refused to place the order, telling the Y company liquor representative that if he wanted to make it a fifth case to send over a case of scotch.

3. On May 15 a fruit dealer approached me and said he would like to expand his dealings with the restaurant. He added he wanted to send a basket of fruit to my home. Even though I told him it was unnecessary, a large basket of apples, oranges, honeydew melons, and cantaloupes was delivered to my house several days later.

4. On the same day I was approached by the meat salesman of Z company who told me: "I've done business with the restaurant before. I've been in and out selling meat to this outfit for my present company and other meat houses. Here's the story. Work it any way you want. Five or ten per cent of billings—you can name your own price. I want to get the business and stay in once I get it."

And so it went. During the six-week period, some thirty different salesmen, managing directors, executives and vice-presidents proferred between $2,500 and $3,000 in kickbacks and gratuities including cash, based on purchases, weekend outings to country clubs and hotels, choice theater tickets, fishing trips, and an almost constant shower of gifts.

After the dossier had been completed, the head of the restaurant again approached the landlord, presented the evidence and said he was prepared, if need be, to bring legal action against the firms who could only do business by offering graft. The landlord, in turn, advised the head of the restaurant that if he even so much as attempted to end the kickback system he would do well to look for another site, for the restaurant's lease would not be renewed. The landlord feared that any new tenant would be blacklisted by the trade. In addition, the landlord, a well-known corporation, knew that its hands were far from clean and that the public washing of the vendors' dirty laundry would undoubtedly result in a community cleansing, a spectacle which the corporation had no desire to see take place. The head of the restaurant did the only thing he could; he put away the dossier and promised not to war on the vendors who gave kickbacks. A short time later the landlord agreed to negotiate the restaurant's lease.

The cases just described illustrate two of the types who foster business graft, Stanley Sternberg, the greedy buyer, and the dishonest vendor. There is however, a third type besides the taker and giver who is responsible, though indirectly, for the exchange of tens of thousands of dollars in kickbacks. He is the employer who takes his own employees for granted. By saving a few dollars in salaries, he may lose thousands in bribes which he unwittingly pays for through padded invoices. As amazing as the following may seem, such cases occur with surprising frequency.

It was 1916 when a man I'll call Morgan first joined one of the nation's largest textile manufacturers. Morgan was twenty-five at the time and a clerk. Over the years he won a series of promotions until he eventually became head of the traffic department, a position that made him responsible for the routing, shipping and delivery of all the firm's raw cotton and finished products between the firm's factories and warehouses as well as delivery to the company's customers. It was a multimillion-dollar operation and as traffic manager Morgan was accountable for seeing that every item—there were hundreds of thousands—arrived at its assigned destination whether it was shipped by truck, air, rail or boat. Yet despite the burden of his responsibilities, Morgan never received more than $9,000 a year. As Morgan himself later put it:

"I have always been close to the head of the firm since we grew up in this business together. On the other hand, as the company grew larger he became occupied with many other problems, and my end of the business and its problems sort of got lost in the shuffle. I am not expressing myself properly, but somehow our daily contact with each other became less and less frequent, and I wasn't able to command his attention as I used to be able to do. I also know that other people holding jobs like mine, with similar responsibilities and volume, were earning two and three times what I was getting from my employer. I just about made with my kickbacks what they make on salary."

During a fifteen-year period, Morgan received more than $100,000 in kickbacks from at least five different transportation companies. The largest cornucopia of graft was a trucking company that first got its start with the textile manufacturer. Beginning with three or four trucks, this firm originally did ninety-five per cent of its business with Morgan. During the ensuing years the trucking company burgeoned until it owned more than 300 vehicles and handled seventy-five per cent of the textile manufacturer's over-the-road deliveries. Besides helping the trucking company become established, Morgan allowed the firm to collect on duplicate bills and had the textile company pay the insurance claims which were actually the trucking company's responsibility, since the freight carrier was self-insured. To show its gratitude the trucking firm paid Morgan $1,000 on the first Monday of every month. The traffic manager explained the payoff this way:

"Most of my deals were arranged through a dummy corporation. Checks were made payable to this outfit, which was under my control, and I would cash them. Considerable sums of money were also handed to me. At our annual company affair I always invited the heads of the trucking company and they would usually pay me in cash there. Also, we often met at conventions, and I was taken care of there by them and others. I suppose you think it was foolish for me to have the checks mailed to my office, but this was the way it started and I guess we just continued our arrangement. In the beginning, I was afraid that my wife might open one of these letters if they were mailed to my home, so I had them sent to the office. It was addressed to me—personal and confidential—which my secretary does not open. However, just the other month when she was ill another clerk took her place for a few days, and one of these envelopes was opened in error. I have been so worried about this, that I have hardly been able to sleep since then."

Ironically, Morgan knew that he was being watched several months before his whole kickback system was exposed, but he could do nothing about it. The accounting department had suddenly begun making an unusual number of inquiries concerning the traffic manager's method of operations. Morgan, though, couldn't have his books show a big change in costs from previous years, because any sizable reduction would have only increased the accountants' suspicions. Eventually, though, the evidence became so overwhelming that Morgan was forced to admit his wrongdoing. Over the years he had collected more than $100,000 in kickbacks while the textile manufacturer had unwittingly paid out twice the sum through padded bills. Morgan himself owned a $28,000 summer home, over $25,000 in cash which he kept in a safe deposit box, stocks whose value ran into five figures and a $100,000 life insurance policy.

When the head of the company was presented with the report on his traffic manager, he called Morgan into the office and told him the following: "I was at your wedding. I know your wife, your children; we've gone through a lot together in a lifetime, so I will give it to you without any preliminaries. Just straight and simple. It's true you might have been entitled to more money. It's also true that you more than made up for it through the money in kickbacks you've collected. But unfortunately in doing so you've cost me over a quarter of a million dollars in padded invoices and unnecessary expenses. But I want to be fair and just to you and your family. I don't want the full amount returned. I want you at my lawyer's office within forty-eight hours. I'll assume fifty per cent of the loss. I want the other fifty per cent returned."

The conversation lasted less than five minutes. Out of his sixty-eight years, Morgan had spent forty-three working for the textile company. In two more years he would have retired on a pension. In less than forty-eight hours he entered the attorney's office and handed him his entire life savings.

The burden that kickbacks place on the economy whether contracting or expanding is perhaps more serious than most people realize. What with rising costs and shrinking profits, the average businessman today cannot afford to lose hundreds of thousands in padded expenses which pay for the graft his employees receive. Take the case of a large Midwest variety chain store and its cosmetics and notions buyer who was responsible for the purchase of several million dollars worth of merchandise. Several vendors were forced to rely on the buyer for sales ranging from $150,000 to $250,000 a year and they bowed to his demands for kickbacks. To insure a larger take, the buyer did the following. One, he permitted vendors to pad invoices, a percentage of this padding accruing to the buyer. Two, he instructed a manufacturer to substitute cheaper ingredients in his product, but told him to charge the company the usual price. The difference in cost price went to the buyer. Three, he overshipped to some of the chain store's outlets and thus increased volume with certain vendors. The result was a larger income for the buyer. And four, he falsified stock-on-hand records downward to justify an increase in purchases from certain vendors, thereby gaining additional kickbacks.

The vendors, in turn, rewarded the buyer with cash gratuities, paid his monthly tab at the local bookie, opened charge accounts at several fashionable stores and completely outfitted the buyer's kitchen and den. Over a four-year period the cosmetics' buyer received the equivalent of $35,000 in kickbacks. The cost to the variety chain store in falsified inventories, lost sales, unsalable merchandise and excessive markdowns exceeded $100,000.

In another instance, the purchasing agent for a New England manufacturer let it be known that he would soon marry. The dowry he received, though, didn't come from his intended's family. It was paid for by the firms which supplied his own employer. One vendor picked up the total tab of the newlywed's six-week honeymoon, including the plane tickets, the hotel expenses and the bills run up at the hotel's fancy shops. Two more vendors "loaned" the purchasing agent $4,000 and $3,000, but never brought up the subject of repayment. A fourth vendor kicked in the down payment on the buyer's new home, and several others donated $2,500 in government bonds as wedding presents. When the purchasing agent was asked how he could explain this sudden display of affection on the part of his employer's suppliers, he replied: "What the hell, most people only get married once in a lifetime." A further investigation, though, showed that he had been receiving a similar amount in kickbacks over the past eight years. Unwittingly, his employer had indirectly paid the cost of the kickbacks several times over through the chiseling the purchasing agent had done in behalf of the vendors.

I might add that the acceptance of kickbacks is easy to rationalize. One buyer I knew, received over $10,000 in kickbacks each year. The buyer, who earned $14,000 plus a bonus freely admitted pocketing five to seven per cent of billings. He explained that since he personally placed his orders directly with manufacturers whom he knew personally, he saw nothing wrong in accepting kickbacks equivalent to what the manufacturers would have had to pay their own salesmen. The fact that as a buyer he was obligated to pass on to his own firm any savings he had made on purchases had escaped him.

Incidentally, I don't know which leads to worse complications, the buyer who puts unethical demands on the manufacturer or the manufacturer who tries to obligate the buyer. In either case one may receive temporary benefits, but ultimately both are the losers.

Here is a striking example of such a case. The president of a furniture manufacturing company telephoned the president of a major department store and wanted an explanation of why the store had refused a $17,000 shipment in spite of the fact it was a confirmed order. The store president replied that he knew the order had been confirmed, but that he was still refusing to accept it.

The manufacturer pressed the issue, saying, "I must admit that as a favor to the buyer I agreed to accept the merchandise prior to the store's inventory. I did that with the understanding that I could ship the merchandise back thirty days later. In fact, I also paid the freight charges."

The store president replied, "I am aware of all this. And I am still refusing the order."

Then the manufacturer, ever more upset, blurted out, "Mr. President, this merchandise doesn't even belong to me. It belongs to another manufacturer. I did this only as a favor to your buyer. It means a $17,000 loss to me, plus the freight charges."

"That's your worry, not mine," replied the store president. "But that's the price you have to pay for helping my buyer be dishonest. I have a solution, though. Why don't you try collecting out of my buyer's bonus?"

As costly as kickbacks are for the businessman, the individual who bears the greatest brunt is the consumer. For almost inevitably the cost of graft is tacked on to the price the consumer pays. In fact more often than not the consumer is paying two, three and four times the amount paid in kickbacks to the dishonest buyer or purchasing agent. For example, in a restaurant where the menu items are priced so that food costs account for thirty-three per cent of the sale dollar, the consumer would pay three times the amount of the kickback. To put it another way, the cost of a food item to the owner of a restaurant is thirty-three cents. Ordinarily on your check that thirty-three cents will be tripled and you will pay ninety-nine cents. Now add an additional two cents in kickbacks to the thirty-three cents the item cost the owner of the restaurant. Instead of just tacking on the additional two cents to the consumer's bill, that sum is multiplied three times and the consumer ends up paying six cents on two cents in graft. In department or retail stores which generally operate on a forty to fifty per cent mark-up, the consumer pays about two times the kickback. And at bars where liquor costs are twenty-five per cent of the selling price, the customer unwittingly pays four times the kickback.

These examples actually represent only the top of the kickback spiral. Where kickbacks occur in earlier stages of the production and distribution cycle, the toll multiplies, for there is a pyramiding effect as each entrepreneur attempts to recover the purchase cost increase that results from the kickbacks he paid out. Mark-ups are added to mark-ups in a chain reaction, which, unless the cumulative cost of the initial kickback is absorbed out of profits, can reach a staggering total by the time the final product is bought by the consumer.

The problem in business graft is not so much greed but what I would call the "kickback cycle." Whether we like the fact or not kickbacks are essentially an outgrowth of our highly competitive economy. Each year thousands of new products are put on the market while thousands of others already established are battling either to retain or increase their sales. For example, John Jones decides to manufacture corrugated boxes. To break into this highly competitive field, he will offer a purchasing agent a kickback if he will only buy his product so that it will be offered to the public. Once the purchasing agent has taken several orders, the new manufacturer will pay more graft either to retain or increase his sales. Then a new kickback cycle, of course, begins.

Recently, *Sales Management*, a marketing magazine, posed the problem to its Sales Leadership Panel consisting of two hundred sales executives. The panelists were asked: Why do prospects or customers resort to shakedowns? The panelists replied that their customers have sought payoffs from their salesmen in order to make it possible for the salesmen:

1. To break into the prospect's firm. A whopping fifty-five per cent report this to be true.

2. To obtain a bigger share of business. A very large fifty-one per cent contend that this is the reason.

3. To retain the business. This is true for twenty-nine per cent of the panelists.

(Note that the percentages add up to more than 100 per cent because the panelists checked one or more of the three possible answers.)

The big question, and one that must be answered positively, is: Can the kickback cycle be broken? I think it can and has in many instances. But it depends upon two things, the business-man's attitude and a concrete system of controls.

First of all, management must not accept the philosophy that kickbacks are a standard practice in the trade and therefore must be tolerated. There are many companies that have been able to withstand business graft and still be as successful as their competitors. It is worth noting that while thirty-five per cent of *Sales Management*'s panelists said they lost business when they turned down requests for payoffs, the remaining sixty-five per cent reported they still got the same amount of business.

Secondly, management should make clear that it expects its employees to maintain proper business relationships and will not tolerate situations in which the integrity of its buyers or agents is likely to be compromised. Employees should be told not only orally but in writing that they risk dismissal and pos-sible prosecution when they accept gratuities. Buyers and pur-chasing agents must also be shown that management can and does find out about kickbacks and can prove their existence no matter how carefully the graft is hidden.

How can this be done? The following measures, if methodi-cally and earnestly put into practice, should solve the kick-back problem for almost every business no matter how large or small.

1. Buyers and purchasing agents should be told not to pur-chase from vendors who are relatives or from firms in which they have a financial interest unless they have management's approval.

2. They should not be allowed to buy from financially risky suppliers without the consent of management.

3. Employees should not be permitted to accept or solicit loans from vendors or arrange for advertising allowances without company authorization.

4. Upon employment or promotion or whenever manage-ment deems necessary, buyers or purchasing agents should authorize the company to check on their financial resources in-cluding bank accounts, investments and real estate holdings. Full disclosure of financial resources is demanded by banks

when extending credit amounting to several thousand dollars on a home purchase or even an installment credit loan for a few hundred dollars. For management to be timid about requiring similar disclosures from employees entrusted with the purchase of millions of dollars' worth of merchandise a year is not only shirking responsibility but is downright foolhardy. It is far more important to deter destructive practices before they begin than it is to take corrective action after the violation occurs.

5. At holiday time, vendors and purchasing agents should be reminded that employees are prohibited from accepting substantial gratuities (even token gifts do not truly foster the holiday atmosphere). If management wants to allow the acceptance of token gifts, written notices should also point out that these gifts must be delivered to the place of business and not the employees' homes. Mail room personnel should be instructed to record all packages addressed to the attention of buyers or the purchasing department, indicating for whom, from whom, and where possible, a description of the article. After January 15, buyers should be required to provide management with a list of vendors from whom they received gratuities, listing each item and its value.

6. Management should let vendors know it will hear their complaints that they cannot make any headway with the buyer even though they are competitive in every way with other vendors.

7. Wherever practicable, competitive bids should be required on large purchases of homogeneous products. Procedures should be established to detect order splitting calculated to avoid competitive bids.

8. Management should also spot check the quality, accuracy and promptness of incoming shipments and vendor returns. It is important to note whether the incoming merchandise meets the order specifications and whether the goods are equal in quality to previously submitted samples.

9. Purchasing and receiving functions should be kept entirely separate. A study should be made of the pattern of a buyer's relationships with personnel engaged in the processing

of shipments and invoices. A serious breach of control occurs when buyers are allowed to participate or interfere with the orderly processing of shipments.

These are the basic preventive measures which, if instituted by an alert management, can end much of the business graft existing today. By taking a firm stand on kickbacks, management insures there will be no misunderstanding of company policy and that whatever rationalization a buyer may make is just that, a lame excuse for dishonesty. Employees should be shown that kickbacks hurt not only their own company, but themselves. For once a gratuity is accepted, it is a rare buyer who can stop. Finally, by placing himself in a position where his professional judgment might be compromised out of indebtedness to a person who hands out kickbacks, the buyer risks his standing in the company, in his profession and in his community.

Chapter 12

The People's Choice

PERHAPS THE highest price of all that we pay for white collar crime is the corruption of our most sacrosanct area of trust, government. Whether it be outright theft or an imprudent act, the inevitable exposure must result in a mounting cynicism and loss of faith in the democratic process.

During the past decade and a half, at least fourteen persons, most of whom have held highly responsible positions in either the Truman or Eisenhower administrations, have committed acts ranging from fraud to so-called ethical indiscretions. They have included such important personages as T. Lamar Caudle, once head of the tax division of the Justice Department, and Matthew J. Connelly, President Truman's White House appointments secretary. Both men were convicted of conspiracy to defraud the government by fixing a tax case. Joseph D. Nunan Jr., Commissioner of Internal Revenue from 1944 to 1947, was convicted of evading taxes during the time he held the government's top revenue job. More recently you will recall the names of Harold E. Talbott, former Secretary of the Air Force, and Sherman Adams, once assistant to President Eisenhower and the second most powerful man in the nation. Both resigned as the result of congressional investigations.

Talbott quit after the Senate questioned the propriety of his telephone calls and letters with a firm which did business with defense contractors. Talbott was a partner in the firm. Adams, the Righteous Puritan, bowed out after admitting that Bernard Goldfine, a Boston textile millionaire and old friend, had given him a vicuna coat, "loaned" him an oriental rug and paid $2,171.62 in Adams's hotel bills, Although he denied using any influence in Goldfine's behalf, Adams did admit communicating with two federal agencies on three occasions regarding cases involving the millionaire.

The cases just mentioned are representative of what I would call one of America's most crucial problems: the relentless destruction of our code of fair play and honesty. A Senate subcommittee several years ago explored the problem of gift giving to government officials and came to this conclusion: "The morals of official conduct may be distinguished, but certainly not separated from the public morals generally. The moral standards of the country, indeed, provide the ethical environment which in turn conditions the standards of behaviour of public officials."

A dramatic illustration of the Senate subcommittee's statement is the case of a man who once was seriously considered as a candidate for the highest honor this country could bestow. Until the last two months of his life he had convinced hundreds of thousands of his honesty. And it was only from his grave that he was to admit his guilt—the embezzlement of $300,000. This is the story of the late Harold Giles Hoffman, one-time Republican governor of New Jersey.

Hoffman was the Horatio Alger of New Jersey politics. A jovial, stocky, intensely loyal man, there were few things that he ever attempted during his life that he didn't accomplish. Indeed, many of his great public successes can only be explained by an amazing personal popularity.

His meteoric career began in the town of his birth, South Amboy, a peaceful railroad community along the Raritan River. Born in 1896, he decided by the time he was twelve that he would go into newspaper work and immediately landed a job as suburban correspondent for several city papers. Two years later he quit school, joined the Perth Amboy *Evening News* and worked up to assistant city editor. With the outbreak of World War I, he joined the Third New Jersey Infantry, saw action at the battle of Verdun and rose from private to captain. He returned to South Amboy as the town's most famous hero. So it was only natural that he should help form the town's new bank, the South Amboy Trust Company, serving as treasurer. In 1925 he ran for mayor of South Amboy. His victory left the community's political pundits bug-eyed. He not only received the largest majority ever given up to that time, but won on a write-in vote. At twenty-nine he had become the youngest mayor in the state. Harold Giles Hoffman had found his forte.

During the next nine years, he continued his climb up the political ladder, collecting friends, votes and offices with the agility of a Billy Sunday gathering in souls. By 1934 he had already served in the New Jersey State Assembly, had two terms in Congress and was head of the State Motor Vehicle Commission when he bagged the governorship, another amazing victory considering the depression and the Democratic tide. At thirty-eight Harold Giles Hoffman had done it again. This time he had become the youngest governor in the history of the state of New Jersey.

As governor Hoffman displayed a rare courage. Early in his administration he pushed through one of the most unpopular laws New Jersey ever had, a two per cent sales tax. An anti-New Deal Republican, he obtained the aid of Democratic boss Frank Hague of Jersey City to get the law passed after many of his own party members refused to back him. Hoffman hoped that the sales tax would help pay some of the huge relief costs of New Jersey's 600,000 unemployed. The sales tax, like prohibition, was openly flouted. It lasted only four months. At its demise, Hoffman warned: "This means financial trouble ahead. It means unbalanced budgets and maybe hungry people."

At about this time, when Hoffman was being boosted for President by his fellow Republicans, he deliberately ruined his own political career by an act that his defenders say was only an attempt to see justice done. His three-year term as governor covered the trial of Bruno Richard Hauptmann, the kidnap-murderer of Charles A. Lindbergh, Jr., the famous flier's first baby. He was convinced that the German carpenter had an accomplice and that the State police under H. Norman Schwarzkopf had "bungled" the case. Hoffman even gave Hauptmann a two-month reprieve with the hope that his "accomplice" could be found. Although he eventually allowed the kidnaper to go to the electric chair, Hoffman was twice threatened with impeachment for ordering the postponement. On the twentieth anniversary of the kidnaping, the former governor still defended his actions. He told an interviewer: "I believe that the crime was committed by more than one person. I believe it would have been difficult to execute that crime without the assistance of someone who was inside either the Lindbergh or the Morrow household. I believe that the police, once Hauptmann had been apprehended and the lone wolf pattern of prosecution was decided upon, not only failed to make, but made every effort to hinder further investigation that might have brought others to the bar of justice." Nearly twenty years later Hoffman's convictions remained unchanged, although they had effectively ended a brilliant political career.

For the next fifteen years he served as director of the state Division of Employment Security, which handled during his tenure one billion dollars in unemployment funds. As governor Hoffman received a salary of $20,000. His top salary in his new position never was more than $13,500 a year. Despite his setbacks—he unsuccessfully tried for the GOP gubernatorial nomination in 1940 and 1944—Hoffman remained the ebullient, glad-handing, joke-telling politician. He became president of the Circus Saints and Sinners, an organization of fun-loving circus, movie, stage and radio stars. A witty, affable after-dinner speaker, he was in such demand that he began charging for his appearances and had an agent arrange his bookings. His schedule eventually became so heavy—he would often put in twenty hours a day—that he suffered several heart attacks. But he still wouldn't slow down. Something was driving him. For Hoffman not only had embezzled $300,000 early in his political career, but had spent the next twelve years hiding his thefts by juggling $16,000,000 in state funds.

One can only imagine the moments of awareness when life confronted Harold Giles Hoffman with the small ironies that were to form the hairshirt of his conscience. Once he claimed a

newspaper had damaged his career when they printed an editorial concerning his allowance of $1,700 in salary increments
to executive office employees shortly before his term as governor
ended. Hoffman filed a libel suit and New Jersey's highest court
of law upheld the $30,000 award. In his unsuccessful bid for the
Republican gubernatorial nomination in 1944, he offered to
defend his personal and public record against his opponent,
Alfred E. Driscoll, later elected governor. At one time friends
suggested that Hoffman, whose thefts originated in a bank
account, would be the perfect candidate for the post of state
banking and insurance commissioner. Perhaps the most ironic
event of all occurred during World War II when Lieutenant
Colonel Harold Giles Hoffman was chosen to play the part
of the prosecutor in the Union Horse Society's 131st annual
mock trial in Philadelphia. According to custom, the defendant
is always found guilty of horse stealing and sentenced to "hang."

Hoffman's difficulties began during the successful 1953 gubernatorial campaign of another young, aspiring candidate. Robert
B. Meyner noticed that whenever he promised a group of
workers they would no longer have to wait six or seven weeks
to receive their unemployment checks, if he were elected governor, he almost invariably received a thunderous ovation. Shortly
after he was sworn into office, Meyner asked two Prudential
Insurance Company officials to check on Hoffman's division of
Employment Security. Meyner, a Democrat, thought highly of
the former Republican governor and he assumed that the two
Prudential officials would come up with some minor recommendations for streamlining the agency. He certainly didn't
expect a report detailing widescale malpractices within the
agency itself. However, when the two businessmen laid their
information before Meyner, the governor acted swiftly. On
the following day, March 18, 1954, he called Hoffman and told
him he was being suspended. He also asked H. Norman
Schwarzkopf, the man whom Hoffman had accused of "bun-
gling" the Lindbergh case, to take over the investigation. Meanwhile, State's Attorney General Grover C. Richman dispatched
twenty state troopers to the agency's midtown Trenton offices
and two warehouses. The troopers were put on a twenty-four-

hour security watch to insure that no documents were removed without the investigators' authorization.

Although Meyner at first refused to make any public charges,
he did tell Hoffman's attorney some of his investigators' findings. Among other things Hoffman was accused of transferring
$3,427,000 in state funds from interest-bearing accounts to non-
interest-bearing accounts in the Trenton Trust Company. The
investigators added Hoffman had deposited $300,000 of State
Disability Funds in his own South Amboy Trust Company
bank in December, 1949, and that the money had drawn no
interest for the state. Hoffman also was accused of using his
agency's artists and other employees to paint and transport the
scenery used by the Circus Saints and Sinners at their monthly
New York luncheons. Finally he was charged with favoring
certain printers and of cheating the state out of thousands
through a special lease-purchase plan involving several of his
agency's field buildings.

On the afternoon of June 4, 1954, Governor Meyner and
Harry Green, Hoffman's friend and attorney, met in Trenton
where Hoffman was to join them. Two and a half months had
passed since the ex-governor's suspension. When Hoffman didn't
appear at 3:00 P.M., the scheduled meeting time, Green called
the Blake Studio Apartments in New York. The phone rang
several times but there was no answer. While Governor Meyner
and Harry Green continued to discuss the Hoffman case in
Trenton, the maid at the Blake Studio Apartments informed
V. H. Watson, the manager, that she was unable to get into one
of the rooms. At 4:15 P.M. Watson climbed down the fire
escape, opened the window and discovered the body of Harold
Giles Hoffman. He was dressed in his shorts, socks and a single
shoe. He had suffered a heart attack while dressing and had
been dead for more than nine hours.

Friends and foes, Democrats and Republicans, indeed all
those who knew him, expressed shock and sorrow upon hearing
about Hoffman's death. Said former U.S. Senator H. Alexander
Smith of New Jersey: "I have always admired him for his ex-
ceptional grasp of governmental operation and his adeptness
in his knowledge of human relations in relation to government."

Commented State Senator Frank S. Farley: "There was nothing of pretense or sham about him . . . In my humble opinion he had the ability to be president of the United States." And from Union County Clerk Henry C. Nulton: "I soldiered with Harold Hoffman. A better guy could never have lived. He was a great American."

They buried him three days later, in the town of his birthplace, the town that he had made famous, South Amboy. It took five hours for the 4,000 mourners to pass his bier, which was set on the stage of the auditorium of the high school named in his honor. An additional 2,000 stood outside listening to the hour-long services over a public address system. The honorary pallbearers included Meyner, and two former governors, Alfred E. Driscoll and Walter E. Edge. After the services a winding funeral procession made up of marching war veterans, firemen of Hoffman's volunteer Independence Engine and Hose Company and several hundred cars slowly moved through the streets of South Amboy to the Christ Church Cemetery. There in a hillside family plot overlooking the Atlantic Ocean, the casket containing the body of Harold Giles Hoffman was lowered into the earth while an Army bugler blew taps. The former governor had been laid to rest, his lips forever sealed. Yet he was to speak once more, with words jolting the state and the nation like an electric shock.

The morning after the funeral, Hoffman's daughter, Mrs. Ada Leonard went to a safety deposit box in Madison, New Jersey, and took out a letter her father had sent her about a month before his death. The legend on the envelope read: "Do Not Open Until My Death. To Be Read, Considered, and Destroyed." Mrs. Leonard, almost overcome by grief, showed the letter to two of her father's close friends, Harry Green and Mrs. Mary Roebling, head of the Trenton Trust Company, both of whom advised that its contents should be made known to the authorities. Finally after destroying the original, Ada Hoffman Leonard at the request of Attorney General Richman recalled the substance of the message "eliminating only such mechanical details as may have slipped my mind." Here is the letter her father sent her as reconstructed by Mrs. Leonard:

There is one thing, Hon, which I have done that cannot be condoned, although I had always the highest intentions about it and exerted the utmost efforts over it.

I first became involved in monetary difficulties when, as a very young man and a very poor man, I ran for congress. A certain wealthy elder candidate, who is now deceased, promised to finance my campaign if when "stumping" my own district, I would also speak on his behalf. We both were elected but when I presented him with my expense account, instead of the essential $17,000 I had expected, he gave me $2,500—$1,000 each for Middlesex and Monmouth, $500 for Ocean. Meanwhile, I had made previous commitments which I "temporarily" covered by drawing from inactive accounts at the South Amboy Trust Company.

What with the high cost of Washington living, the maintenance of two homes, and what I can only label as the expensive naivete of a newcomer congressman, things, instead of bettering, got worse.

Then during the gubernatorial primary and general election, I suffered further disappointments at the hands of friends who promised to pay election expenses, but, it subsequently developed, only at the price of state favors which I considered impossible to grant.

Things got deeper and deeper until, in 1938, I found myself involved to the extent of $300,000. The disability funds where this amount may not appear to be were not established until a much later date. Not a single dollar has been taken by me since 1936, and to the best of my knowledge, no single person has actually been hurt by my default.

It is also my understanding that the trust company's insurance covers losses of this kind up to the amount of $175,000, with individual deposits secured to the amount of $10,000.

I must tell you too, one time I knew that an amount of state money was about to be suddenly withdrawn and would reveal my guilt. I was obliged to go to a certain state official, unnamed but dead, explain my whole situation and plead for his help. He "helped" alright—but from that time on he "borrowed" money from me to lavish on certain gambling operations of his own. This money, he assured me, would in turn win money enough to enable me to clean the slate at the bank. I was opposed to this scheme—protesting that all I had wanted was time in which to pay off these monies by some honorable means—I never did gamble, or bet, or even speculate, you know that. However this "friend" insisted and furthermore threatened to expose me and he blackmailed me into giving him something like $150,000, all told—just about half again the amount of my debt. Ada, dear, had it not been for that devastating setback, I really think that by this time I could have repaid my obligation.

For these many years, as you may well imagine, I have lived in constant fear that George Kress [1] (who is in my opinion a highly honorable and fine fellow, and who knew absolutely nothing of my predicaments and deals) would somehow discover the serious shortage.

But, until rather recently, I have always lived in hope that I would somehow be able to make good, to set everything straight.

Now, I must leave it, dear, to you to do what you know must be done. Mother is and has always been a devoted and frugal person, has known nothing of my financial plight and has in no way contributed to it. However, Mother also is a very honorable woman and I know she will want to contribute everything she possibly can, above her actual subsistence needs, to see this thing through for me.

It is a sad heritage I leave to Mother, to Hope [another daughter] and to you and to the wonderful grandchildren, but I pray it may somewhat be softened by the knowledge that I do love you all so much.

DADDY

State investigators began checking into Hoffman's records in an attempt to reconstruct the series of embezzlements and fantastic manipulations that he used to cover up his thefts. The mystery of how he managed to hide his defalcations for nearly twenty-five years was unraveled when they stumbled into a record room in a state capital warehouse belonging to the

[1] Vice-president and treasurer of the South Amboy Bank.

Division of Employment Security, Hoffman's agency. The room contained the records of more than forty banks including the South Amboy Bank. This is what had happened.

In April, 1930, Hoffman was appointed Motor Vehicles Commissioner for a four-year term. He remained as a holdover after his term ran out and was nominal head of the division for a year after becoming governor. At the same time Hoffman became Motor Vehicles Commissioner, that agency opened an account in his name at the South Amboy Bank where Hoffman also was secretary-treasurer. Hoffman began dipping into the Motor Vehicle account in December, 1931, taking $60,000. During the succeeding four years he embezzled an additional $205,000, removing most of the money in bi-monthly $10,000 clips. Between 1936 and 1937, when he was governor, an additional shortage of $35,000 was created, bringing Hoffman's total thefts to $300,000.

During the succeeding twelve years Hoffman covered up his embezzlements by switching and juggling nearly $16,000,000 in state funds. His manipulations included the Motor Vehicle fund, the General State fund, the School Relief fund, the Motor Fuels Tax fund, the Highway System account, the Grade Crossing Elimination fund, and the General Treasury account. His method was simple. He would take the money from one of the other funds and transfer it to the Motor Vehicle account so that the $300,000 shortage would be covered. Then to hide the shortage in the School Relief Fund, for example, he would deposit money from the Highway System account. Many times Hoffman evaded exposure by shifting funds just before the accounts were checked. By 1942 there was a shortage of $950,-000 in the Highway System account, but an excess of $300,000 in the Motor Fuel Tax fund and a $350,000 surplus in the General State fund, making a deficit of $300,000. By the following year the shortage was concentrated in the General State Fund and the Grade Crossing Elimination fund. By 1947 when all state money was placed in the General Treasury account, it was $300,000 short. Over the years Hoffman's manipulations included sixty-eight bank deposits and withdrawals involving $15,801,197.74. The deposits and withdrawals were signed or endorsed by three former state treasurers and a deputy state treasurer.

Hoffman's last maneuver occurred in December, 1949, when he withdrew $300,000 from his Employment Security Division Disability Funds and deposited that sum in the South Amboy bank's General Treasury account, where the shortage had been concealed for two years. From 1949 until his death Hoffman annually sent the state treasurer certificates which stated that the missing $300,000 in the disability benefits funds was on deposit in the funds' account at the South Amboy bank. The name on these certificates was George A. Kress, vice-president and treasurer of the bank. Over the years Hoffman had forged Kress's name fifty-three times including the certificates he sent to the state treasurer.

What amounts to Hoffman's testament was a series of letters which he sent to his oldest daughter. Composed in the grubby Blake Studio Apartments shortly before he died, they perhaps best reveal the tragedy of his life. The misfortune is not that he died a poor man after thirty years of public service—he left little more than $1,000—nor that for nearly two decades he violated the trust placed upon him. The real tragedy is that the world in which he lived is no less guilty than he. In a sense the words that follow make up the last will of Harold Giles Hoffman:

Never let any of your sons, if you can prevent it, enter politics. At best it is a "lousy" game. In order to be elected you must necessarily accept favors from a large number of people. If you attempt to repay them later, after being elected to office, it becomes wrongdoing. If you do not try to help those who have helped you, you become an ingrate.

There is a peculiar fascination about public life. As you know, I have had lots of opportunities to take higher-paying civilian jobs. In spite of this I stuck to government; it was a field with which I was familiar, and I think that part of this attachment grew out of the fact that I could help so many people do so many different things.

No poor man, in particular, should ever get in the field of

elective politics. Today it costs a great deal to get elected; you must necessarily receive financial support. Not all, but most, of those who help you look afterward for some favors. It generally happens that those for whom you do the most, and whom you help build up to financial or political prominence, do the least for you. You know of one case. In the depression days, when I was running for Governor, I took on a fellow who was about to lose his job, which was selling electric irons and such. He received $35 a week. When I was elected I kept on putting him in one job after another, and finally he became an assistant to the State Highway Commissioner. He switched his allegiance, when it became expedient to be with the "winner" and was rewarded by being made State Highway Commissioner at, I think, $18,-000 a year. In addition, he became Chairman of the Garden State Parkway Commission, which job he presently holds. While he was still Highway Commissioner, I understand, he was also drawing down $600 a month for his services to the Garden State Parkway Commission. To the best of my recollection he has never sent me a Christmas card.

I could recite many almost similar cases.

"Morality," in its ultimate determination, is a funny thing. If, as a public official, I spend a couple of days, or afternoons, each month at the Circus Saints & Sinners, which has been my hobby—an organization that exists just to provide funds and to do good for needy people—I am wrong. If other governmental officials or employees elect to go to the race track (which I seldom, if ever do, simply because I do not care for the "sport of kings") it is perfectly all right, and the accepted thing. If I use a little State truck to bring over a few pieces of scenery for the Saints & Sinners, to New York, I become reprehensible, but if some other State official uses a State car and a State employee to take him out to play golf, that is okay—simply because hundreds of 'em do it.

I remember, a few years ago, that the then Governor, Al Driscoll, received a lot of favorable editorial comments because he had returned passes for the Garden State and Monmouth Park race tracks. He didn't like horse racing. But, he does like to ride on trains, for free, so he accepted the pass for railroad transportation.

It's the old story! The guy who has it can go to Wall Street and gamble a million dollars a day. Little Mrs. Murphy, who goes to a parish bingo party and spends fifty cents, is conspiring to break the law. The fellow who can afford it can go to the race track and gamble a thousand dollars a day on the horses; little Joe Doakes who can't afford to take a day off, and who gambles a buck a day through his neighborhood barber, is a crook. Without attempting to excuse my own derelictons, which are admitted, I claim that if gambling is morally wrong, you can not make it legally right by legislation designed to provide taxes for the State or Federal Government. The fellow who can afford to bet a million dollars a day in the market, in my opinion, shouldn't look down on the little fellow who gambles five dollars in a crap game. They are both trying to get something for nothing.

And you know that I have never been a gambler! Had I been, I might have been far better off. I have had—and this may be beyond the comprehension of a lot of people, an almost uncontrollable urge to help other people, particularly people who are in trouble. Within this field, most of my earnings and most of my "misappropriations" have gone. I am not trying to create any alibis, but the fact remains that after twenty-five years in public life, I am a poor man.

No one knows this, Honey, better than you. When I left the Governor's office, branded as "New Jersey's Most Expensive Governor," I had to borrow, within three weeks—as I recall it —$400, to pay your tuition at N.J.C. (New Jersey College for Women).

A check of the records would be interesting. I was supposed to be a "big spender." The Governors who succeeded me—and this is only a guess—had expense accounts that were three, four, or five times the amount that was allowed me. A check of the records will reveal that the total expenditures of the State of New Jersey today are many millions of dollars above the total when I was Governor, striving sincerely to keep down the expenses of the State.

Many people think that the method of financing government is very complex. Actually, it is very simple. *This generation finances the debts of the last generation by borrowing money for the next generation to pay.* Because I believed that this is a dubious and costly principle—because I believed that we should pay as we go—through the sales tax, for instance—I was branded as being a "Spendthrift Governor."

While I was Governor, we not only paid off over $26 million in bonds that had been levied in former administrations, but we did not borrow a dollar, and we not only lived within the income of the State, but had a surplus at the end of each year. It would be interesting to compare this record with that of any succeeding Governors.

Chapter 13

The Man in the Single-Breasted Union Suit

ONE OF America's most exclusive clubs has recently fallen under the spotlight of some of the decade's most disturbing headlines. The members of the club are in a sense an anomaly in our society. Although their function is integral to the American way of life, they are often shunned as pleaders of radical or even alien concepts. Despite their power—in a few instances it surpasses that of the head of General Motors—they are rarely considered successes because of the work they do. This club forms the latest addition to America's growing white collar class. Its members are the nation's labor leaders.

In 1957 the Select Committee on Improper Activities in the Labor or Management Field, United States Senate, held its now-famous hearings on corruption. It investigated the activities of fifty companies and seven labor unions with a total membership of two million. The seven labor unions represented a small percentage of the 190 unions in the United States with a membership of over seventeen million.

Chairman McClellan noted in his interim report:

"In attempting to assess the multitude of facts presented to it over the past 12 months, the committee has been keenly aware of the inherent dangers of generalization. Much that is shameful and unsavory has been uncovered about the behaviour of certain elements in both labor and management. This sort of information has necessarily been spotlighted, but it is in no way intended to reflect on the overwhelming majority of the labor unions and businessmen of this Nation, of whose integrity the committee is firmly convinced.

"By the same token, no honest man, in these vital sectors of American life should want to tolerate the existence of evil in his midst. To blunt, if not eradicate, the effectiveness of this evil should be his urgent aim, for however small a proportion of society the miscreants may form, their influence far exceeds their number."

This is the story of one of the unions the committee investigated. It dramatically illustrates what happens when corruption and dishonesty get a strangle hold on an important segment of the labor movement. The union involved is the Bakery and Confectionery Workers International Union of America, one of the oldest in the nation. Although a relatively small union —at the time of the investigation it had 160,000 members—the Bakers' operations are vital. The nation's very staff of life, our daily bread, is dependent upon thousands of its members. The union also wields jurisdiction over many of the American people's gastronomic pleasures ranging from the production of biscuits and pretzels to cakes, cookies, pies and pastries.

The Bakers' Union can look back on a proud and ancient history. Bakers' Union refers to the original union still headed by James G. Cross. A new union, American Bakery and Confectionery Workers International Union, AFL-CIO, was formed after Cross's union was expelled from the AFL-CIO on charges of corrupt domination. Founded on January 13, 1886, by representatives of twenty-five independent unions who met in Pittsburgh, the Baker's Union joined the then-fledgling American Federation of Labor a year later. Conditions that beset the baking industry at the time were medieval. It was not uncommon for a bakery worker to labor sixteen hours a day seven days a week in dirt-infested kitchens. His wages were often pitifully meager. He was forced to board with his employer so that it was a rare bakery worker who even saw his own wedding cake. The Bakers' Union helped change all that. Today the nation's 160,000 organized bakery and confectionery employees work a five-day forty-hour week in sanitary plants or shops. Over the years the Bakers' Union amassed a $6,300,000 pension fund and a $2,000,000 welfare fund. The Bakers' lot has indeed improved. However, somewhere along the way this once-proud union was undermined by corruption. The Select Senate Committee named three men—Max Kralstein, George Stuart and President James G. Cross—as being largely responsible for the union's current plight.

Let us begin with Max Kralstein, a little man with skimpy, graying hair and a high, thin voice. Kralstein, president in charge of District 1, New York, was once described as a man who came into this world "with a smudge of flour on his cheek and a bagel for a teething ring," a man who still felt a "close emotional kinship with the bagel bakers," and a man among whose "least-known virtues because he carefully conceals it" are an "innate shyness and sense of modesty." This eulogy of modest Max appeared in the glossy souvenir journal printed for a testimonial dinner given in his honor in June, 1956. It would appear, however, that words could not fully express the gratitude due Kralstein, for this man of "innate shyness" also was presented with a portrait costing $1,447.21, a $1,650 fur piece for his wife and a check for $57,818.94. A short time later modest Max, who according to one of the dinner planners lived in "such a modest home," purchased another for $40,000.

The point that aroused the Select Senate Committee's curiosity was the method in which the money was raised. After all, the committee later said, "neither testimonial dinners nor gifts to guests of honor are unfamiliar phenomena on the American social scene." The collection methods used, however, was a different kind of testimony. Among the contributors to the Kralstein affair were a number of bakery owners. Most of the twenty solicitors who approached them were union business agents. The employers were given the opportunity of buying tickets for the dinner at a cost of $25 apiece or ads in the souvenir journal. The ads cost a minimum of $50. Five employers who donated sums varying between $50 and $200 later testified that they had neither known Kralstein nor had been told the ultimate use to which the money would be put.

In its interim report the Committee later wrote:

"Additional chapter and verse on the dilemma confronting the bakery-shop owner solicited for a contribution was given to the committee by Joseph Kramer of Manhattan. Kramer reported that he was no stranger to difficulties with the union; at one period, prior to his agreement to a contract, his store had been picketed for 7 months, departing customers had had cakeboxes knocked out of their hands and a Pennsylvania farmer who had supplied eggs to the shop had been warned that unless he ceased deliveries his farm would be burned down.

"Against this background, Kramer received a visit from a business agent named Hart:

"Mr. Hart approached me in the bakery shop and he was very nice, and he did not threaten me in any way, and he said, 'We are having a dinner, and we are going to have a dinner for Mr. Kralstein.'

"I said, 'Who is Mr. Kralstein? I never heard of Mr. Kralstein.' He said, 'Well, he is with us and he did a good job by merging the union, and we want to give him a dinner.'

" 'Well,' I said, 'That is all right, but I am not interested in that.' He said, 'Well, look, do you want to give us an ad, about $50?' And I said, 'I will give you $25,' and he said, 'Well, no, $50 is the minimum.'

"I said, 'I have to think that over.' I said, 'I don't know whether I am interested in that.' Well, about 4 weeks later, he came back and he asked me and I said, 'Well, I have been thinking it over. I will give you $100.'

"Kramer's generous change of heart, which he testified grew out of a fear that 'something would happen again,' resulted in a somewhat florid representation in the Kralstein journal:

MR. KENNEDY (*Chief Committee Counsel*): I notice in the ad that you got in the book, you put here, "Best wishes to Max, whom we love and respect." Did you send that in?
MR. KRAMER: No, no; I did not.
MR. KENNEDY: That was not made up by you?
MR. KRAMER: No.
MR. KENNEDY: It says, "Kramer's Pastries."
MR. KRAMER: No; I did not. I never seen that.

"Kralstein, himself, who appeared before the committee voluntarily, asserted that testimonial dinners were an old story
for the bakers' union. He ticked off an impressive list of similar
past occasions at which largesse was bestowed upon international officers and their kin; a dinner for President Cross where
he was presented with a Buick and his wife with 'an appropriate
gift'; another Cross dinner which netted him $10,000 or $11,000
to cover a mortgage on his home; a dinner for former President
Schnitzler, at which he was given 'a Caddie car' for $4,052 and a
clock, and his wife 'a little token, a ring for $398.' President
Emeritus Herman Winter on one occasion had received a car,
'his lovely daughter a bracelet.' Secretary-Treasurer Curtis
Sims was given a diamond ring. Kralstein, himself, at an earlier
dinner, had been presented with a Chrysler and a 'few thousand
dollars.' "

According to Kralstein the same methods of solicitation were
used in each case.

As for the $60,000 modest Max received, he explained he did
not think the munificence of the sum was important. "To me,"
he said, "it is not the amount, if it is $10 or $100,000. It is the
principle of the thing."

As columnist Murray Kempton put it: "The principle of
the thing, in Max Kralstein's morality, is that everybody does it.
Only Max Kralstein does it more."

It is perhaps more than incidental that modest Max paid no
taxes on his booty, although many of the employers charged off
their donations as business expenses. This means that the
Federal government and eventually the taxpayer became Kralstein's benefactors.

As stale as the Bakers' loaf may have tasted in New York, it
had turned almost completely to mold in President Cross's Midwest domain. For the area that borders America's bread basket
seemed to offer some of the juiciest pickings for Cross and his
chief henchman, George Stuart, vice-president in charge of
District 6.

Stuart, a chunky man in his fifties, "personally misused approximately $40,000 in union funds" in the Chicago area, according to the Committee. His methods made modest Max look the soul of benevolence. Part of Stuart's riches grew out of a system common in the labor movement, the trusteeship. A trusteeship is a device whereby an international union may take over management of a local if it feels that the local is not being operated properly. One of the locals that fell into Stuart's grasp was Chicago Local 100. The Senate Committee noted "Local 100's trusteeship was imposed on it early in 1955 after allegations of malfeasance against its president, Gilbert Mann, who told the Committee he had been given no hearing at all by the international. His separation from his post, Mann recalled, was a simple matter; he walked into his office one morning to find George Stuart, accompanied by an auditor, '. . . sitting behind my desk with a gun. It was my gun, he had taken it out of the drawer, left there by my brother while he was in the hospital.' "

MR. KENNEDY: What did he say to you at that time?

MR. MANN: He told me then that I must resign and he showed me a telegram from the president of the Bakery and Confectionery Workers International Union where we had been placed in trusteeship.

MR. KENNEDY: Who was the president at that time?

MR. MANN: James Cross.

Mann who was sixty-nine had put in eighteen years as an officer of Local 100. When he was summarily booted out by Stuart he was not only broke but owed $1,450 on a mortgage on his home. Stuart promised Mann fifteen weeks' pay, but Mann said he never received it. Stuart, however, obligingly offered to have the Bakers' take over Mann's mortgage on a reduced payment plan. Mann, whose total monthly income consisted of a $98.50 social security check, paid $50 a month on the mortgage. The payments were sent to Stuart's bank. Committee Investigator George M. Kopecky was later called on to testify.

MR. KENNEDY: Does that $50 payment end up in the bank account of Mr. George Stuart or does it end up in the bank account of the local union?

Mr. Kopecky: That sum winds up in the personal savings account of George Stuart at the American National Bank.

Mann himself later testified:

". . . I thought maybe I would like to have a checkup in the hospital at my age, but I thought I had better question the union regarding it.

"I hadn't received any policy. So I asked the officers of Local 100 now, after they have merged, about my policy and they told me that the union had paid for my policy until April and that they got a letter from the international union that they shouldn't have paid for that because I would have to work 24 hours a week in a shop and they said I have no insurance whatsoever now.

"However, they said to me, they returned $8 of my money that I had been paying on the withdrawal card and told me to take out a retirement card and that I would receive $500 at death. I was talking to one of the other officers yesterday here, and he said if I don't hurry up and die, I won't get that $500 either."

George Stuart's activities didn't stop with Gilbert Mann.

During 1955, Locals 100 and 300 appropriated $10,500 for an "organizing drive" at the Salerno Biscuit Company, which, according to Anthony Conforti, then secretary of Local 300 "had about forty-three per cent of the cookie business in the Chicago area." The drive was to be a "quiet" one. As it turned out only George Stuart and a few cronies knew of its existence. George Salerno, president of the target company, indicated in an affidavit that the so-called organizing attempt had been so quiet that to his knowledge no effort whatsover had been made ". . . either from within the plant by paying workers presently employed, or from outside the plant by having pickets or other individuals distribute literature, or in any way contact the workers."

Stuart's zeal for secrecy was unique in the history of the labor movement. In his reports to the international he never once mentioned that an attempt was being made to organize Salerno. Anthony Conforti later explained his superior's reticence. The following is from the Senate investigators' interim report:

"Access to the $10,500, Conforti told the Committee, was made easy by an arrangement by which Stuart had Conforti deposit the weekly $500 contribution of the two locals in a special bank and withdraw cash from it periodically. Occasionally, the money would accumulate when Stuart, who then lived in Kansas City, did not appear to pick it up. At Stuart's eventual suggestion, Conforti said, he set up a special account at his own bank in which his personal funds and the union funds were commingled, and cash withdrawals continued from there . . ."

Stuart's financial manipulations not only benefited George Stuart but others, including the master baker himself, James G. Cross. On December 28, 1955, Teamsters Joint Council 43 in Detroit purchased two Cadillacs for $13,100.18. Two days later Local 100, which was still under Stuart's tutelage, mailed out a check to the Teamsters Council. The check was for $13,100.18, the exact sum the Teamsters paid for the two Cadillacs, which, incidentally, were registered under the names of George Stuart and James G. Cross. Meanwhile Stuart, who had been appointed guardian of Local 100's affairs, brazenly explained the local's expense by writing in the day book: "Teamsters Joint Council No. 43, Joint Organization Expenses, $13,100.18." Brothers Stuart and Cross apparently understood the benefits of joint organization.

The case of James G. Cross is perhaps the most tragic and ironic. Once a pan greaser and fruit cook by trade, Jimmy Cross rose in the ranks to become head of the nation's Bakery and Confectionery workers. A boy wonder in union politics, his was a heritage of militant unionism. The mold that shaped the early character of Jimmy Cross was a town called Gillespie, in southern Illinois. There Cross's father labored in the soft coal fields with other Scottish and Welsh immigrants. As a youngster, Jimmy was raised on a heady diet of Old World socialism, militant unionism, Scottish thrift and a spartan Presbyterianism. Young Cross's first commitment was to John L. Lewis and the United Mine Workers. However, when a group of miners rebelled over some of John L's high-handed tactics, Cross switched his allegiance to a rival group, the newly formed Progressive Miners. It wasn't long before this handsome, blond son of a miner was plucked from the fold and sent to Brookwood Labor College at Katonah, New York, where he received a year's training as a union organizer and leader.

The depression was in full swing when Jimmy Cross graduated. Then twenty-one, he began searching for the leaven of a militant unionist. He returned to the coal fields of Illinois and eventually drifted to Detroit where he met another young labor leader by the name of James Hoffa. They were to become close friends.

It was 1935 when Cross took his first big step as a union organizer. A series of sit-down strikes had swept through the Detroit area. The bakery workers at the plant where Cross was employed locked themselves in and demanded a wage increase. When the employer agreed to a five-cent-an-hour increase, Cross exhorted the workers first to join the Bakers' Union, then bargain. They quickly agreed and won a ten-cent-an-hour increase. Soon after Cross was elected president of the local comprising the five hundred workers at the plant. He was all of twenty-three.

Young Jimmy's rise in the union hierarchy was meteoric. From local president he moved on to head the Bakers' entire Midwest organizing drive. At twenty-nine he was elected to his first national office, industry vice-president representing the country's biscuit and cracker workers. Nine years later he became secretary-treasurer, the number two man in the union, and within two years, president. At forty Jimmy Cross had joined the ranks of the select, those 190 men who lead the nation's international labor unions.

Starting four years later the name of James G. Cross was to rock across the country in a series of headlines that would shock even the jaded. For this once militant and idealistic son of a coal miner had betrayed the yearnings and dreams of all those who had believed in him. His public damnation was to be proclaimed in ringing words by the Senate Committee that investigated his activities. Said the Committee:

"As one of the oldest organized labor groups in our national life, the Bakery and Confectionary Workers International Union of America has witnessed many a historic moment in labor's climb up the economic ladder. After its own 72 continuous years in existence, the union should by now have reached new peaks of progress. Such, however, is not the case. Instead, retrogression has been the bakers' lot, a grim fact directly traceable to the ruinous stewardship of International President James G. Cross.

"Stewardship, is, in fact a misnomer for the Cross brand of administration, for it implies accountability, of which the bakers have had less and less, to the vanishing point, since Cross took over in 1953. In its place they have had double-talk and dishonesty; their constitution has been abused and perverted; their hard-earned funds have been plundered; tyrannical and swindling trusteeships have crushed their local freedoms.

"As an exemplar of a labor autocrat, Cross, in the opinion of the committee, conjures up few rivals. Such has been his cynical and rapacious grasp on the bakers union that in all the misdeeds uncovered by the committee's hearings he seldom plays other than a starring role; in the instances when he does not, his handpicked henchmen do. The committee is of the emphatic belief that the culpability of James G. Cross is central to the corrosion of the bakers union."

The key to Cross's power is lodged in the International's general executive board which had the responsibility of making union policy and approving the activities of the president. Since the Bakers' Union holds its international convention once every five years, the executive board serves as the overseer of the organization's day-to-day activities. This is how Cross was able to control the executive board and thus the union.

Under the constitution, Cross not only had the authority to appoint international representatives of the union but also fixed their salaries. The executive board, which approves both their appointments and salaries, includes among its seventeen members thirteen of these selfsame international representatives. During the 1956 convention the delegates gratuitously gave him the sole right not only to select but to remove the international representatives who made up seventy-five per cent of the executive board. Added frosting on the cake was supplied by the convention which previously set the salaries of the president and secretary-treasurer. Under the new rule the salaries were to be fixed by the executive board, three-quarters of whom customarily had their salaries fixed by the president.

The Select Senate Committee was to note in its interim report: "No sooner had the convention adjourned than a special meeting of the board voted Cross a salary increase from $17,500 to $30,000, and Secretary-Treasurer Curtis Sims an increase from $15,000 to $22,500. Cross returned the compliment a few weeks later by instituting raises in varying amounts for the entire board and all international organizers."

These were not the only constitutional changes made at the 1956 convention. Previously the rank and file elected the international officers by secret ballot in referendum held after the convention. This rule, however, was changed so that the convention itself nominated and elected the international officers. The change came about through the adoption of identical resolutions submitted by locals representing 2,989 of the 5,557 votes. One clause in the resolution read: "Whereas, to continue such an outmoded and outdated procedure [a rank and file referendum] can no longer be considered a democratic process, specially costing many thousands of our dollars which is a definite waste of the membership funds."

Ironically, just four years before the convention threw out the rank and file election referendum, Cross, then secretary-treasurer, had this to say in the union's official journal:

"Our organization retains the basis of pure democracy, even more so than that of the Nation itself. We vote directly for the candidates, where in the Nation we vote for electors pledged to vote for certain candidates. We maintain more democracy than many labor unions who elect their officers by the votes of delegates at their convention."

Needless to say one of the 1956 convention's first acts after abolishing "pure democracy" was to re-elect James G. Cross International President.

The tightfisted control that Cross maintained over the union apparatus formed an ironic contrast to his loosefisted expenditure of funds. In 1956 alone Cross's expenses came to nearly $40,000 or more than twice his salary. More than half was spent on entertainment, dinners, birthday parties, gratuities and personal expenses. Cross had not offered a single bill to support the $25,000 in vouchers that he had submitted.

And what were some of these expenses, all paid from the dues of the union members? Here are just samplings taken between 1955 and early 1957: A two-day trip to Portland, Oregon, in October, 1955, costing $963.53; a ten- or eleven-day trip soon afterward to New York, $4,069.75, including among other items, $214 for twenty-two football tickets paid in advance for the Rose Bowl game and $130.13 for a hotel room which, said Cross, "was used for playing poker for the rest of the general executive board members"; a six-day trip to Miami in February, 1956, $2,980.15, including daily room rent of $44 and cabana rent of $50, but excluding a separate $1,079.58 item at this time for driving from Washington to his home at West Palm Beach; a six-day trip to Paris and London in September, 1956, accompanied by his wife and daughter, $4,261.48; another trip to Palm Beach and Miami in January and February, 1957, $4,431.17, including a $331.31 item for a hotel bill to Elsie K. Lower.

The case of Elsie K. Lower, described in testimony as "Mr. Cross' girlfriend, so to speak," came as close as is possible to incinerating the character of the Bakers' president. According to police records, Miss Lower had been arrested fourteen times on charges ranging from grand theft and drunken driving to offering and residing in a house of ill fame. A slim, dark-haired woman in her middle twenties, Miss Lower repeatedly claimed her answers might tend to incriminate her when asked about her relations with Cross. The Bakers' president said that he had met Miss Lower at an AFL cocktail party at the Ambassador Hotel in Los Angeles in the fall of 1954. Under Committee questioning Cross admitted that Miss Lower had taken a number of trips including journeys to Portland, New York, Denver and two trips to Miami Beach. He explained their presence together by insisting that Miss Lower had come only to discuss union business. One may infer that the discussions were upon occasion prolonged, for at least in one instance Cross and Miss Lower registered in adjoining rooms with a connecting door.

And what was this union business which took up so much of Brother Cross's time and cost the Bakers' upwards of $10,000 including some $2,300 in transcontinental phone calls? According to the testimony presented to the Committee Miss Lower had been hired to help organize Van de Kamp's bakery, a large southern California company, which had consistently withstood the Bakers' more arduous organizing efforts. Miss Lower's job was to obtain the names and addresses of the people working in the plant. There were between eight hundred and nine hundred people employed there. According to John Nelson, assistant trustee of Los Angeles Local 37, Miss Lower supplied the union with fifty names at $20 a name. Miss Lower, however, was more modest in her attainments as an organizer. She told the Committee that she had been to Van de Kamp's bakery perhaps once, maybe twice, and that she had talked to no other employee except the head baker, "a very good friend of mine." Committee Counsel Kennedy then asked her if she could remember his name. In a rare flight of eloquence, Miss Lower replied:

"I can't even remember. He is a Mexican fellow. He is married to a woman named Margie. That is all."

But that wasn't all, at least not for Cross. The most damaging testimony was still forthcoming. According to the Senate probers it "went to the heart of the committee's inquiry into collusive labor-management relations."

As young union organizer Cross found himself spending much of his time in meetings with employers, certainly a routine function for most union leaders. One of the employers he came to know was a man named Martin Philipsborn, Sr., then acting head of Zion Industries, a large baking and candy manufacturer in Zion, Illinois. It was not long after their first meeting in 1938 or 1939 that Cross and Philipsborn developed a warm personal relationship. Cross himself was later to testify that Martin Philipsborn's attitude was one of "paternal fondness." Between 1944 and 1948 Cross recalled that it was his job to negotiate company contracts with the elder Philipsborn. Then Cross yielded to his first recorded temptation. For it was in 1948 that James G. Cross obtained through Philipsborn's good offices, a $16,000 mortgage on his Chicago home. The firm was known as the H. F. Philipsborn Mortgage Company. The owner was Martin Philipsborn's brother.

During the ensuing years the elder Philipsborn's "paternal fondness" deepened with the union leader's burgeoning power and needs. Around February 3, 1955, Martin Philipsborn, Sr., lent Cross and his wife $57,600 for the purchase of a home in Washington. On or about August 27, 1956, the elder Philipsborn came across with another loan, this one for $40,000, so that Jim and Ruth Cross could buy a home in West Palm Beach, Florida. Cross eventually repaid the loans. The Committee, however, charged that the Bakers' president "sold a group of his members down the river by secretly conniving to extend a substandard contract they abhorred with a man to whom he was then personally indebted" directly and indirectly to the munificent sum of more than $97,000. The Committee also found that the action of the man with whom Cross connived, Martin Philipsborn, Sr., was "equally reprehensible."

How did Cross meet his obligations? First, a word of explanation. The Zion Industries, which the Philipsborn family owned, consisted of a bakery and candy plant. Cross's union had already organized the bakery workers, but not the candy employees. The shell game begins with the bakery workers.

Early in September, 1956, Local 1 in Chicago began negotiations for a new contract for Zion's bakery workers. Negotiations bogged down and on October 1 the local's secretary-treasurer, Peter Carbonara, wired Cross for permission to strike the plant. Carbonara noted that a strike vote taken by the Zion bakery workers showed 110 in favor and only 8 opposed.

Four days later Cross wrote a letter to Anthony Conforti, president of Local 1. In the letter Cross granted strike permission "if final adjustment efforts fail." Local Secretary-Treasurer Carbonara testified that a couple of weeks later he had a phone call from Vice-President George Stuart who was attending the union convention in San Franscisco. Stuart, he said, announced that he wanted to retract the strike permission; he asked the surprised Carbonara to mail back the Cross letter, indicating he would mail a new strike permission after a get-together of the union's general executive board.

Carbonara was to receive no new strike permission. For shortly after the San Francisco convention Cross and the ubiquitous George Stuart lunched with Philipsborn in Washington. The luncheon, held in November, 1956, came just two months after Philipsborn's $40,000 loan to Cross.

Cross was to deny later that he discussed the terms of the proposed Zion bakery contract. He then testified:

"I agree with Mr. Philipsborn and Mr. Stuart that if he could withdraw his opposition to the organization of the candy plant, I would then instruct Mr. Stuart to go to the local union and its membership meeting and see if he could sell those [bakery] workers on the idea of extending their contract under the, terms negotiated by Carbonara in exchange for this candy plant that we had been unable to organize for over 20 years."

Cross's version of the meeting was to say the least incomplete. For, in a letter to Stuart, the elder Philipsborn noted the points discussed and agreed upon. One of them included an extension of the bakery workers' contract to fifteen months from the expiration of the old contract. This extension would contain no new benefits to the workers. Cross, as you remember, had denied that terms of the bakery workers' contract had even been discussed.

The Committee was to note: "Thus, despite denials by Cross, it was plain that he had negotiated a contract with the man to whom he was heavily and personally indebted without consulting either the officers or members of the local whose economic future was involved."

This substandard contract which was to last until December 31, 1957, was abruptly terminated and a new three-year contract granting wage increases was negotiated and signed in the summer of 1957. This change of heart came only after the Senate Committee had begun investigating Cross and the Bakers' Union.

As far as the organization of the candy workers was concerned Cross's claim to victory was directly contradicted by
John Klansek, international representative of the union. In
an affidavit dated June 12, 1957 (eight months after the Cross-
Philipsborn meeting), Klansek declared that "the candy plant
is not organized to my knowledge."

Klansek's affidavit also recalled an experience he had had in
negotiating back in 1954 with Martin Philipsborn, Jr., for a
new contract for the bakery workers:

". . . From time to time, Philipsborn indicated to me that
he was a personal and intimate friend of Cross and that Cross
would be displeased with the fact no progress was being made.
Further, Philipsborn told me that his father had a mortgage
of about $20,000 on the house which Cross owned."

Klansek was to testify later that the day following the reading of his affidavit, Cross had countermanded all his assignments as an international representative.

A subject that piqued the Committee's curiosity was how
the Bakers' chief repaid the $40,000 loan made to him just a
few months prior to his appearance before the Senate investigators. A Washington bank, Cross said, gave him a $10,000
mortgage on the Florida home. He himself put up collateral for
a $16,000 loan. The remaining $14,000 was lent to him by an
old friend, modest Max Kralstein.

By the time the Committee concluded the major portion of
its hearings on the Bakers' on July 17, 1957, Cross was a dis-
credited man. A short time later the AFL-CIO expelled the
old Bakery and Confectionery Workers Union from its ranks
for corrupt domination and granted a charter to a rival union
set up by five former international officers. These five top-
ranking union officials had already formed a "committee of
integrity."

On October 6, 1958, Cross was indicted by a Federal grand
jury on a perjury charge. The perjury indictment, the first
to stem from Select Senate Committee hearings, was based on the
testimony of Mrs. Nathan Ehrlich, a grandmother and the
wife of a dissident Bakers' leader. Mrs. Ehrlich testified that

Cross, George Stuart and two goons had stormed into the San Francisco hotel room she and her husband occupied during the 1956 convention. The attack, she said, occurred in the early hours of a Sunday morning. "And as I saw Mr. Cross hitting my husband," she declared, "I went out from bed and I started to pull him by the jacket and he pushed me down on the bed and then when I slipped down, he was kicking me with his feet." Cross stoutly denied being present at the time of the attack, claiming that he was taking a shower in his own room in the presence of his male secretary.

A little more than four months later Cross was acquitted. United States District Judge Richmond B. Keech ruled that no legislative purpose could be served by questioning the union leader about his previous denial that he was present during the assault. Cross incidentally is still head of the old Bakers' Union.

A question that remains unanswered is what corrupted James G. Cross?

To answer that question let us briefly examine some of the dramatic changes that have taken place in the labor movement in the last three decades. As A. H. Raskin, brilliant labor reporter for *The New York Times,* recently put it:

"Before Franklin D. Roosevelt started the New Deal in 1933, payless paydays were common for union officials—from president to mimeograph clerk. Two or three rooms in a down-at-the-heels building served as headquarters, and electric bills piled up so high that candles were kept handy for use in the frequent periods when the current was turned off. Delegates to union conventions passed the hat in their factories to raise enough money for coach fare and a bed at the Y.M.C.A. Some had to hitchhike or steal rides in freight cars. The Automat was their idea of a high-class restaurant."

Today, the average union leader looks upon those times as the pioneer era, similar to the settling of the West, a romantic period of heroic accomplishment. A union leader would no more think of riding the rails to a labor convention than the average American would envision crossing the Great Divide in a wagon train. And for good reason. Besides the obvious contributions of the Wright brothers, the labor movement can afford to give its leaders the best.

Consider for a moment the fiduciary state of the nation's blue collar organizations. The treasuries of all local and international unions hold one billion dollars. The annual income from membership dues and assessments comes to more than 600 million dollars. Add to that, additional billions that are pouring into collectively bargained pension and welfare funds. When used for good works the condition is admirable. However, in unions like the Bakers' the absence of membership control over the expenditure of union funds turns the treasury into an embezzler's dream. Imagine what would happen if the retiring president of a bank tossed out the bank's records, unlocked the vault, threw away the key and then admonished his successors to preserve their integrity. With such conditions prevalent in much of the labor movement, what is amazing is not the amount of corruption, but the high proportion of honesty that does exist.

The millennium of wealth and power which befell organized labor has resulted in another factor which, in part, explains some union chieftains' misdeeds. Although the officials of the nation's 190 unions still publicly identify their cause with the sweat and toil of their seventeen million members, their private aspirations are distinctly middle and even upper class.

Such yearnings have occasionally resulted in the incongruous. Not long ago eight labor leaders arrived at the White House. Their means of conveyance—a limousine with liveried chauffeur. Their mission—to plead the cause of the unemployed. Or as one union official explained his appearance at the bargaining table, "If the man sitting across the table from me wears a diamond ring," he told a congressional committee, "I think I am entitled to the same thing. I represent my people on the same level."

C. Wright Mills succinctly summed up this social paradox in his book *The New Men of Power: America's Labor Leaders.* "In the arena of power," he wrote, "the labor leaders are newly risen men; no matter how much bluster some of them may employ, they feel the gap. They reveal their feelings in their general tendency to imitate the standard middle-class, business-like mode of living, and by the resentment they show when they talk about business's lack of respect for labor. This craving for status and respect is often a strong undercurrent of their lives.

"Thirty years ago many labor leaders were willing to sacrifice such social esteem as they might have felt due them in return for the power and income they enjoyed. Today, many of the newer leaders want social esteem because they already have an income that is generally respectable and power which is not to be scorned. In their long struggle to win a more secure position for unions and more respect for the workers, the labor leaders in America have also been waging a fight for more security and respect for themselves."

The fight, however, has been a losing one. Despite the power he represents, the average labor leader has been singularly unsuccessful in his attempt to attain the public prestige, acceptability and social privileges that are literally thrust upon his business counterpart. (How many business leaders were born on the seedy side of the tracks, had little formal education, hew to the Democratic Party and swear by the closed shop? This is the portrait of almost every union leader in the country.)

One can perhaps understand, if not excuse, the actions of the labor leader who, after years of hardship and struggle, is accepted as an equal at the bargaining table but not the dinner table. Indeed, the wound of nonacceptance can fester to the point where the union official may compensate with an eighteen-room Georgian house, a Fleetwood and even a mistress. Since most top labor leaders rarely make more than $25,000, he may dip into that unguarded sea of membership dues and pension and welfare funds.

What, of course, makes his violation of trust seem so reprehensible is the very nature of his livelihood. The labor leader's job is to better the working conditions and existence of the union's members. Unlike the manufacturer or retailer who is primarily concerned with the sale of commodities, the product he represents is human labor. Thus, for the union leader to profit personally from the people he represents— and the only way he can is by theft—is perhaps the most immoral act that can be committed in the gray flannel world of white collar crime.

Let us return to the riddle of James G. Cross. According to at least six people who have been intimate observers or participants in the affairs of the Bakers' Union corruption of the union itself started long before Cross became president. He simply imitated the evil of others, the only difference being that Cross was more thorough and operated on a grander scale. Secondly, as Cross himself began to hobnob with business leaders he developed a taste for material luxury, his seduction in a sense was only human.

These answers, however, are incomplete. For we are still left with the basic enigma: How was it possible for this once militant unionist to deny his own heritage and embrace all those evils which he had so fervently battled? The answer to that question can only come from James G. Cross.

Chapter 14

The Solution to White Collar Crime

SHOCKING AS it may seem, the people chiefly responsible for the increase in white collar crime are those who could do the most about ending it. Indeed the fault lies with top management and not with lower- or middle-rung employees. To put it simply, the majority of American businessmen are asleep at the switch. They not only lack awareness of the seriousness of the problem but fail to realize that they themselves are the main contributors to their own employees' dishonesty. Strong words? Let us examine a few facts.

Despite the gravity of the situation, only between ten and fifteen per cent of the nation's manufacturers, wholesalers and retailers have bothered to bond their employees against theft. (This does not include banks, probably all of whom have honesty insurance.) The majority of employees who are covered by fidelity or honesty insurance are those who deal with cash. Generally not covered are employees who handle merchandise. Yet the theft of goods is often greater than the embezzlement of cash. It is not uncommon to find a firm's treasurer, a man who never stole a penny, to be covered by honesty insurance, while thirty other employees, none of whom are bonded, are systematically stealing $3,000 a week in merchandise.

Even more important the small percentage of firms which carry honesty insurance are usually the biggest concerns, companies which not only have better control systems but can more easily afford the losses due to internal theft. Small- or medium-sized companies rarely bond their employees. This point was dramatically made in a survey published by the Surety Association of America. More than 20,000 businessmen and executives participated in the study. The survey broke down the percentages of typical commercial establishments protected by fidelity bonds against those not protected and came up with these amazing results:

	Protected	Not Protected
Hardware	6%	94%
Contractors	8%	92%
Appliance Stores	7%	93%
Groceries	3%	97%
Restaurants	4%	96%
Clothing	5%	95%
Drug Stores	7%	93%

Contrast this lack of protection, just a sample, against the losses to American business through embezzlement, missing inventory, manipulation and falsification of records. These losses, which incidentally do not include such items as padded overtime, theft of company secrets, and customer ill will, exceed four million dollars a day, every working day of the week, every week of the year. In 1957 alone fidelity bonding companies paid in claims and operating expenses more than they received in premiums. To put it another way, bonded losses rose from thirteen million dollars in 1946 to thirty-five million in 1957, a 270 per cent increase in honesty insurance claims. Add this startling fact: Only one-thirtieth of the losses due to employee dishonesty are actually recovered. Finally, an estimated 200 firms are scheduled to go into bankruptcy in 1960 as the result of internal thefts. To sum up: If the American businessman doesn't awake to the problem, he will discover the white collar thief has not only picked his pocket but stolen his pants.

So far we have examined the businessman's lack of awareness of the situation. Perhaps even more alarming is the fact that he unwittingly fosters dishonesty through poor business practices. Conversely the existence of employee dishonesty is the barometer for how well an organization is being run. Take this classic case from our own files. The owner of a chain of carpet, linoleum and tile marts called us one day. There appeared to be a minor tile shortage at one of the chain's stores. The store's sale performance, he added, was excellent. The manager was hardworking. The eight salesmen were the best. The missing tiles, though, troubled him. Would we check?

This is what we found. The store's so-called star salesman took frequent two-hour naps in the sun. His resting place—the main display window whose floor had a downy foot-thick covering of carpets. Other members of the sales staff spent between three and four hours a day playing poker and gin. Usually, only one man was left to take care of the customers. Invariably, he was the least experienced of all, the one salesman who needed constant guidance. The store's staff, all men between twenty-five and forty, decided to lighten the burden of their working day by setting aside one full hour for unabated merrymaking. The revelry took the form of daily water fights, each man bringing his own toy pistol. The climax came the day after the assistant manager was bested in one of the battles. He decided to surprise the marksman who had given him a particularly thorough drenching. The next day the assistant manager came to work with toy tommy gun which he loaded with water. Hiding behind a large roll of rugs, he waited until the rival salesman approached with a customer, a woman who happened to be pregnant. As the rival salesman unrolled the rugs, the assistant manager leaned forward, screaming an Indian war cry and madly pumping the water-filled tommy gun. The woman screamed that people were coming out of the walls. The assistant manager, though, had got his revenge. He not only left the rival salesman dazed but dripping.

And where was the store manager during all these shenanigans? He was inside his office, the door closed, busily doing paper work.

The tiles, of course, had been stolen, as we had expected. A stock clerk who had been with the firm only three months had handed the tiles over to a contractor who nonchalantly pulled his truck up to the shipping platform and hauled the loot away. When asked why he had helped steal the tiles, the stock clerk replied, "Look at the way they act around here. Nobody gives a damn what you do."

Incidentally, this case had an ironic aftermath. Six months later we received a phone call from the owner of the same chain of carpet marts. He was having trouble in another store. Each week some $700 worth of tiles were missing. We asked him the name of the store manager. "Oh, you know him," he said. "He was the assistant manager of the store you once surveyed." The owner of the chain had decided that all the tommy-gun-packing employee needed was a good tongue lashing. He felt he was too good a salesman to lose.

The point that needs stressing is that management's lack of awareness of what actually takes place in it's own bailiwick serves as prime cause of much white collar crime. According to bonding companies' statistics, fifty per cent of all employees are subject to temptation, depending upon circumstances. If they are given the opportunity to steal, they will do so. And they are given the opportunity because top management frequently has lost touch with the actual conditions in its factories, warehouses, offices or stores.

One reason for this is that executives often diagnose their firm's well being by relying solely on statistics, reports, charts and profit and loss statements. The patient, according to these figures, is bursting with "health." Actually, one reason the business world finds itself engulfed by a wave of dishonesty is its lack of concern with so-called "healthy" operations. When our management engineers are sought on engineering projects involving a survey of systems, materials handling, plant layout, and inventory controls—with no hint of dishonesty— in over fifty per cent of the cases they find some form of dishonesty, whether it be falsification of records, inventory manipulations or outright theft.

Companies, I might add, spend thousands in periodic audits of their books. But in complex business operations, accounting audits are rarely able to penetrate operations with enough depth to guarantee disclosure of all significant irregularities and cleverly concealed inefficiency. The very information on which the audits are based may be invalidated by manipulations hidden to even the most thorough accounting techniques.

I would add accountants are frequently not given sufficient fees or the time necessary for exhaustive investigations. At the same time they are often made the scapegoats of management's errors.

The reason should be quite obvious. Yet management rarely seems to be aware of it. To put it simply: Validity of accounting figures is no better than their source. And their source is people's reliability, accuracy, carefulness, good judgment, morale, memory and *honesty*. No one can sit in an office and determine the validity of figures or know what is happening unless he goes down to those places where the figures originate. Yet the average businessman patiently waits for a mass of charts, ledgers, statements and declarations. If the figures balance, everything is fine. But it is so easy to make them balance.

Indeed, it has been our experience that on the very day inventory is counted, more than fifty per cent of the departments are actually manipulating their inventory figures, a fact that top management discovers too late. According to the 1958 report on Merchandising and Operating Results of the Controllers Congress, stores with less than a one million annual sales volume experienced over a ninety per cent increase in inventory shortages between January 1957 and January 1958, (from .6 to 1.15 per cent of sales). This increase has not only wiped out profits in many instances, but forced a number of smaller stores into bankruptcy. Here is just a partial list of techniques used in retail establishments to manipulate inventory figures, manipulations which bookkeeping records may not show: falsifying prices, concealing how long merchandise has been in stock, inflating counts, destroying documents, misrepresenting the stock's quality, and hiding damaged and salvageable merchandise. Such malpractices occur not only daily but affect small as well as large concerns.

Inventory shrinkage, of course, is also a big problem in industry. When inventory is a big balance sheet item, when materials, tools and supplies are costly, when goods undergo a long, complicated routing through different departments, there are innumerable opportunities for fraud, deceit and outright theft. Although management may believe otherwise, these losses do not appear as identifiable inventory discrepancies. Waste and scrap records, for example, are regularly used for concealing diverted or stolen goods. Old rejects or obsolete parts help build up a given day's output by being counted as part of current production. In fact we have frequently found that abnormally high waste and scrap figures are accepted by management as normal and valid simply because they have been on the same level for years. Yet those very figures were being used to hide a whole series of manipulations.

I might add that industry's reliance upon traditional devices for controlling inventory of materials, tools and work in process is sometimes the very reason for their vulnerability. The fact that there is perpetual control of finished stock and parts is hardly a deterrent to malefactors. During the year a dishonest employee can find numerous ways of putting through adjustments that serve to reconcile discrepancies between physical counts and book records.

A case from our files that dramatically illustrates how easy it is to manipulate figures involves the manufacturer of wooden doors and frames and a one-penny pencil. By inserting the pencil in a meter that counted the number of units produced, a group of dishonest employees inflated the production figures and reaped $175,000 in fraudulent incentive earnings.

Another ingredient in this potpourri of internal dishonesty is management's failure at the point of hiring. Instead of intelligently interviewing a prospective employee, many employers make a cursory inspection of his job qualifications, his high school or college degrees, his dress and the way he carries himself. Concerned only with surface impressions, they do not take the pains to probe the depths. As the result of this lax attitude an interviewer may find that because an extra ten minutes seemed too precious to spare he has cost his company thousands of dollars in losses and has created a white collar thief.

For example, no effort is made to investigate the potential employee's financial needs, his debts, family or personal expenses, whether they be alimony, outstanding loans, mortgages, medical bills or a large number of dependents. In too many instances management refuses to realize that the employee who cannot live on the salary the company can afford to pay will almost inevitably compensate by falsifying output, or overtime, or expense accounts, or solicit kickbacks. Eventually he will turn to outright theft. Yet you would be surprised at the number of employers who do not bother to protect themselves or the white collar workers they hire.

Although it's important to check the references of all employees, it may be noted that habitual criminals play no part in ninety-nine per cent of all white collar crime. In one suburban store recently we found twenty-nine part-time employees involved in theft. Of the twenty-nine, twenty-one had college degrees while four were attending college. Two were elementary school principals, one a parochial school principal, another a credit manager of a large company, still another an insurance adjuster and so on. The merchandise they voluntarily returned exceeded $50,000. Total loss to the store—over $200,000. Most of the employees involved held two jobs so that they could afford to live in the new suburban area surrounding the store. The store carried all the items they needed in their new homes. These employees soon developed a community spirit. As they helped each other steal, one would say to the other, "Be my guest."

Still another contributing factor to the increase in white collar crime are the inadequate control systems management relies on. A case from our files that dramatically points this up involves a mammoth basic metals processing plant. Management was aware that the plant was losing $500,000 a year due to internal thefts. Yet the top executives were actually shocked when we informed them their security system made an excellent setting for a comic opera.

The value of the precious metals and ores processed at this plant can best be illustrated by the following: the *by-product* of just one operation came to $10 million a year. Over a four-year period the plant lost nearly $2 million in precious metals. The firm's executives fired numerous memos to the guard force and other employees calling for the strictest enforcement of all security measures. The memos, though, didn't seem to help. Finally, the company called us in. The firm's profits had taken a decided dip due to the recession, and that annual $500,00 loss had begun to take on a new meaning.

This is what we discovered. Guards were either asleep or drunk while on duty. Neither employees nor visitors who entered the plant were questioned. In fact, a stranger could wander with complete immunity into the building where the precious metals were stored.

When we gave this information to management, we were politely told that we had overstated the case, that the situation simply couldn't be that bad. In fact, the comptroller who worked in the executive offices two hundred miles from the plant decided he would personally test our findings.

It was 3:00 A.M. when the comptroller, dressed in a business suit, began his safari. His first step was to search for a hole under the fence that we had described in our report. He quickly found it, crawled through the hole and approached the locked gate. He started to rattle the chain. When no one stopped him, he took a sledge hammer and pounded a hollow metal post. He was greeted with silence. Next he entered the building where the precious metal was stored. The first person he met was a guard. Although the comptroller carried no identifying badge and was not in working clothes, the guard didn't even nod. The comptroller continued on his way, wandering from office to office making phone calls, kicking waste paper baskets and slamming doors. Still no one came. By this time he was standing only ten feet from the vault where the precious metal was kept. And whom should he meet? The same guard he had passed before. For a moment the comptroller's heart fluttered. At last, he thought, he was going to be stopped.

But the guard continued past him. Angrily, he approached the guard and asked him, "Do you know who I am?" The guard replied blankly, "No. I don't." Then while the guard dumbly stood by, the comptroller picked up a phone, called the firm's general manager with whom he had planned the escapade, and told him about what he had found. After the initial shock, the general manager blurted, "I want action." And that's just what he got.

The same scene two months later. The guard force has been doubled. An expert in police detection has just spent the two months training the guard force in everything from sabotage to search and seizure. Huge spot lights dotted the area. The building that housed the precious metals refinery was turned into a veritable vault. Special locker rooms were constructed where all employees and visiting dignitaries stripped and changed into work clothes that were combed for valuable dust. Even the water used in showers was filtered for filings. The overall cost for these super security measures—more than $200,000.

Again a member of top management set out to check on the plant's security. This time the investigator was the refinery superintendent or chief of plant operations, a new man on the job who worked only during the day. It was 4:00 A.M. when he started out. According to the regulations the main gate was not only supposed to be locked but guarded every minute of the day and night. The superintendent found the gate open and the guard fast asleep. Half the value of the plant's new security system or $100,000 had just been thrown out the window. The superintendent awakened the guard with two words, "You're fired." He moved on to the precious metals buildings. Like his predecessor, he was dressed in a business suit and wore no identification. At four o'clock in the morning he couldn't have been more conspicuous. Each time he met an employee he asked the same question, "Do you know me?" And each time he got the same answer, a blank stare. By the time he had finished wandering through the building, the plant superintendent had fired six men.

The moral to this story is simple, yet time and again I have seen management ignore it. Security programs are meaningless when management relies solely on a system of controls but pays no attention to the employees who are supposed to enforce them. Originally, the guard force was untrained and undisciplined, a dumping ground for the slightly disabled, the incompetent and those who had been put out to pasture. In fact, not only the guard force itself but other plant employees were totally demoralized. They lacked pride in the company they worked for as well as themselves. In effect, they didn't give a damn. It would have taken a miracle for management to have built up sufficient morale and discipline in only two months.

What then is the answer to white collar crime? Some suggest more criminal prosecution. Currently there is very little. According to *Fortune* magazine, "Only about one out of ten discovered defaulters is ever brought into court, and many of these received light or suspended sentences." There are a number of reasons why most employers shy away from law enforcement agencies and the courts. For one, they fear that publicity attached to prosecutions will give their firm a bad name by holding them up to public ridicule plus loss of face among board directors, stockholders and competitors. A second fear is the danger of "flareback," the prosecution that boomerangs. Juries often find a complicated embezzlement too difficult to understand. A jury acquittal in a criminal prosecution may leave the employer facing a civil damage suit. Finally, employers run into difficulty with law enforcement agencies. In many instances they simply do not have the skilled manpower to make the depth interviews and to investigate crime as complicated as white collar theft. In addition, the main concern of many law enforcement agencies is getting a grand larceny conviction. In most states a grand larceny conviction can cover a theft as low as $100. If a charge covering $200, for example, can be successfully prosecuted, the law enforcement agency may ignore thousands of dollars of embezzled money and perhaps ten years of dishonesty.

I might add that prosecution inevitably is a last resort. The crime has already been committed, with restitution difficult. It is, of course, more important to prevent the theft from taking place. But how?

We like to use the term preventive management in describing the solution to white collar crime. This means management must take preventive measures without waiting for the symptoms to appear. It is the constant search for malignant conditions for which there is no surface evidence. It is the establishment of an atmosphere under which the white collar employee knows that management is alert, that management cares, that management is aware of what is going on. It is thinking and planning ahead to avert possible catastrophes. Just as in preventive medicine, so in preventive management, it is far cheaper and more effective to cure a minor ailment before it becomes dangerous than to take corrective measures later.

Here are some general guideposts used in preventive management. (For a more detailed plan of action, see the addendum.)

Don't Act Impulsively. I want to emphasize the importance of not striking out at the first person, or the first procedure or practice that is associated with something that has gone wrong. I have seen the same system thrown out and replaced several times in the same organization because of impulsive action. I have also seen supervisors, purchasing agents and even top-level executives fired from their jobs without affecting to the slightest degree the conditions causing their separation. Even when a given loss is uncovered, many high-ranking executives are content to discharge the culprit and file a claim for the loss without a complete investigation. For one, such a probe may disclose even greater losses. Secondly, without such an examination no intelligent action can be taken to help to prevent such fraudulent practices from happening again. I might add the impulse to act emotionally instead of calmly is not only fatal but ironic. For as so often happens the executive or supervisor who clamors for discharge, arrest and prosecution is the individual who is to blame for the malpractice taking root. It is as simple as the case of Sleepy Jones, the man who operates the incinerator in the Wide Awake factory. When Jones spends four hours each day wandering through the plant collecting

$200 daily in bets, who is *really* responsible for gambling on the premises. Is it Jones? Or the Wide Awake supervisor who has never questioned Jones' whereabouts or activities?

Set Fair Standards of Performance. An important factor in white collar crime are the pressures management imposes on its own associates as well as lower echelon employees. The average white collar worker too frequently is expected to meet unreasonable quotas or budgets. Straddle such people with impossible tasks, and they are bound to manipulate as a means of self-protection. This situation is particularly true among supervisory and executive personnel who are subject to two kinds of pressures. They are either called upon to beat last year's sales or production records or to keep costs down. And when these goals are excessive and unreal the result is a manipulation of records. When people begin to cheat a little more here and there, it is only a short step to manipulations on a larger scale. It might be interesting to note that sixty per cent of all the losses that we have uncovered are directly attributable to supervisory and executive personnel. Management must remember that although its reports may look good, the company is suffering from losses that do not reflect in its books. We call it: "losses books don't show." It's what you don't know that can hurt you.

Maintain Good Communications. Efficiency depends to a great extent on employee reaction to the rules, procedures and general conditions under which they work. The maintenance of good communications is essential if management is to discover the very causes of low profit margins, dishonest manipulations and gross inefficiency. This also means that management must descend from its walnut paneled tower and utilize its own eyes and ears to learn what's going on.

Know the Status of Employee Morale. Management must recognize that poor morale causes employees to resort to every variety of covert inefficiency. Indeed, nothing creates shortages so rapidly and so surely, or reacts quite so adversely on customer goodwill, as resentful and disgruntled personnel. Whenever low morale exists, the invariable result is theft on the one hand and bad customer relations on the other. Incidentally,

one company I know has a program called, "Tell It To Tom."
Tom is an employee with long service who not only has the
confidence of his fellow workers but management as well.
Tom's job is to listen to his co-workers' complaints and personal problems, whether they concern the company or their
own private lives. He brings the gripes to the attention of
management and can marshal the firm's forces in helping an
employee who is having personal difficulty. He will also call
on public and private agencies to lend a helping hand.

To sum up: The problem of white collar crime is essentially
a moral one. If allowed to flourish, it not only can destroy
honest employees, thriving businesses, entire communities, but
even our values of decency and fair play. Indeed the businessman and the executive must bear the final responsibility. For
it is within their power to excise what has become our most
dangerous moral malignancy.

Addendum

A System of Preventive Management

WHAT SPECIFIC concrete steps can the American businessman take to deal with the problem of white collar crime, a problem that not only cuts deeply into his profits but is ruining the lives of many once honest, hard-working employees. The following is the system of preventive management that we have selected and developed over a period of thirty years. This system of controls or preventive measures can aid businessmen in learning the facts about the thing they need to know most, how their own business functions. I firmly believe that although such a system cannot end white collar crime (no system of controls could do that), it could, if instituted by enough companies, save millions of dollars in unnecessary losses.

Let us begin with a quick summary of the fundamental steps in a control system:

I. Selection of strategic control points.

The selection of strategic control points or specific areas to be checked by management is vital if an optimum use is to be made of the manpower and funds available for the control system. To safeguard inventory and supplies, control over three areas—receiving, shipping and exits—is of paramount importance. (Essential precautions concerning those three areas are often neglected.)

II. Develop standards of performance.

Control is impaired unless steps are taken to measure results against anticipated standards of performance. These indicators point up situations requiring attention by management. Some indicators to establish: production efficiency standards, sales quotas, overtime allowances, open-to-buy limits, inventory levels, cash budgets.

III. Checking and reporting on performance.

    A. Control of overall operations must be firmly held by executives ultimately responsible for the company's goals.

    B. Secure information on performance.

There are three basic ways of obtaining information on performance: direct observation of activities; conferences with personnel responsible for work being done; reports from supervisory personnel, auditors, management consultants.

    C. Promptly report information on performance.

Delays in compiling performance information are frequently used to cover up all kinds of abuses. For example, many companies receive important operating reports at least three months after the time covered in the report. Should significant inventory discrepancies be reported, management is burdened with the almost impossible task of verifying the accuracy of its reported inventory shrinkage as well as locating the cause of the shortage. The sheer number of transactions that have transpired in the interim make any attempt to reconstruct the company's inventory status almost foolhardy. Contrast this situation with companies who receive operating reports within hours or days of a specific operation. Not only practical steps can be taken for the verification of results in the report, but opportunities for malefactors to doctor figures and manipulate inventory are greatly reduced.

IV. Take corrective and disciplinary action. Employees quickly learn that they must pay a price for malpractices. At the same time they will realize that management intends to keep its word and that there are limits to an employee's activities. Finally, swift but just corrective and disciplinary action serves as a warning to employees throughout the company.

So far I have suggested just the overall functions of preventive management. The following seven points will show in more detail how these controls against internal dishonesty can be made to work. The seven points are: 1. Dual responsibility. 2. Manualization and definition of organization. 3. Set realistic standards of performance. 4. Create an element of mystery. 5. Spot checks. 6. Periodic inspections. 7. Created errors.

Dual Responsibility

Protection from fraud demands that work be subdivided so that no employee has complete control over any record or transaction. Responsibility is allocated so that, without duplicate effort, an employee verifies the work of others in the normal course of his duties. This check and review which is inherent in any good system of control, greatly reduces the possibility that errors or fraud remain undetected for inordinate periods.

The following are examples of how dual responsibility is maintained over typical work functions:

1. The preparation of the payroll and the payment of employees is handled by two different groups of employees, especially if employees are paid in cash.
2. Persons who maintain inventory records are not allowed to participate in the actual physical counting of inventory.
3. Persons approving payments on invoices or customers' bills are not allowed to participate in the actual receiving of supplies or merchandise.
4. Shipping records are matched against billings to customers by employees in two different departments.
5. Wrappers in stores compare items and prices on saleschecks made out by salesclerks with the items to be wrapped.
6. Employees in sensitive positions are rotated from one job to another. For example, branch managers should be periodically shifted to different stores, warehouses, sales offices. Truck drivers' routes can be changed. Factory foremen and supervisors should be rotated. Payroll and accounts receivable clerks who handle alphabetical listings should be shifted from say a, b listings to e, f listings.

Definition of Organization and Manualization

It is essential that management define in *writing* the company's overall policies, as well as procedures governing each job function and operation of the firm. For example, if a firm has a no-kickback policy, this policy should be put in writing and distributed to all employees concerned. In addition specific procedures used to prevent employees from accepting kickbacks should also be written down and distributed. (For a list of such procedures note Chapter 11.) I might add all positive business procedures will prove useless if a firm permits double standards among its employees.

There are four reasons why company policies and job procedures should be defined clearly in *writing:* 1. All employees will have the same interpretation. 2. Policies and procedures can be reviewed and changed to meet current conditions. 3. They can be checked for compliance and understanding. 4. They will not become obscure in time.

Any attempt to list all the procedures different kinds of firms might use to prevent dishonesty would fill an encyclopedia. However, to illustrate what I mean, here is a list of directives concerning the purchasing function of a large retail organization.

I. Purchase Orders
    A. No commitment for merchandise may be made without, or at variance with, a properly written, signed, and approved purchase order.
    B. Approval Regulations
       1. General Rules
         a. Items costing up to $100 must be approved by the assistant buyer.
         b. Up to $300 need buyer's approval.
         c. Over $300, merchandise manager must approve.
         d. Over $1,000 for delivery after thirty days, need executive officer's approval.
       2. Merchandise Manager or executive officer must approve all orders in overbought departments (departments overstocked with inventory). The exception: customer special orders and orders that sell well (fill-in orders) up to $200.

    3. Any alteration of purchase orders after approval must be reapproved. Changes and reapproval must appear on all copies of the order.

    4. Arbitrary splitting of order to circumvent approval limits must be considered a violation of company policy subject to disciplinary action.

I would like to add that initial employee training, especially among supervisors, is too often haphazard, thus proving one of the weakest points in maintaining effective control. Even where manuals are available and procedures defined, procedural abuse or evasion is common, particularly because of a so-called "emergency" or "lack of time." Management is frequently responsible for the supervisor's failure because it has not emphasized the need for following proper procedures. It pays too much attention to things and not enough to people even though human failures are the prime cause of loss.

Good communication between management and employees is essential if management hopes to discover the causes of low profit margins, manipulations, poor morale, and gross inefficiency. I cannot stress too strongly the importance of telling each employee, on each operational level, his or her specific responsibilities for the protection of the company's assets. Given clear and concise policy and procedural directives, employees will be made aware of their individual roles in preventing losses. They, in turn, will be better equipped to cooperate in the drive against malpractices and internal dishonesty.

Set Realistic Standards of Performance

Standards of performance are not merely a set of figures on a piece of paper, but an estimate of human capabilities. Management cannot make such estimates by accounting methods alone. It requires a realistic evaluation of what management expects from its employees. To be required to meet a specific goal while being denied the means to achieve this end, leaves an employee with an impossible choice, to fail—or to be dishonest.

Here is just one example of a situation where performing standards are unrealistic. The receiving department in every hotel must have scales capable of weighing the supplies being delivered. Yet in many instances these scales are infrequently checked for accuracy or the variety of scales used are inadequate. As a result, receiving personnel run into innumerable discrepancies between weights stipulated on the invoices and those reported on the scale. They soon grow indifferent and fall behind in their work. It is only a step from making the weights of different items conform with the invoices to having a receiving manager work out a deal with the truck driver to cover up "short" shipments. Many hotels have paid dearly for such "oversights."

An Element of Mystery

Inject an element of mystery into the control system. Employees should not know all the controls, checks and reviews used at subsequent stages of an operation. Management can capitalize on this element of mystery to deter malpractices or poor work performances.

For example, sales clerks are told they must submit prenumbered sales checks in sequence at the end of each working day. Unknown to the sales clerks, a small random sample (about ten per cent) can be made of the submitted saleschecks. If any of the checks are found to be missing, this should immediately be brought to the attention of the salesclerk responsible. An explanation, of course, should be demanded. The result—the salesclerk and her friends will assume that all checks are being scrutinized and will think twice before contemplating a fraudulent act.

Spot Checks

Frequent, unannounced spot checks should be made of all employee operations. Employees should know that these spot checks are a normal part of management control. If morale is high, such checks will not only serve as a significant hindrance to temptation but will provide a positive incentive towards a high level of performance.

Here are several examples of how spot checks can be made. When perpetual inventory records are maintained by an employee outside the stockroom, it is possible to exercise effective control over *withdrawals* from the stockroom through the use of pre-numbered requisitions. A selective physical count of certain items in stock can then be made at frequent intervals and then compared with the balance shown on the perpetual inventory records. If the stock on hand doesn't jibe with the recorded figures, it is time for a thorough investigation.

Similarly, in retail establishments, spot checks can be made to ascertain the reliability of price changes. Select a department and take a random sample (ten to twenty per cent) of price changes recorded on remark or markdown sheets. Then compare these price changes with the actual price tickets on merchandise to verify whether the correct changes, if any, were made. Also price tickets on merchandise should be inspected at random. The buyer should then be challenged to present the appropriate document supporting the prices listed on the price tickets.

Periodic Inspections

Responsible executives should also make formal, periodic inspections of work areas to assure prompt follow-up of managerial instructions. The vital areas to be inspected include: receiving, document processing, housekeeping and stockkeeping, security controls. The results of these inspections should be turned over to top management.

Here is a check list that can be used in any periodic inspection program:

1. Merchandise in unguarded areas.
2. Excessive exposure of goods to pilferage.
3. Merchandise in unauthorized areas.
4. Merchandise in shipping areas with no covering documents.
5. Inadequate security devices like fences in disrepair or failure to restrict truck drivers to receiving and shipping platforms.
6. Failure to use security devices already provided.
7. Security devices (alarms, locks to stock areas) that need repair.
8. Large accumulation of damaged or salvage merchandise.
9. Accumulation of merchandise to be returned to vendor.
10. Documents in unauthorized areas. Examples: shipping documents, customer credit and refund documents, invoices, requisitions.

11. Unprocessed documents (documents covering an operation that has been completed). Examples: delayed invoices, salescheck or order accumulations, vendor returns, receiving records, shipping records, purchase orders, bills of materials.

Created Errors

A created or controlled error is one that is deliberately inserted into an employee's or department's operation. This is an extremely valuable tool in evaluating the accuracy and care with which personnel carry out their assigned tasks. To cite just a few areas in which created errors can be profitably utilized:

1. To test purchasing agents deliberately post erroneous entries in copies of purchase journals which are periodically checked by the purchasing agents themselves. Thus, invoices might not be listed, fictitious ones added, vendor returns omitted, figures transposed, and invoices for other purchasing agents included. (Of course, a careful record must be kept so that the necessary corrections can be made. This record also provides a basis to measure the attention which the purchasing department devotes to making these checks.)

2. Purposely create discrepancies on shipping documents covering inter-company or inter-departmental transfers of merchandise or supplies. For example, incorrect prices, quantities or department numbers would be recorded as a check on the personnel handling the arrival of these items.

3. Arrange with vendors to ship-short or overship on a specific shipment to ascertain whether receiving personnel detect discrepancies in quality or quantity received. Of course, the amount of over or under shipments must be prearranged and the cooperation of vendors assured.

Innumerable created errors tests can be developed. But if the department being tested fails to catch the errors, the tests must be followed up with quick, corrective action by management.

The essence of preventive management is good business practices. For every dollar that is lost due to dishonesty at least twice that amount is dissipated as the result of the poor business practices that are responsible for white collar crime. By protecting your assets you not only cut losses due to dishonesty but increase profits by making your company and its employees work with maximum efficiency.